T0366342

Foundations and Applications of the Time Value of Money

The Frank J. Fabozzi Series

Foundations and Applications of the Time Value of Money

PAMELA P. DRAKE
FRANK J. FABOZZI

John Wiley & Sons, Inc.

Published by John Wiley & Sons, Inc., Hoboken, New Jersey.
Published simultaneously in Canada.

For general information on our other products and services or for technical support, please
contact our Customer Care Department within the United States at (800) 762-2974, outside
the United States at (317) 572-3993 or fax (317) 572-4002.

Wiley also publishes its books in a variety of electronic formats. Some content that appears in
print may not be available in electronic formats. For more information about Wiley products,
visit our Web site at www.wiley.com.

Library of Congress Cataloging-in-Publication Data

Peterson Drake, Pamela, 1954–
  Foundations and applications of the time value of money / Pamela P. Drake
and Frank J. Fabozzi.
      p. cm.—(The Frank J. Fabozzi series)
  Includes index.
  ISBN 978-0-470-40736-3 (cloth)
  1. Finance—Mathematical models.   2. Money—Mathematical models.
  3. Business mathematics.   4. Time—Economic aspects.   I. Fabozzi, Frank J.   II. Title.
  HG106.P48 2009
  332.4′1—dc22

                                                              2009014330

Printed in the United States of America

10 9 8 7 6 5 4 3 2 1

Contents

Preface

We wrote this book for those who want to understand more about the math of the time value of money. We wrote this book for the novice by starting with the basics. We also take the time value of money mathematics to a more advanced level for readers who are brushing up on their finance skill in the time value of money, readers who want to learn how to perform these calculations using spreadsheets or financial calculators, and readers who are just curious how this all works.

You don't have to have a financial calculator or scientific calculator with financial functions to learn this stuff, but it helps. You don't have to have access to computer spreadsheet programs to perform the calculations, but it's not a bad idea to see how it all works in this software. You don't have to be a math genius to perform the time value of money skills. All it takes is being comfortable with basic math.

We've included some examples from personal finance situations so that you can see how you can apply these skills to help you make better financial decisions. Though this is not a personal finance book, we do at least arm you with the basic skills to approach most any financial problem that involves the time value of money.

About the Authors

PAMELA PETERSON DRAKE, PhD, CFA, is the J. Gray Ferguson Professor of Finance and Department Head, Department of Finance and Business Law in the College of Business at James Madison University. She received her PhD in finance from the University of North Carolina at Chapel Hill and her B.S. in Accountancy from Miami University. She earned the designation of Chartered Financial Analyst. Professor Drake previously taught at Florida State University (1981–2004), and was an Associate Dean at Florida Atlantic University (2004–2007). She has published numerous articles in academic journals, as well as authored and co-authored several books. Professor Drake's expertise is in financial analysis and valuation. She has been teaching students about the time value of money for almost 30 years. She has been teaching so long that she can remember when a spreadsheet was columnar yellow paper with green lines, and the only calculator was a 10-key adding machine.

FRANK J. FABOZZI, PhD, CFA, CPA, is Professor in the Practice of Finance and Becton Fellow at the Yale School of Management. Prior to joining the Yale faculty, he was a Visiting Professor of Finance in the Sloan School at MIT. Professor Fabozzi is a Fellow of the International Center for Finance at Yale University and on the Advisory Council for the Department of Operations Research and Financial Engineering at Princeton University. He is the editor of the *Journal of Portfolio Management* and an associate editor of the *Journal of Fixed Income* and *Journal of Structured Finance*. He earned a doctorate in economics from the City University of New York in 1972. In 2002, Professor Fabozzi was inducted into the Fixed Income Analysts Society's Hall of Fame and is the 2007 recipient of the C. Stewart Sheppard Award given by the CFA Institute. He earned the designation of Chartered Financial Analyst and Certified Public Accountant. He has authored and edited numerous books in finance. He has been writing and teaching about finance for over 35 years, so long that if he had invested $1 in an account earning 5% when he first started teach, it would be worth over $5.51 today. He recently tossed out the computer punch cards used for his doctoral dissertation.

Introduction

The most powerful force in the universe is compound interest.
—Albert Einstein

Understanding financial transactions, whether involving investing, borrowing, or lending, requires understanding the time value of money. The purpose of this book is to help you understand the time value of money and all the financial mathematics that go with it.

If we think about the most common transactions in someone's personal finance, we can see some of the basic financial mathematics. Consider a few examples:

- A home mortgage involves an annuity of mortgage payments to pay off the borrowed amount.
- Leasing a car involves an annuity of lease payments, along with a down payment, for the use of a vehicle for a specified period.
- Saving for retirement involves an annuity—typically in terms of the periodic saving for retirement and the periodic withdrawals from savings during retirement.
- Comparing loan terms among different financial arrangements involves determining the effective annual rate for each loan so that you can choose the lowest cost loan.

In this book, we cover the financial math that you need to address these and other financial transactions so that you can make the better, more informed financial decisions.

OUTLINE OF THE BOOK

In Part One, we cover the fundamental math. In Chapters 1 and 2, we deal with the compounding and discounting of lump sums—that is, translating single values through time. In Chapter 3 we show how valuing a series of cash flows is a simple extension of discounting or compounding lump sums. We show you how to value these cash flows today and at any point in time. In addition to valuing cash flows, we address how to calculate yields on financial transactions, which are useful when comparing different investment opportunities or financing arrangements. In Chapter 4, we demonstrate how to calculate the annual percentage rate, the effective annual rate, and the internal rate of return for financial transactions.

In Part Two, we look at different applications of the time value of money mathematics. In Chapter 5 we examine loans and how loans are amortized. We show you how you can take a payment on a loan and break it into the interest and principal repayment components. In Chapter 6, we focus on deferred annuities, which are typically associated with the retirement issue: How do we reach a specific goal? How do we save money to satisfy our needs in retirement?

In Chapter 7, we show you how you can value a bond using the mathematics involving lump sums and annuities. We also show you how you can calculate the yield on a bond and examine the sensitivity of a bond's value to a change in interest rates. In Chapter 8, we focus on the valuation of stock. We look at how simple models, which assume that dividends on a stock grow at a constant rate, can characterize the value of a stock. We also show you how to modify this simple model to capture other dividend patterns of stock to arrive at a valuation. We close the book in Chapter 9, where we look at how the time value of money mathematics has been applied to three scenarios: evaluating whether to get an MBA; deciding whether to lease or buy a car; and whether gold is a good investment. We chose these three applications so that we could demonstrate how the time value of money mathematics can be used to address personal financial planning issues. Although this is not a personal finance book—and we do not purport to give financial advice—we do want you to take away with you the basic tools and techniques that allow you to address financial problems that interest you.

We advise you to read through—and work through—Part One before attempting Part Two. Part One lays the foundation that you need for Part Two, and you may be a bit lost in Part Two without that foundation. Once you finish Part One, it won't be a problem if you skip around Part Two and take these chapters in any order that you wish.

OUR APPROACH

Throughout the book, we use alternative approaches to most every problem. We work examples using the pure mathematics—with all the gory formulas.

We do this because some readers may be able to look at the equation and realize "Oh, yeah, now I get it!" But then other readers may look at an equation and think "Oh, no, how do I stop the pain?!" For these readers, we offer calculations in table format, with calculators, with spreadsheets, and plenty of graphs. Hopefully, one of these methods will enable you to understand what is going on.

Calculators

We offer calculator and spreadsheet steps along with many of the examples. We do this because not everyone is a math purest and most everyone is practical: The calculators and spreadsheets are there to help us. We do suggest, however, that you do attempt to learn the math that lies behind the calculator program just in case a financial problem comes your way that does not fit neatly into a calculator or spreadsheet program.

We show the steps for two calculators throughout the book—the financial calculator, the Hewlett-Packard 10B and the scientific calculator, the Texas Instruments TI-83 (which is similar to the Texas Instruments TI-84 model, which is why we refer to these calculators as TI-83/84). The Hewlett-Packard 10B calculator (HP 10B) is the simplest to learn and the steps required to perform calculations are very similar to most of the other financial calculators. However, we do provide instruction in Appendix A on several other financial calculators so that you can find some instruction for your financial calculator or one similar. In addition to these financial calculators, we provide additional instruction on the TI-83/84 in this appendix as well.

If you encounter problems when using your financial calculator, check the Tips and Troubleshooting that we offer in this appendix. If you keep getting answers that disagree with ours, check to see that you set up your calculator properly and that you are executing the functions correctly.

Spreadsheets

In addition to the calculator explanations, we also provide information on how to use the financial functions in spreadsheets to perform the calculations. We refer to Microsoft Excel throughout the book, but as we explain in Appendix B, the functions operate the same as those in the free Google Docs' spreadsheet, which is available at www.google.com. We encourage you to learn how to use the spreadsheets for financial calculations because, when you begin to apply time value of money mathematics to your personal financial decision making, you may need some of the tools that these spreadsheets can provide, including graphing.

Formulas

We cannot avoid using formulas in a book that covers the time value of money mathematics. We include all the relevant formulas within the chapters—whether you want to work through these or not. We also include the formulas in Appendix C, which is a summary of the notation and of the formulas by chapter.

Problems and Examples

When you read a chapter, you will encounter three different types of problems:

- *Examples*, which are brief problems that demonstrate the calculation that was just discussed in the text. These problems are numbered sequentially throughout the chapter and the answers, including an explanation of how to get the answer, are included right there.
- *Try it! problems* are problems that you can work on your own. You can find detailed answers to these problems at the end of each chapter summary.
- *End-of-chapter problems*. There are 10 problems at the end of each chapter. We provide the detailed solutions to these problems in Appendix E, at the back of this book.

We encourage you to work all of these problems. You will notice that one chapter will build upon another chapter, so it is important for you to have a good understanding of a chapter before moving on to the next.

Glossary

Along with the math comes a bunch of terminology, so we've tried to sort it out for you. In Appendix D, we include a glossary of the terms used in this book.

THE KEYS TO LEARNING THE TIME VALUE OF MONEY

We would like to leave you with a couple of suggestions for learning the time value of money mathematics:

- **Focus on the basics.** The basic valuation equation, which we introduce you to in Chapter 1, is the heart of all of the time value of money. Learn this and you've got it made.

- **Learn at least two ways to do each problem.** You are more likely to learn the mathematics of the time value of money if you can see it from at least two angles. Learn to do each problem with at least two of the three approaches that we offer: basic math, financial calculator, or spreadsheet.
- **Practice, practice, and practice.** There is no substitute for this.

Foundations and Applications of the Time Value of Money

The Basics of the Time Value of Money

The Value of Compounding

Remember that time is money.
—Benjamin Franklin
Advice to a Young Tradesman (1748)

Most people are familiar with the Seven Wonders of the World: the Great Pyramid of Giza, the Hanging Gardens of Babylon, the Statue of Zeus at Olympia, the Temple of Artemis at Ephesus, the Mausoleum of Maussollos at Halicarnassus, the Colossus of Rhodes, and the Lighthouse of Alexandria. Supposedly, when Baron von Rothschild was asked if he could list the Seven Wonders, he said he could not. However, he did respond by saying that he could name the Eighth Wonder of the World: compound interest. Actually, labeling compound interest as the Eighth Wonder of the World has been attributed to other notable figures: Benjamin Franklin, Bernard Baruch, and Albert Einstein. Regardless of to whom we attribute this label, as you will see in this chapter, the label is appropriate.

One of the most important tools in personal finance and investing is the time value of money. Evaluating financial transactions requires valuing uncertain future cash flows; that is, determining what uncertain cash flows are worth at different points in time. We are often concerned about what a future cash flow or a set of future cash flows are worth today, though there are applications in which we are concerned about the value of a cash flow at a future point in time.

One complication is the *time value of money*: a dollar today is not worth a dollar tomorrow or next year. Another complication is that any amount of money promised in the future is uncertain, some riskier than others.

3

Compounding

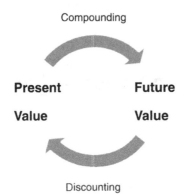

Present   **Future**

Value   **Value**

Discounting

Moving money through time—that is, finding the equivalent value to money at different points in time—involves translating values from one period to another. Translating money from one period involves interest, which is how the time value of money and risk enter into the process.

Interest is the compensation for the opportunity cost of funds and the uncertainty of repayment of the amount borrowed; that is, it represents both the price of time and the price of risk. The price of time is compensation for the opportunity cost of funds—what someone could have done with the money elsewhere—and the price of risk is compensation for bearing risk. That is, the riskier the investment, the higher the interest rate.

Interest is *compound interest* if interest is paid on both the principal—the amount borrowed—and any accumulated interest. In other words, if you borrow $1,000 today for two years and the interest is 5% compound interest, at the end of two years you must repay the $1,000, plus interest on the $1,000 for two years and interest on the interest. The amount you repay at the end of two years is $1,102.50:

Repayment of principal		$1,000.00
Payment of interest on the principal—first year	5% of $1,000	50.00
Payment of interest on the principal—second year	5% of $1,000	50.00
Payment of interest in the second year on the interest from the first year	5% of $50	2.50
Total amount repaid at the end of the second year		$1,102.50

You can see the accumulation of values in Exhibit 1.1. The $2.50 in the second year is the interest on the first period's interest.

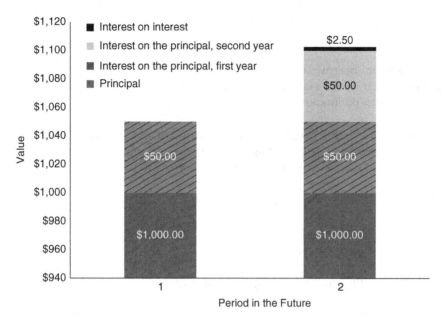

EXHIBIT 1.1 Components of the Future Value of $1,000 Invested at 5% for Two Years

We refer to translating a value today into a value in the future as *compounding*, whereas *discounting* is translating a future value into the present. The future value is the sum of the present value and interest:

$$\text{Future value} = \text{Present value} + \text{Interest}$$

Most financial transactions involve compound interest, though there are a few consumer transactions that use *simple interest*. Simple interest is the financing arrangement in which the amount repaid is the principal amount and interest on the principal amount. That is, interest is paid only on the principal or amount borrowed. For example, if you borrow $10,000 at 5% simple interest and repay the loan after two years, you must repay the $10,000, plus two periods' interest at 5%:

$$\text{Repayment with simple interest} = \$10,000 + [\$10,000 \times 2 \times 0.05]$$
$$= \$11,000$$

In the case of compound interest, the amount repaid has three components:

1. The amount borrowed
2. The interest on the amount borrowed
3. The interest on interest

The *basic valuation equation* is the foundation of all the financial mathematics that involves compounding, and if you understand this equation, you understand most everything in financial mathematics:

$$FV = PV(1 + i)^n$$

where: FV = the future value
PV = the present value
i = the rate of interest
n = is the number of compounding periods

The term $(1 + i)^n$ is the *compound factor*. When you multiply the value today—the present value—by the compound factor, you get the future value.

We can rearrange the basic valuation equation to solve for the present value, PV:

$$PV = FV\left[\frac{1}{(1 + i)^n}\right] = \frac{FV}{(1 + i)^n},$$

↑
Discount
factor

where $1 \div (1 + i)^n$ is the *discount factor*. When you multiply the value in the future by the discount factor, you get the present value.

In sum,

$$\frac{\text{Future}}{\text{value}} = \frac{\text{Present}}{\text{value}} \times \frac{\text{Compound}}{\text{factor}}$$

$$\frac{\text{Present}}{\text{value}} = \frac{\text{Future}}{\text{value}} \times \frac{\text{Discount}}{\text{value}}$$

The focus of this chapter is on compounding—that is, determining a value in the future. We look at discounting in the next chapter.

OF INTEREST

The word *interest* is from the Latin word *intereo*, which means "to be lost." Interest developed from the concept that lending goods or money results in a loss to the lender because he or she did not have the use of the goods or money that is loaned.

In the English language, the word *usury* is associated with lending at excessive or illegal interest rates. In earlier times, however, usury (from the Latin *usura*, meaning "to use") was the price paid for the use of money or goods.

COMPOUNDING

We begin with compounding because this is the most straightforward way of demonstrating the effects of compound interest. Consider the following example: You invest $1,000 in an account today that pays 6% interest, compounded annually. How much will you have in the account at the end of one year if you make no withdrawals? Using the subscript to indicate the year the future value is associated with, after one year you will have

$$FV_1 = \$1,000\,(1 + 0.06) = \$1,060$$

After two years, the balance is

$$FV_2 = \$1,000\,(1 + 0.06)\,(1 + 0.06) = \$1,000\,(1 + 0.06)^2$$
$$= \$1,000\,(1.1236) = \$1,123.60$$

After five years, the balance is

$$FV_5 = \$1,000\,(1 + 0.06)^5 = \$1,000\,(1.3382) = \$1,338.23$$

After 10 years, the balance is

$$FV_{10} = \$1,000\,(1 + 0.06)^{10} = \$1,000\,(1.7908) = \$1,790.85$$

You can see the accumulation of interest from interest on the principal and interest on interest over time in Exhibit 1.2.

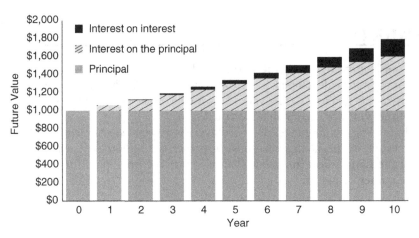

EXHIBIT 1.2   The Accumulation of Interest and Interest on Interest of a $1,000 Deposit with 6% Compound Annual Interest

If you invest $1,000 today and receive $1,790.85 at the end of 10 years, we say that you have a return of 6% on your investment. This return is an average annual return, considering compounding.

 TRY IT 1.1: SAVINGS

Suppose you deposit $1,000 in an account that earns 5% interest per year. If you do not make any withdrawals, how much will you have in the account at the end of 20 years?

What if interest was not compounded interest, but rather simple interest? Then we would have a somewhat lower balance in the account after the first year. At the end of one year, with simple interest, you will have:

$$FV_1 = \$1,000 + [\$1,000\,(0.06)] = \$1,060$$

After two years:

$$FV_2 = \$1,000 + [\$1,000\,(0.06)] + [\$1,000\,(0.06)]$$
$$= \$1,000 + [\$1,000\,(0.06)\,(2)] = \$1,120$$

FINANCIAL MATH IN ACTION

Analysts often come up with estimates of growth in revenues and earnings for publicly traded companies. We can use these estimates to make projections.

Consider the Walt Disney Company. At the end of fiscal year 2008, analysts expected Disney's earnings to grow at a rate of 12.19% per year, in the long-term.* If Disney's earnings for fiscal year 2008 were $2.2788 per share and if we concur with the analysts, we can estimate the earnings per share for fiscal years into the future. For example, the estimate for the earnings per share for 2009 is

$$\$2.2788\,(1+0.1219) = \$2.5566 \text{ per share}$$

The estimate for 2010's earnings is

$$\$2.2788\,(1+0.1219)^2 = \$2.8682 \text{ per share}$$

The estimate for 2011's earnings is

$$\$2.2788 \times (1+0.1219)^3 = \$3.2179 \text{ per share}$$

*Estimates from Reuters.com/finance, accessed December 25, 2008.

After five years:

$$FV_5 = \$1,000 + [\$1,000\,(0.06)\,(5)] = \$1,300$$

And after 10 years:

$$FV_{10} = \$1,000 + [\$1,000\,(0.06)\,(10)] = \$1,600$$

You can see the difference between compounded and simple interest in Exhibit 1.3, in which we show the growth of $1,000 at 6% using both types of interest.

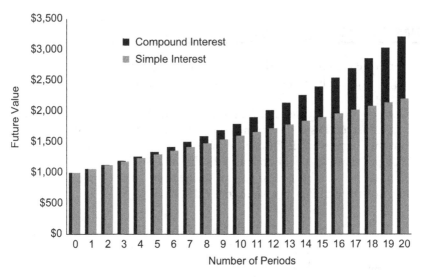

EXHIBIT 1.3   Future Value of $1,000 at a 6% Interest Rate

The difference between the future value with compounded interest and that with simple interest is the interest-on-interest. For example, at the end of 10 years the interest on interest is

Future value with compound interest	$1,790.85
Less future value with simple interest	$1,600.00
Interest on interest	$190.85

Most financial transactions involve compound interest. If the method of calculating interest is not stated, you should assume that the interest is compound interest.

Example 1.1

Suppose that you invest $100,000 today in an investment that produces a return of 5% per year. What will the investment be worth in two years? Answer: **$110,250.**

We calculate the future value at the end of the second year, FV_2, as

$$FV_2 = \$100,000 \, (1 + 0.05)^2 = \$100,000 \, (1.1025) = \$110,250$$

Example 1.2

Suppose you have a choice between two accounts, Account A and Account B. Account A provides 5% interest, compounded annually and Account B provides 5.25% simple interest. Which account provides the highest balance at the end of four years? Answer: Account A provides the higher balance at the end of four years. Consider a deposit of $10,000 today (though it really doesn't matter what the beginning balance is). What is the difference in the values of the two accounts? Answer: **$55.05.**

Account A: $FV_4 = \$10{,}000 \times (1 + 0.05)^4 = \$12{,}155.06$

Account B: $FV_4 = \$10{,}000 + (\$10{,}000 \times 0.0525 \times 4) = \$12{,}100.00$

The difference, $55.06, is the interest on interest.

 ### TRY IT 1.2: LOAN REPAYMENT

If you borrow $10,000 and the interest on the loan is 8% per year, all payable at the end of the loan, what is the amount that you must repay if the loan is for four years?

CALCULATOR AND SPREADSHEET SOLUTIONS

The calculations are easier with the help of a financial calculator or a spreadsheet program. The calculator's financial functions assume compound interest. If you want to perform a calculation with simple interest, you must rely on the mathematical programs of your calculator.

The future value of $1,000, invested for 10 years at 6%, is $1,790.85, which we can calculate using a financial calculator or a spreadsheet with the following key strokes:

TI-83/84 Using TVM Solver	HP10B	Microsoft Excel
N = 10	1000 +/− PV	=FV(0.06,10,0,−1000)
I% = 6	10 N	
PV = −1000	6 I/YR	
PMT = 0	FV	
FV = *Solve*		

CALCULATION TIP

You will notice that we changed the sign on the PV when we put this information into the calculator. This is because of the way the calculator manufacturers program the financial function: assuming that the present value is the outflow. The changing of the sign for the present value is required in most (but not all) financial calculators and spreadsheets.

In the calculators, PV is the present value, N is the number of compound periods, I% or I/YR is the interest rate per period, and FV is the future value.

In Microsoft Excel®, the future value calculation uses the worksheet function FV:

= FV (rate per period, number of periods, periodic payment,
    present value, type)

Where "type" is 0 (indicating cash flows and values occur at the end of the period).[1] Using notation similar to that found on calculators, this command becomes

=FV(i,N,PMT,PV,0)

Because there are no other cash flows in this problem, PMT (which represents periodic cash flows, such as a mortgage payment) is zero. To calculate the FV, the function requires the following inputs:

=FV(.06,10,0,−1000,0)

CALCULATION TIP

In the financial functions of your calculator, the interest rate is represented as a whole number (that is, 6 for 6%), whereas in the math functions of your calculator and in spreadsheet functions, the interest rate is input in decimal form (that is, 0.06 for 6%).

---

[1]If we leave off the 0, this is assumed to be an end-of-period value.

If we want to use the math functions instead of the financial program of a calculator, you would need to use a power key, such as y^x or $\char94$ and input the interest in decimal form:

TI-83/84	HP10B	Microsoft Excel
$(1+.06)\char94 10$	$1+.06=$	$=1000*(1.06\char94 10)$
ENTER	N y^x	
X1000	10 y^x	
ENTER	X 1000	
	ENTER	

WHY CAN'T I CALCULATE THE FUTURE VALUE WITH SIMPLE INTEREST USING MY CALCULATOR FUNCTIONS?

Calculators' time value of money programs are set up to perform calculations involving compound interest. If you want to calculate the future value using simple interest, you must resort to old-fashioned mathematics:

Simple interest = Principal amount × interest rate per period

× number of periods

or

$$\text{Simple interest} = \text{PV}\,in$$

The future value of a lump-sum if interest is computed using simple interest is, therefore

$$\text{FV}_{\text{simple}} = \text{PV} + \text{PV}\,in = \text{PV}\,(1 + in)$$

If the present value is \$1,000 and interest is simple interest at 5% per year, the future value after four periods is

$$\text{FV}_{\text{simple}} = \$1,000 + \$1,000\,(0.05)\,(4)$$

$$\text{FV}_{\text{simple}} = \$1,000\,(1 + 0.2) = \$1,200$$

The interest paid on interest in compounding is the difference between the future values with compound and simple interest.

Why not always use the financial functions in your calculator or spread-sheet? Because not every financial math problem fits neatly in the standard program and you may have to resort to the basic financial math.

We provide additional information on using calculators for financial mathematics in Appendix A. We provide additional information on using spreadsheets for financial mathematics in Appendix B.

FREQUENCY OF COMPOUNDING

If interest compounds more frequently than once per year, you need to con-sider this in any valuation problem involving compounded interest. Consider the following scenario.

You deposit $1,000 in account at the beginning of the period, and interest is 12% per year, compounded quarterly.

This means that at the end of the first quarter, the account has a balance of

$$FV_{1st\,quarter} = \$1,000 \left(1 + \frac{0.12}{4}\right) = \$1,000 \left(1 + 0.03\right) = \$1,030$$

We calculate the quarters' balances in a like manner, with interest paid on the balance in the account:

$$FV_{2nd\,quarter} = \$1,030.00 \left(1 + 0.03\right) = \$1,060.90$$
$$\Downarrow$$
$$FV_{3rd\,quarter} = \$1,060.90 \left(1 + 0.03\right) = \$1,092.73$$
$$\Downarrow$$
$$FV_{4th\,quarter} = \$1,092.73 \left(1 + 0.03\right) = \$1,125.51$$

Therefore, at the end of one year, there is a balance of $1,000 $(1 + 0.03)^4 = \$1,125.51$.

We show the growth of the funds in Exhibit 1.4.

When an interest rate is stated in terms of a rate per year, but interest is compounded more frequently than once per year, the stated annual rate is

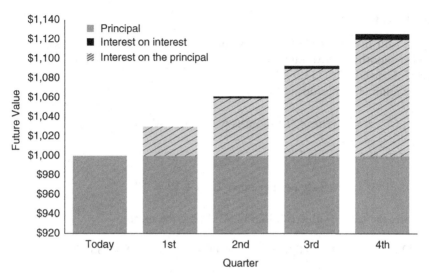

EXHIBIT 1.4 Growth of $1,000 in an Account with 12% Interest per Year, Compounding Quarterly

referred to as the *annual percentage rate* (APR), but the actual calculation requires using the rate per compound period and the number of compound periods. For example, if a loan of $5,000 for three years has an APR of 10% and interest compounds semi-annually, the calculation of the future value at the end of three years uses:

$$i = \text{rate per compound period}$$

$$= 10\% \div 2 = 5\% \text{ per six months}$$

$$n = \text{number of compounding periods}$$

$$= 2 \text{ per year} \times 3 \text{ years} = 6 \text{ periods}$$

and, therefore,

$$FV_3 = \$5,000 \, (1 + 0.05)^6 = \$6,700.48$$

Notice that this future value is more than if we had ignored compounding of interest within a year, which would have produced a future value of $5,000 (1 + 0.10)^3 = $6,655.

Example 1.3

Suppose you invest $20,000 in an account that pays 12% interest, compounded monthly. How much do you have in the account at the end of 5 years? Answer: **$36,333.93.**

The number of periods is 60:

$$n = 5 \text{ years} \times 12 \text{ months per year} = 60 \text{ months}$$

and the rate per period is 1%:

$$i = \text{Rate per period} = 12\% \div 12 = 1\%$$

Therefore, the future value is $36,333.93. Using the math,

$$\text{FV} = \$20,000\,(1 + 0.01)^{60} = \$20,000\,(1.8167) = \$36,333.93$$

Using the financial calculator or spreadsheet time value of money functions:

TI-83/84	HP10B	Excel
PV −20000	20000 +/− PV	=FV(.01,60,0,−20000,0)
I 1	1 I/YR	
N 60	60 N	
FV Solve	FV	

 ## TRY IT 1.3: FREQUENCY

Suppose you have a choice of borrowing $1 million with the following terms, with interest paid at the end of the loan:

10% APR, quarterly interest

10.5% APR, semi-annual interest

11% APR, annual interest

Under which loan terms would you have the largest payment at the end of four years?

FINANCIAL MATH IN ACTION

Credit card companies allow customers with balances to pay a minimum amount, instead of the full amount each month. What remains unpaid accumulates interest at sometimes quite high interest rates. Suppose you have charged $1,000 and choose to pay the minimum balance of 2% at the end of each month. And suppose your credit card company charges 29.99% APR interest, with monthly compounding.

How much will you owe after using the strategy of paying the minimum? Interest on unpaid balances is 29.99% ÷ 12 = 2.4992% per month:

Month From Now	Starting Balance	Interest for the Month	Balance Owed	Minimum Payment	Ending Balance
1	$1,000.00			$20.00	$980.00
2	$980.00	$24.49	$1,004.49	$20.09	$984.40
3	$984.40	$24.60	$1,009.00	$20.18	$988.82
4	$988.82	$24.71	$1,013.54	$20.27	$993.27
5	$993.27	$24.82	$1,018.09	$20.36	$997.73
6	$997.73	$24.93	$1,022.66	$20.45	$1,002.21
7	$1,002.21	$25.05	$1,027.26	$20.55	$1,006.71
8	$1,006.71	$25.16	$1,031.87	$20.64	$1,011.23
9	$1,011.23	$25.27	$1,036.50	$20.73	$1,015.77
10	$1,015.77	$25.39	$1,041.16	$20.82	$1,020.34
11	$1,020.34	$25.50	$1,045.84	$20.92	$1,024.92
12	$1,024.92	$25.61	$1,050.53	$21.01	$1,029.52

In other words, you will end up owing more at the end of the month.

What we have seen so far with respect to compounding is discrete or periodic compounding. However, many financial transactions, including credit card financing, involve *continuous compounding*. This is the extreme of the frequency of compounding, because interest compounds instantaneously. If interest compounds continuously, the compound factor uses the exponential function, e, which is the inverse of the natural logarithm.[2] The compound factor for continuous compounding requires the stated rate per year (that is, the APR) and the number of years:

$$e^{(\text{Annual interest rate}) \times (\text{Number of years})} = e^{\text{APR } n}$$

If annual interest is 10%, continuously compounded, the compound factor for one year is

$$e^{0.10} = 1.1052$$

For two years, the factor is

$$e^{0.10 \times 2} = e^{0.20} = 1.2214$$

For 10 years, the factor is

$$e^{0.10 \times 10} = e^1 = 2.7183$$

The formula for the future value of an amount with continuous compounding is:

$$FV = PV\left[e^{\text{APR } n}\right]$$

The compound factor is $e^{\text{APR } n}$.

You can view continuous compounding as the limit of compounding frequency. Consider a \$1 million deposited in an account for five years, where this accounts pays 10% interest. With annual compounding, this deposit grows to

$$FV_{5,\text{ annual compounding}} = \$1,610,510$$

With continuous compounding, this deposit grows to

$$FV_{5,\text{ continuous compounding}} = \$1,648,721$$

You can see the difference between annual compounding and continuous compounding in Exhibit 1.5. At the end of 40 years, the difference between continuous compounding and annual compounding is over \$9 million.

---

[2]The "e" in the exponential function is also referred to as Euler's e, or the base of the natural logarithm. The numerical value of e truncated to 10 decimal places is 2.7182818284. We will see more of Euler's e in Chapter 4.

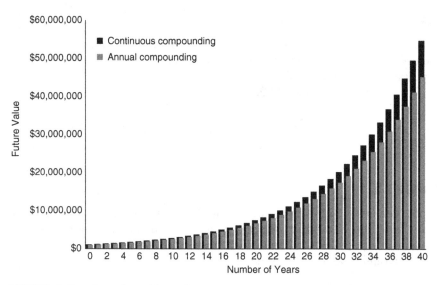

EXHIBIT 1.5 The Value of $1 Million at 10% Interest, Compounded Annually vs. Continuously

Using a calculator, you can find e^x in the math functions. For example, suppose you want to calculate the future value of $1,000 invested five years at 4%, with interest compounded continuously. The future value is:

$$FV_5 = \$1,000\ e^{0.04 \times 5} = \$1,000\ e^{0.2} = \$1,000\ (1.2214) = \$1,221.40$$

Using Microsoft Excel, you use the exponential worksheet function, EXP:

$$= 1,000 * EXP(0.04 * 5)$$

where the value in parentheses is the exponent.

CALCULATION TIP

The programmers of financial calculator and spreadsheet financial functions set these up for discrete compounding. You will need to use the math functions of the calculator or the spreadsheet to perform calculations for continuous compounding.

Example 1.4

Suppose you invest $1,000 today in an account that pays 9% interest, compounded continuously. What will be the value in this account at the end of ten years? Answer: **$2,459.60.**

The future value is $2,459.60:

$$FV = \$1,000 \, e^{0.09 \times 10} = \$1,000 \, e^{0.9}$$
$$= \$1,000 \, (2.4596) = \$2,459.60$$

Example 1.5

Suppose you invest $5,000 in an account that earns 10% interest. How much more would you have after 20 years if interest compounds continuously instead of compounded semi-annually? Answer: **$1,745.34.**

You would have $1,745.34 more:

$$FV_{\text{continuously}} = \$5,000 \, e^{0.1 \times 20}$$
$$= \$5,000 \, (7.3891) = \$36,945.28$$
$$FV_{\text{semiannually}} = \$5,000 \, (1 + 0.05)^{40}$$
$$= \$5,000 \, (7.0400) = \$35,199.94$$
$$\text{Difference} = \$36,945.28 - 35,199.94 = \$1,745.34$$

 TRY IT 1.4: CONTINUOUS COMPOUNDING

If you borrow $10,000 and the interest on the loan is 8% per year, compounded continuously, what is the amount that you must repay at the end of four years?

SUMMARY

Understanding how compounding works helps you understand financial transactions, including how investments grow in value over time. The basic valuation equation, $FV = PV \, (1 + i)^n$, is the foundation of all of the financial math that you'll encounter in finance. What we will do in the following chapters is build upon this basic valuation equation, and help you to understand how to translate future values to the present, calculate the yield or return on investments, calculate effective interest rates, amortize a loan, and value stocks and bonds.

Throughout this book, we show you how to use the fundamental math behind the calculations, as well as the financial calculator and spreadsheet functions. While calculators and spreadsheets are very helpful, it is also important to understand the underlying math—because you might just encounter a financial transaction that doesn't fit neatly into one of these functions.

"TRY IT" SOLUTIONS

1.1. Savings

$$\text{Amount on deposit} = \$1,000 \, (1 + 0.05)^{20} = \$2,653.30$$

1.2. Loan Repayment

$$\text{Amount of repayment} = \$10,000(1 + 0.08)^4 = \$13,604.89$$

Using a financial calculator: $PV = -10000; i\% = 8, n = 4.$Solve for FV

1.3. Frequency of Compounding
The 10.5% with semiannual compounding requires the largest repayment:

$$FV_{10\% \text{ APR, quarterly compounding}} = \$1,000,000(1 + 0.025)^{16}$$
$$= \$1,484,505$$
$$FV_{10.5\% \text{ APR, semiannual compounding}} = \$1,000,000(1 + 0.0525)^8$$
$$= \$1,505,833$$
$$FV_{10.75\% \text{ APR, annual compounding}} = \$1,000,000(1 + 0.1075)^4$$
$$= \$1,504,440$$

1.4. Continuous Compounding

$$\text{Amount of repayment} = \$10,000 \, e^{(0.08)(4)} = \$10,000 \, e^{0.32}$$
$$= \$13,771.28$$

PROBLEMS

1.1. If you invest $10,000 in an account that pays 4% interest, compounded quarterly, how much will be in the account at the end of five years if you make no withdrawals?

1.2. If you invest $2,000 in an account that pays 12% per year, compounded monthly, how much will be in the account at the end of six years if you do not make any withdrawals?

1.3. Suppose you invest $3,000 in an account that pays interest at the rate of 8% per year, compounded semi-annually. How much will you have in the account at the end of five years if you do not make any withdrawals?

1.4. Suppose you invest $100 for 20 years in an account that pays 2% per year, compounded quarterly.
  a. How much will you have in the account at the end of 20 years?
  b. How much interest on interest will be in the account at the end of 20 years?

1.5. If you deposit $100 in an account that pays 4% interest, compounded annually, what is the balance in the account at the end of three years if you withdraw only the interest on the interest each year?

1.6. Suppose you invest €100 today in an investment that yields 5% per year, compounded annually. How much will you have in the account at the end of six years?

1.7. Which investment of $10,000 will provide the larger value after four years:
  a. Investment A earns 5% interest, compounded semiannually.
  b. Investment B earns 4.8% interest, compounded continuously.

1.8. What will be the value in an account at the end of 12 years if you deposit $100 today and the account earns 6% interest, compounded annually?

1.9. What will be the value in an account at the end of six years if you deposit $100 today and the account earns 12% interest, compounded annually?

1.10. What will be the value in an account at the end of 10 years if you deposit $1,000 today and the account earns 7% interest, compounded continuously?

For solutions to these problems, see Appendix E.

CHAPTER 2

Don't Discount Discounting

Remember, that money is of the prolific, generating nature. Money can beget money, and its offspring can beget more, and so on.

—Benjamin Franklin,
Advice to a Young Tradesman (1748)

Much of what is done in valuing an asset, a company, a share of stock, or a bond, involves translating a future value to the present. We refer to translating a value back in time as *discounting*, which requires determining what a future amount or cash flow is worth today. Discounting is used in valuation because we often want to determine the value today of some future value or cash flow (e.g., what a bond is worth today if it promised interest and principal repayment in the future).

DISCOUNTING

The equation for the present value is a rearrangement of the basic valuation equation that we saw earlier, in Chapter 1:

$$PV = \frac{FV}{(1+i)^n},$$

where: PV = the present value (today's value)
FV = the future value (a value or cash flow sometime in the future)
i = the interest rate per period
n = the number of compounding periods

From this formula for the present value we know that:

- As the number of discount periods, n, becomes larger, the discount factor becomes smaller and the present value becomes less.

■ As the interest rate per period, i, becomes larger, the discount factor becomes smaller and the present value becomes less.

The discount rate is similar in concept to the interest rate in compounding values into the future—but with discounting, we are bringing values from the future to the present. For example, if you have some funds you want to put into an account today so that you have a specific balance in an account at a given time in the future, the discount rate is the interest rate that you would have to earn on the funds you set aside today so that you reach this goal.

In investing, the discount rate represents the *opportunity cost of funds*—that is, what you could have earned for the same level of risk. In other words, what else could you have done with the money?

i, r, k ... WHAT'S THE DIFFERENCE?

In this book, we use the lowercase "*i*" to indicate the interest rate. If you look at other books and web site documents related to our topic, you will see other notations for the interest rate, including r for return or the required rate of return, and k for the cost of capital. These really represent the same concept: the time value of money.

We use "*i*" (despite our word processor's attempt to turn every lowercase *i* into the first-person singular pronoun, "*I*") to keep it simple and to remind you that it means interest. When we refer to the calculator functions, we use the notation that is closest to what appears on the calculator key, which is often I/YR.

We represent the time value of money by different notations, and by different names, depending on the application. For example:

Name	Common Application
Interest rate	Compounding
Discount rate	Discounting
Required rate of return	Return expected by investors, used in valuing securities, such as stocks and bonds
Cost of capital	Evaluating capital investments (e.g., buying a new plant), reflecting the cost of funds provided by bondholders and shareholders
Opportunity cost of funds	Evaluating competing investment opportunities

Example 2.1

Suppose that you wish to have $20,000 saved by the end of six years. And suppose you deposit funds today in an account that pays 3% interest, compounded annually. How much must you deposit today to meet your goal?

You are given: FV = $20,000; $n = 6$; $i = 3\%$.

Solve for the present value, PV:

$$PV = \$20,000 \div (1 + 0.03)^6 = \$20,000 \div 1.1941 = \$16,749.69$$

Example 2.2

Suppose that you wish to have $1 million forty years from now. If you deposit funds today in an account that pays 5% interest, compounded annually, what amount must you deposit today to reach your goal? You are given the following data inputs:

FV = $1,000,000
$n = 40$
$i = 5\%$

The present value is

$$PV = \$1,000,000 \div (1 + 0.05)^{40} = \$142,045.68$$

Looking at this same concept in terms of the opportunities, consider the type of problem in which you are promised a specific amount of funds at some future point in time. How much would you be willing to pay now for this investment considering what you could otherwise do with these funds in terms of investing? For example, suppose someone offered you an investment that would pay a lump sum of €10,000 five years from today. If your opportunity cost of funds is 5%, you should be willing to pay

$$PV = €10,000 \div (1 + 0.05)^5 = €10,000 \div 1.2763 = €7,835.26.$$

To check this, consider the investment of €7.835.26 for five years in an account that pays 5% interest. The future value is

$$FV = €7,835.26 \times (1 + 0.05)^5 = €10,000$$

If instead of 5%, your opportunity cost is 10%, the present value of this investment is

$$PV = €10,000 \div (1 + 0.10)^5 = €10,000 \div 1.6105 = €6,209.21$$

The discount rate affects the present value: the greater the discount rate, the lower the present value. The number of periods also affects the present value: the greater the number of discount periods, the lower the present value.

Consider another problem. Suppose we discount $1 million to the present. If we discount this $1 million for five periods at 4%, the present value is

$$PV = \frac{\$1,000,000}{(1 + 0.04)^5} = \frac{\$1,000,000}{1.2167} = \$821,927.11$$

Discounting this same future value 10 periods at 4% produces a smaller present value:

$$PV = \frac{\$1,000,000}{(1 + 0.04)^{10}} = \frac{\$1,000,000}{1.4802} = \$675,564.17$$

We graph the present value of $1 million for different numbers of discount periods in Exhibit 2.1. As you can see in this graph, the slope of the relation between the present value and the number of discount periods is steeper, the greater the discount rate

We also graph the present value of $1 million for a different number of periods in Exhibit 2.2. As you can see in this Exhibit 2.2, the greater the number of discount periods, the more sensitive is the present value to the discount rate.

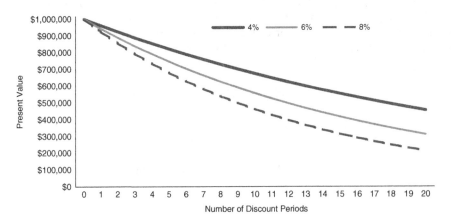

EXHIBIT 2.1   Present Value of $1 Million for a Different Number of Discount Periods and Different Discount Rates

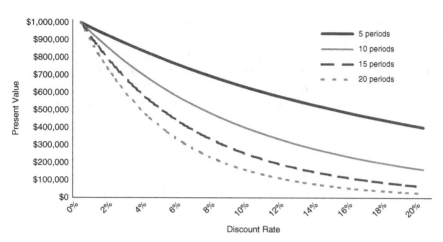

EXHIBIT 2.2   Present Value of $1 Million for a Different Number of Discount Periods and Different Discount Rates

Calculator and Spreadsheet Solutions

Calculate the present value of $6,000 to be received in eight years if the interest rate is 5% per year:

$$PV = \frac{\$6,000}{(1.05)^8} = \$4,061.04$$

The present value is $4,061.04. Using a financial calculator or spreadsheet, we need to input the number of periods, the interest rate, and the future value. In Microsoft Excel® we use the present value function:

$$= PV(RATE, NPER, PMT, FV, type)$$

where: RATE = the interest rate, stated in decimal form
NPER = the number of periods
PMT = 0 in this case because we are assuming no other cash flows
FV = the future value
type = reflects the timing (0 or end of period, the usual assumption, and 1 for the beginning of the period)

The last argument in the function, *type*, is optional. If you leave this off the list of arguments, the program assumes that the cash flows occur at the end of the period instead of the beginning of the period.

When you use a calculator, the order in which you enter the known values of PV, i, n, and so on, does not matter. However, when using a spreadsheet function, it is important to enter the arguments (the rate, the number of periods, etc.), in order. Providing the inputs in the wrong order will guarantee a wrong answer.

Using our notation, the present value function in Microsoft Excel is

$$= \text{PV}(i, n, \text{PMT}, \text{FV}, \text{type})$$

Using financial calculators or a spreadsheet, the calculation of the present value of \$6,000 discounted eight periods at 5% is the following:

TI-83/84 Using TVM Solver	HP10B	Microsoft Excel
N = 8	8 N	=PV(.05,8,0,60000,0)
I% = 5	5 I/YR	
FV = 6000	6000 FV	
PMT = 0	PV	
PV = Solve		

If you are using a financial calculator or spreadsheet, you will notice that the calculated present value is displayed as a negative number. This has to do with the way the program is written for the calculator; it is written such that $0 = \text{FV} - \text{PV}(1 + i)^n$. Think of the calculation in the following way: If you invest \$4,061.04 (which is a cash outflow) today, you get \$6,000 in the future (which is a cash inflow). We will refer to values in the positive, but if you are using a calculator or spreadsheet, you will need to mentally or actually multiply the resulting present value by negative one for a cleaner interpretation.

CALCULATION TIP

If you want to take a value to power (e.g., 1.05^8), you generally key in the base (e.g., 1.05) and then use the key marked as $\wedge$ or y^x: $(1 + 0.05)^8 = 1.4775$. To invert a value (e.g., $1 \div 1.4775$), use the key marked 1/x: $1 \div 1.4775 = 0.6768$.

TRY IT 2.1: DISCOUNTING

What is the value today of $500,000 to be received in 10 years, with an interest rate of 7 percent?

Frequency of Compounding

Suppose that interest compounds more frequently than annually. We must therefore adjust both i and n to reflect this more frequent compounding. Consider an example: calculate the present value of $10,000 due at the end of five years if the annual interest rate is 6 percent, compounded semiannually. If the annual rate is 6 percent, the semiannual rate is 6% ÷ 2 = 3%. The number of semiannual periods is five years × 2 times per year = 10. Therefore, the present value of this $10,000 is

$$PV = \$10,000 \div (1 + 0.03)^{10} = \$10,000 \div 1.3439$$

$$= \$10,000 \times 0.7441 = \$7,440.94$$

TRY IT 2.2: DISCOUNTING AND FREQUENCY OF COMPOUNDING

Which of the following requires the least amount of a deposit today?

- A balance of $10,000, four years from today that has grown from a sum deposited in an account that pays 8 percent interest, compounded quarterly.
- A balance of $10,000, five years from today that has grown from a sum deposited in an account that pays 7 percent interest, compounded annually.
- A balance of $10,000, 10 years from today that has grown from a sum deposited in an account that pays 4 percent interest, compounded continuously.
- A balance of $10,000, eight years from today that has grown from a sum deposited in an account that pays 4 percent interest, compounded semiannually.

If interest compounds continuously, the present value is

$$PV = \frac{FV}{e^{APRn}}$$

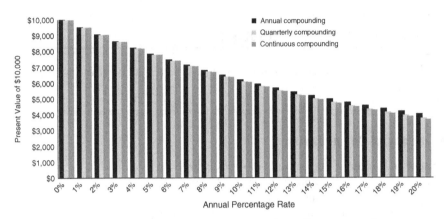

EXHIBIT 2.3 Discounting $10,000 for Five Years for Different Annual Percentage Rates and Different Frequencies of Compounding

where APR is the annual percentage rate, n is the number of years, and e is the base of the natural logarithm. For example, what is the present value of $10,000 due at the end of five years if the interest rate is 6%, compounded continuously? The answer is $7,408.18, that is,

$$PV = \$10,000 \div e^{0.06 \times 5} = \$10,000 \div e^{0.30}$$
$$= \$10,000 \div 1.3499 = \$10,000 \times 0.7408 = \$7,408.18$$

We can see the difference the frequency of compounding makes in Exhibit 2.3, in which we expand this last example to include quarterly and continuous compounding. For a given annual percentage rate, the greater the frequency of compounding, the greater is the effective interest rate and the smaller is the present value. But as you can also see in the Exhibit 2.3, the difference may be quite small.

Example 2.3

How much would you have to deposit today in an account that pays 4% annual interest, compounded quarterly, if you wish to have a balance of $100,000 at the end of 10 years? You are given the following data inputs:

FV = \$100,000
$i = 4\% \div 4 = 1\%$
$n = 10 \times 4 = 40$ quarters
$PV = \$100,000 \div (1+0.01)^{40} = \$100,000 \,(0.6717) = \$67,165.31$

Example 2.4

How much would you have to deposit today in an account that pays 4% annual interest, compounded continuously, if you wish to have a balance of $100,000 at the end of 10 years? You are given the following information:

$$FV = \$100,000$$
$$i = 4\%$$
$$n = 10 \text{ years}$$
$$PV = \$100,000 \div e^{0.04 \times 10} = \$100,000\ (0.67032) = \$67,032$$

Example 2.5

Suppose you have two investment opportunities that promise $1 million in 20 years:

Investment A: A return of 6% per year, compounded monthly.

Investment B: A return of 5.8% per year, compounded continuously.

Which investment requires a larger investment today to reach your goal? Answer: **Investment B.**

$$PV_A = \$1,000,000 \div (1 + (0.06/12))^{240} = \$302,096.14$$
$$PV_B = \$1,000,000 \times \left(e^{0.058 \times 20}\right) = \$313,486.18$$

 TRY IT 2.3: DISCOUNTING WITH CONTINUOUS COMPOUNDING

Consider an investment, Investment X, which is a promise to pay $10,000 five years from now. You are comparing this investment with another investment, Investment Y, of similar risk, that is a promised yield of 6% per year, compounded continuously, over the same time. What would you be willing to pay for Investment X so that you are indifferent between Investment X and Y? In other words, what would the present value of Investment X have to be to have equivalent value to Investment Y?

DISCOUNTING MORE THAN ONE FUTURE VALUE

In many cases, we need to discount more than one future amount to determine the value of some investment. For example, in the case of a stock, the value of the stock depends on the expected future dividends. As another example, the value of a bond is the present value of the interest and repayment of bond principal expected in the future.

Consider an investment that promises €1,000 at the end of one year, €2,000 at the end of two years, and €3,000 at the end of three years. If the discount rate is 5%, what is the value of this investment today?

Diagramming these cash flows, we see the following:

Today	1	2	3	Period
	€1,000	€2,000	€3,000	Cash flow

Discounting each the cash flows for the appropriate number of periods results in a value today for the investment of €5,357.95:

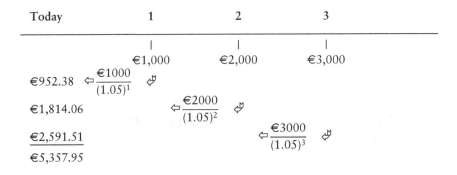

To check our work, we could recognize that discounting these cash flows to the present is equivalent to first determining what these cash flows are worth at the end of three years—similar to a savings problem—and then discounting this value to the present. The future value of the cash flows in this example is:

Cash Flow	Future Value
€1,000	€1,102.50
€2,000	2,100.00
€3,000	3,000.00
Total	€6,202.50

Discounting the €6,202.50 three periods at 5% produces a present value of €5,357.95. What this check on our work shows is that implicit in the discounting calculation is an assumption that when you receive cash flows from an investment, we are assuming that we reinvest these cash flows into another investment that yields the same return—in this case 5%.

Example 2.6

Suppose a friend wants to borrow some money from you and is willing to pay you back $5,000 two years from now and then $7,000 four years from today. If your opportunity cost of funds is 5% (that is, what you could have earned on the money in an investment with similar risk to a loan to your friend), how much are you willing to lend your friend? Answer: $10,194.07.

Period	Cash Flow	Calculation	Present Value
1	$0		$0
2	$5,000	$\dfrac{\$5,000}{(1+0.05)^2}$	4,435.15
3	$0		0
4	$7,000	$\dfrac{\$7,000}{(1+0.05)^4}$	5,758.92
Total			$10,194.07

Calculator Solutions

The calculation of the present value of more than one cash flow is easier with built-in programs. The present value of more than one future cash flow is the net present value.

Using the calculator to determine the value today of a series of future cash flows is straightforward. In a calculator, this requires identifying the cash flows in the future in chronological order. If there are periods in the future in which there are no cash flows, then this needs to be included in the series of cash flows.

Consider the following series of cash flows:

End of Period	Cash Flow
1	$1,000
2	$0
3	$5,000
4	$0
5	$6,000

Texas Instruments TI 83/84 In the TI 83/84 calculators, you create a series consisting of the set of cash flows. Once you save these in the calculator, you then apply the NPV function. What you enter in the NPV function is the following:

$$NPV(5, 0, \{1000,0,500,0,6000\})$$

where the first argument is the whole percentage interest rate, the next argument is the cash flow today (which is zero in this example), and the last argument is the list of cash flows. Alternatively to creating the list using the {} and STO, you can use the LIST function and enter the cash flows as a list and then use the NPV function that resides in the APPS.

Hewlett-Packard HP 10B In the HP10B, you need to input these cash flows one at a time, including the zero cash flows, and then use the NPV function to solve for the present value. Note that we must enter the initial cash flow, that is, today's cash flow, first, followed by each successive period's cash flows.

Microsoft Excel In Microsoft Excel, the function is similar to that used in the TI83/84. You type the values of the cash flows into adjacent cells, then use the NPV function, including the discount rate as the first argument, followed by the list of the cash flows or the reference to the cells that contain the cash flows.[1]

TI-83/84 Using NPV function	HP10B	Microsoft Excel		
2nd {1000,0,5000,0,6000	0 CFj		A	B
STO 2nd L1	1000 CFj	1	Period	Cash flow
ENTER	0 CFj	2	1	$1,000
APPS	5000 CFj	3	2	$0
1:Finance ENTER	0 CFj	4	3	$5,000
7:NPV ENTER	6000 CFj	5	4	$0
5, 2nd L1)	5 i	6	5	$6,000
ENTER	NPV	7	NPV	← = NPV(.05,B3:b7)

---

[1]If there is an initial cash flow (that is, one today), we subtract it after the NPV calculation. For example, if this investment requires a $5,000 initial investment, the net present value would be calculated as: =NPV(0.05,B3:B7) − 5,000.

For more information on using financial calculators, see Appendix A. For more information on using spreadsheet financial functions, see Appendix B.

 TRY IT 2.4: DISCOUNTING WITH MORE THAN ONE CASH FLOW

Joe says that he can pay you $1,000 after one year and $2,000 after three years. If your opportunity cost of funds is 5%, how much are you willing to lend to Joe?

DETERMINING THE NUMBER OF COMPOUNDING PERIODS

Let's say that you place $1,000 in a savings account that pays 10% compounded interest per year. How long would it take the savings account balance to reach $5,000? In this case, we know the present value (PV = $1,000), the future value (FV = $5,000), and the interest rate ($i = 10\%$ per year). What we need to determine is the number of compounding periods.

Start with the basic valuation equation and insert the known values of PV, FV, and i:

$$FV = PV (1 + i)^n$$
$$\$5,000 = \$1,000 (1 + 0.10)^n$$

Rearranging,

$$(1 + 0.10)^n = 5.000$$

Therefore, the compound factor is 5.0000.

We can determine the number of periods either mathematically or by using a financial calculator.[2] Solving the equation mathematically, we start with the following:

$$5 = (1 + 0.10)^n$$

---

[2] In the "olden" days, we used a table of factors to approximate the number of periods We would look at the discount factors and find the factor for 10% interest that is closest to the factor of 5.

We must somehow rearrange this equation so that the unknown value, n, is on one side of the equation and all the known values are on the other. To do this, we must use logarithms and a bit of algebra. Taking the natural log of both sides,

$$\ln 5 = n \times \ln(1 + 0.10)$$

or

$$\ln 5 = n \times \ln 1.10$$

where "ln" indicates the natural log. Substituting the values of the natural logs of 5 and 1.10, which we can calculate using most any calculator, we arrive at

$$1.6094 = n \times 0.0953.$$

Rearranging and solving for n,

$$n = 16.8877$$

which means 17 whole compound periods.

Because the last interest payment is at the end of the last year, the number of periods is 17—it would take 17 years for your $1,000 investment to grow to $5,000 if interest is compounded at 10% per year.

We can develop an equation for determining the number of periods, beginning with the valuation formula:

$$FV = PV\,(1 + i)^n,$$

Using algebra and principles of logarithms,

$$n = \frac{\ln FV - \ln PV}{\ln (1+i)}$$

Suppose that the present value of an investment is $100 and you wish to determine how long it will take for the investment to double in value if the investment earns 6% per year, compounded annually:

$$n = \frac{\ln 200 - \ln 100}{\ln (1 + 0.06)} = 11.8885 \Rightarrow 12 \text{ years}$$

Notice that we round off to the next whole period. To see why, consider this last example. After 11.8885 years, we have doubled our money if interest were paid 88.85% all the way through the twelfth year. But, we stated earlier that interest is paid at the end of each period—not part of the way through. At the end of the eleventh year, our investment is worth \$189.93, and at the end of the twelfth year, our investment is worth \$201.22. So our investment's value doubles by the twelfth period—with a little extra, \$1.22.

But, of course, we could resort to using our financial calculator or spreadsheet functions to arrive at the number of periods:

TI-83/84 Using TVM Solver	HP10B	Microsoft Excel
PV = −100	100 +/−PV	=NPER(.06,0,−100,200,0)
PMT = 0	200 FV	
FV = 200	6 *i*/YR	
I% = 6	N	
N = Solve		

Example 2.7

How long does it take to double your money if the interest rate is 5% per year, compounded annually? Answer: **15 years.**

$$Inputs : PV = \$1; \ FV = \$2; \ i = 5\%$$

Solving for *n*:

$$n = (\ln 2 - \ln 1) \div \ln 1.05$$
$$= (0.6931 - 0) \div 0.0488$$
$$= 14.2029 \Rightarrow 15 \text{ years}$$

Example 2.8

How long does it take to triple your money if the interest rate is 5% per year, compounded annually? Answer: **23 years.**

Inputs: PV = \$1; FV = \$3; *i* = 5%

Solving for *n*:

$$n = (\ln 3 - \ln 1) \div \ln 1.05$$
$$= (1.0986 - 0) \div 0.0488$$
$$= 22.5123 \text{ years} \Rightarrow 23 \text{ years}$$

Example 2.9

How long does it take to double your money if the interest rate is 12% per year, compounded quarterly? Answer: **6 years.**

$$\textit{Inputs}: \text{PV} = \$1; \ \text{FV} = \$2; \ i = 12\% \div 4 = 3\%$$

Solving for n:

$$n = (0.6931 - 0) \div 0.0296$$

$$= 23.4155 \text{ quarters} \Rightarrow 24 \text{ quarters} = 6 \text{ years}$$

 TRY IT 2.5: ARE WE THERE YET?

Suppose you deposit $1,000 in an account paying 9% APR interest, with monthly compounding. How long will it take this deposit to grow, with interest, to reach $10,000?

SUMMARY

The discounting of future values is the foundation of valuation. We use discounting to determine how much we are willing to pay to receive a future amount or how much we need to deposit in an account today to achieve some savings goal. The rate at which we discount relates to the opportunity cost of funds. The greater this opportunity cost, the lower the present value. If the discount rate involves compounding of interest more than once within an annual period, the present value must reflect this compounding.

"TRY IT" SOLUTIONS

2.1. Discounting
Inputs: $i = 7\%$, $n = 10$; FV = 500,000. Solve for the present value: PV = **$254,174.65**

2.2. Discounting and the Frequency of Compounding
The continuous compounding arrangement has the smallest present value:
a. $\text{PV}_a = \$10,000 \div (1 + 0.02)^{16} = \$7,284.46$

    b. $PV_b = \$10,000 \div (1 + 0.07)^5 = \$7,129.86$
    c. $PV_c = \$10,000 \div e^{(0.04)(10)} = \$6,703.20$
    d. $PV_d = \$10,000 \div (1 + 0.02)^{16} = \$7,284.46$
2.3. Discounting with Continuous Compounding
    PV of Investment $X = \$10,000 \div e^{0.06 \times 5} = \$10,000 \div 1.34986 = \$7,409.18$
2.4. Discounting with More Than One Cash Flow
    $PV = [\$1,000 \div 1.05] + [\$3,000 \times (1.05)^3] = \$952.38 + 2,591.51 = \$3,543.89$
2.5. Are We There Yet?
    $PV = \$1,000; i = 9\% \div 12 = 0.75\%; FV = \$10,000$

    $n = [\ln (10,000) - \ln (1000)] \div \ln (1 + 0.0075)$

    $= [9.21034 - 6.90776] \div 0.007472 = 308.16$ months $\Rightarrow$ 309 months

    $= $ **25 years, 9 months**

PROBLEMS

2.1. Complete the following, solving for the present value, PV:

Case	Future Value	Interest Rate	Number of Periods	Present Value
A	$10,000	5.0%	5	_____
B	¥563,000	4.0%	20	_____
C	$5,000	5.5%	3	_____

2.2. Suppose you want to have $0.5 million saved by the time you reach age 30, and suppose that you are 20 years old today. If you can earn 5% on your funds, how much would you have to invest today to reach your goal?

2.3. How much would I have to deposit in an account today that pays 12% interest, compounded quarterly, so that I have a balance of $20,000 in the account at the end of 10 years?

2.4. Suppose I want to be able to withdraw $5,000 at the end of five years and withdraw $6,000 at the end of six years, leaving a zero balance in the account after the last withdrawal. If I can earn 5% on my balances, how much must I deposit today to satisfy my withdrawals needs?

2.5. Using an interest rate of 5% per year, what is the value today of the following cash flows:

Years from Today	Cash Flow
1	£0
2	£0
3	£10,000
4	£10,000

2.6. Which of the following series has the highest present value, assuming an annual interest rate of 5%?

Series	End of First Year	End of Second Year	End of Third Year
A	€0	€0	€500
B	€165	€165	€165
C	€470	€0	€0

2.7. What is the present value of $500 to be received in two years if the interest rate is 4% per year and:
- Compounds daily?
- Compounds continuously?

2.8. What is the present value of £5 million to be received in 10 years if interest is 12% compounded monthly?

2.9. What is the present value of $6,000 to be received in 10 years if interest is 6%, compounded continuously?

2.10. What is the present value of $10,000 to be received in three years if the interest rate is 5%?

For solutions to these problems, see Appendix E.

CHAPTER 3

Cash Happens

Price is what you pay. Value is what you get.

—Warren Buffett

When you value an investment, you compare the benefits of the investment with its cost. The process of valuation involves estimating future cash inflows and outflows, and discounting these future cash flows to the present at a discount rate that reflects the uncertainty of these cash flows. Another way of evaluating investments is to answer the question: Given its cost and its expected future benefits, what return will a particular investment provide? We will look at how to calculate the value and the return on investments, focusing on stocks in this reading.

Suppose your investment advisor suggests the following investment opportunity: Invest $900 today, and you will receive $1,000 one year from today. Whether or not this is a good deal depends on:

- What you could have done with the $900 instead of investing it with the investment advisor.
- How uncertain are you that the investment advisor will pay the $1,000 in one year.

If your other opportunities with the same amount of uncertainty provide a return of 10%, is this loan a good investment? There are two ways to evaluate this. First, you can figure out what you could have wound up with after one year, investing your $900 at 10%:

- Value at end of one year = $900 + (10% of $900).
- Value at end of one year = $900 (1 + 0.10).
- Value at end of one year = $990.

Because the $1,000 promised is more than $990, you are better off with the investment the advisor offers you.

Another way of looking at this is to figure out what the $1,000 promised in the future is worth today. To calculate its present value, we must discount the $1,000 at some rate. The rate we'll use is our opportunity cost of funds, which in this case is 10%:

$$\text{Value today of \$1,000 in one year} = \frac{\$1,000}{(1+0.10)^1} = \$909.09$$

This means that you consider $909.09 today to be worth the same as $1,000 in one year. In other words, if you invested $909.09 today in an investment that yields 10%, you end up with $1,000 in one year. Since today's value of the receipt of $1,000 in the future is $909.09 and it only costs $900 to get into this deal, the investment is attractive: It costs less than what you have determined it is worth.

Because there are two ways to look at this, through its future value or through its present value, which way should you go? While both approaches get you to the same decision, it is usually easier in terms of the present value of the investment.

VALUING A STREAM OF FUTURE CASH FLOWS

We can generalize this relationship a bit more. Let CF_t represent the cash flow from the investment in period t, so that CF_1 is the cash flow at the end of period 1, CF_2 is the cash flow at the end of period 2, and so on, until the last cash flow at the end of period N, CF_N. If the investment produces cash flows for a finite number of periods, N, and the discount rate is i, the value of the investment, the present value, is

$$\text{Present value of investment} = \frac{CF_1}{(1+i)^1} + \frac{CF_2}{(1+i)^2}$$
$$+ \frac{CF_3}{(1+i)^3} + \ldots + \frac{CF_N}{(1+i)^N},$$

which we can write more compactly as

$$PV = \sum_{t=1}^{N} \frac{CF_t}{(1+i)^t}$$

Suppose you have an opportunity to buy an asset expected to give you $500 in one year and $600 in two years. If your other investment opportunities with the same amount of risk give you a return of 5% a year, how much are you willing to pay today to get these two future receipts?

We can figure this out by discounting the $500 one period at 5% and the second $600 two periods at 5%:

$$\text{Present value of investment} = \frac{\$500}{(1+0.05)^1} + \frac{\$600}{(1+0.05)^2}$$

$$\text{Present value of investment} = \$476.19 + \$544.22 = \$1,020.41$$

Using a financial calculator's or spreadsheet's net present value (NPV) function, we can arrive at the same present value.[1] The NPV program requires you to input all cash flow, beginning with the cash flow in the next period, in order, and specifying the interest rate:

TI-83/84	HP10B	Microsoft Excel
{500,600} STO	0 CF$_j$	=NPV(.05,500,600)
listname	500 CF$_j$	
NPV(5,0, *listname*)	600 CF$_j$	
	5 I/YR	
	NPV	

Why didn't we use the spreadsheet or financial calculator time value of money functions and solve for PV? Because we are not dealing with a single cash flow in the future or a series of cash flows that are the same, rather, we have two cash flows and they are of different amounts. We need to use the calculator or spreadsheet's net present value function to solve this problem. Therefore, the present value of these flows is $1,020.41.[2]

---

[1]Because we do not have a cash flow that occurs today in this scenario, we need to indicate the fact that today's cash flow is zero in the financial calculators; zero as the second element in the NPV function, and 0 for the initial CF$_j$ for the HP10B calculator. If there is no cash flow you must input a "0" to hold the time period's place in the program—otherwise, the cash flow will receive an incorrect time value of money.

[2]The *net present value* is the present value of all cash flows, whether they are positive or negative, discounted at the appropriate discount rate. We add the word "net" to "present value" because we are often using these calculations to determine how much value is added, on net, once you consider how much the investment costs and how much value you will get from the investment. Therefore, if this investment cost you $1,000, its net present value is $20.41.

In cases in which you require a present value of uneven cash flows, you can use a program in your financial calculator, the *net present value,* or *NPV,* program.

This investment is worth $1,020.41 today, so you will be willing to pay $1,020.41 or less for this investment:

- If you pay more than $1,020.41, you get a return less than 5%.
- If you pay less than $1,020.41 you get a return more than 5%.
- If you pay $1,020.41 you get a return of 5%.

We can look at this problem from a different perspective, solving for the return on the investment. Suppose you pay $1,000 for the investment that produces $500 at the end of one period and $600 at the end of two periods. What is the return on this investment? Solving for the return involves trial and error; that is, trying different interest rates to find the one in which the cost of the investment (the $1,000) is equal to the present value of the two cash flows.

Try 4%:

$$\$1,000 =? \ \frac{\$500}{(1+0.04)^1} + \frac{\$600}{(1+0.04)^2}$$

$$\$1,000 =? \ \$480.77 + \$554.73$$

$$\$1,000 \neq \ \$1,035.50$$

This tells us that we have not discounted enough (that is, 4% is too low a rate). We know that the present value of these cash flows using a 5% discount rate is $1,020.41 (from our work above), so we should try an even higher rate of 6%.

Try 6%:

$$\$\ 1,000 =? \ \frac{\$500}{(1+0.06)^1} + \frac{\$600}{(1+0.06)^2}$$

$$\$\ 1,000 =? \ \$471.70 + \$534.00$$

$$\$\ 1,000 \neq \ \$1,005.70$$

Repeating this same procedure using 7% gives us a value of the right-hand side of this equation of $991.35. Because $991.35 is less than the $1,000, this means that the rate that equates the cost of the investment (the $1,000) with the future cash flows is between 6% and 7%.

But thank goodness for financial calculators and the financial functions in spreadsheets so that we don't have to use trial and error every time we want to solve for a return based on an uneven cash flow stream. Using a spreadsheet or financial calculator's internal rate of return, IRR, function, we can determine this precisely—and without having to do all the iterations ourselves. Why do we use an IRR function? Because the return on investment, once we consider all the cash flows associated with the investment and the timing of these cash flows, is the investment's *internal rate of return* (IRR).

TI-83/84	HP10B	Microsoft Excel		
{500,600} STO	−1000 CF_j		A	
listname	500 CF_j	1	−1000	
IRR(−1000, *listname*)	600 CF_j	2	500	
	IRR	3	600	
		4		← = IRR(A1:A3)

The interest rate that equates the $1,000 investment with the present value of the two cash flows is 6.39%. This means that if you buy this investment for $1,000 and hold it for two years, and receive the $500 and $600 as promised, you will have a return of 6.39% on your investment.

We can demonstrate this point by looking at this problem from a different angle. Suppose you invest $1,000 and can earn 6.39% on your investment. At the end of the first period, you will have $1,000 × (1 + 0.0639) = $1,063.90. At the end of the second period, you will have $1,063.90 × (1 + 0.0639) = $1,131.883. Your return on this investment is

$$PV = \$1,000$$
$$FV = \$1,131.883$$
$$n = 2$$

Solving for *i* using a calculator or spreadsheet, we find *i* = 6.39%.

Now let's look at the benefit of receiving the $500 and the $600. At the end of the first period, you have $500. At the end of the second period, you have $600 + $500 × (1 + 0.0639) = $1,131.95. Therefore, these are equivalent investments because they have equivalent returns. What is happening here to make this true? The internal rate of return of 6.39% assumes that when there are cash flows from the investment (such as the $500 in this example), these cash flows are reinvested at the internal rate of 6.39%.

FINANCIAL MATH IN ACTION

For years, companies have been taking out life insurance policies on their employees. Sometimes these policies are insurance on key personnel—so-called key-man insurance. Other times these policies are insurance on personnel en masse (often dubbed janitors' insurance). Many of these policies are single-premium insurance—that is, one payment for the lifetime of the insured, so these policies are often in effect after the employee leaves the employer. Under current law, employers must have the employees' written permission to take out these policies, which may reduce their popularity among employees.

Suppose your employer bought a single-pay insurance policy on your life for $8,000 that pays a death benefit of $150,000. If you are 40 years old and your life expectancy is 80 years old, was this a good investment if the company's cost of capital is 8%? The future value of this investment is $150,000, but the present value is $150,000 ÷ $(1 + 0.08)^{40}$ = $150,000 ÷ 21.7245 = $6,904.65. This was not a good investment, because the company spent $8,000 to get something with a value of $6,904.65.

If you are 40 years old and you die when you are 50, was this a good investment? Yes, because the present value of the payoff of the policy is $150,000 ÷ $(1 + 0.08)^{10}$ = $69,479.02, which is more that the company paid for the policy.

Bottom line? The sooner you die, the more valuable the life insurance is to your beneficiary.

 ## TRY IT! 3.1 WHAT'S IT WORTH?

Consider the following cash inflows from an investment today:

Years from Today	End of Period Cash Flow
1	$3,000
2	$0
3	$2,500

If your opportunity cost of funds is 5%, what is this investment worth today?

Moving Values through Time

Consider the following: You plan to deposit €10,000 in one year, €20,000 in two years, and €30,000 in three years. If the interest earned on your deposits is 10%:

- What is the value today of these deposits?
- What will be the balance in the account at the end of the third year?

What is the value of the deposits today? We calculate the value of these deposits today as the sum of the present values, or $48,159.28:

Today 0	1	2	3
€9,090.91	€10,000	€20,000	€30,000
16,528.93			
22,539.44			
€48,159.28 = PV			

Instead of calculating the individual present values and adding them, you can calculate the present value of this series of cash flows using spreadsheet and calculator functions:

TI-83/84	HP10B	Microsoft Excel
Create the list and store it in a list	0 CF	
{CF$_1$,CF$_2$,CF$_3$} STO *listname*	10000 CF	1 10000
{10000,20000,30000} STO L1	20000 CF	2 20000
Use the NPV program in the TVM	30000 CF	3 30000
Solver, NPV(interest rate, CF$_0$, listname)	10 I/YR	4 ← = NPV(.1,A1:A3)
NPV(10,0,L1) ENTER	NPV	

Looking in to the future, we can calculate the balance in the account at the end of the third year as the sum of the future values, or €$64,100:

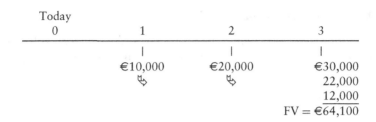

Note that there is no short cut in most calculators and spreadsheets for the future value of an uneven series of cash flows.[3] In most cases, you need to calculate the future value of each of the individual cash flows and then sum these future values to arrive at the future value of the series.

Why would we want to know the future value of a series? Suppose you are setting aside funds for your retirement. What you may want to know is how much you will have available at the time you retire. You'll have to assume a specific return on your funds—that is, how much interest you can earn on your savings—but you can calculate how much you'll have at some future point in time.[4]

Why would we want to know the present value of a series? Suppose you are considering investing in a project that will produce cash flows in the future. If you know what you can earn on similar projects, what is this project worth to you today? How much would you be willing to pay for this investment? We can calculate the present value of the future cash flows to determine the value today of these future cash flows.

Example 3.1

Suppose you deposit $100 today, $200 one year from today, and $300 two years from today, in an account that pays 10% interest, compounded annually.

What is the balance in the account at the end of two years? Answer: **$641**.

$$FV = [\$100 \times (1.10)^2] + [\$200 \times 1.10] + \$300 = \$641$$

---

[3]Exceptions include the Hewlett-Packard 17B and 19B model calculators and the more recent Texas Instruments BA II models.
[4]We cover the mathematics of this in Chapter 7.

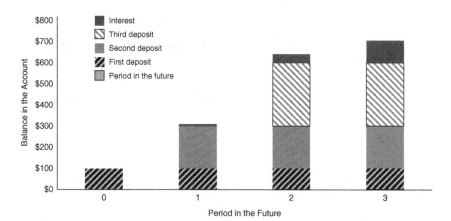

EXHIBIT 3.1 Growth in the Balance of the Account for a Series of Deposits Consisting of $100, $200 and $300, with Interest of 10% per Period

What is the balance in the account at the end of three years? Answer: **$705.10.**

$$FV = \left[\$100 \times (1.10)^3\right] + \left[\$200 \times (1.10)^2\right] + \left[\$300 \times 1.10\right]$$
$$= \$133.1 + 242 + 330 = \$641 \times 1.10 = \$705.10$$

What is the present value of these deposits? Answer: **$569.68.**

$$PV = \$100 + \left[\$200 \div 1.10\right] + \left[\$300 \div (1.10)^2\right]$$
$$= \$100 + 192.31 + 277.37 = \$569.68$$

Example 3.2

Consider three cash flows:

Period	End of Period Cash Flow
20X1	$2,000
20X2	$4,000
20X3	$3,000

If the interest rate is 5%, what is the value of these cash flows at the end of 20X1? Answer: **$8,530.61.**

Period	End of Period Cash Flow	Calculation	Value at the End of 20X1
20X1	$2,000		$2,000.00
20X2	$4,000	$4,000 ÷ (1 + 0.05)	3,809.52
20X3	$3,000	$3,000 ÷ (1 + 0.05)^2	2,721.09
Total			$8,530.61

What is the value of these cash flows at the end of 20X3? Answer: $9,405.

Period	End of Period Cash Flow	Calculation	Value at the End of 20X3
20X1	$2,000	$2,000 × (1 + 0.05)^2	$2,205
20X2	$4,000	$4,000 × (1 + 0.05)	4,200
20X3	$3,000		3,000
Total			$9,405

We can check out work by comparing the present value and future value:

$$FV = PV \times (1 + 0.05)^2$$

$$\$9405 = \$8530.61 \times (\text{discount factor for two years at } 5\%)$$

$$\$9405 \div 8530.61 = (1 + 0.05)^2$$

CHECK IT OUT

You can apply some commonsense checks to your work to make sure that you are at least in the ballpark. Consider the cash flows:

Period	End of Period Cash Flow
1	$10,000
2	$25,000
3	$15,000

If there was no interest (that is, $i = 0\%$), what would be the present value, at the end of period 0, of these cash flows?

$$PV = \frac{\$10,000}{(1+0.00)^1} + \frac{\$25,000}{(1+0.00)^2} + \frac{\$15,000}{(1+0.00)^3}$$

$$= \frac{\$10,000}{1} + \frac{\$25,000}{1} + \frac{\$15,000}{1} = \$50,000$$

In other words, the present value is the sum of the cash flow, or $50,000. If the interest rate is anything above 0%, the present value would be less than $50,000. Therefore, you can think of the sum of the cash flows as being the ceiling for the present value of the cash flows. The present value cannot be greater than this sum.

If there was no interest, what would be the future value, as of the end of period 3, of these cash flows?

$$FV = \$10,000\,(1+0.00)^1 + \$25,000\,(1+0.00)^2$$
$$+ \$15,000\,(1+0.00)^3 = \$50,000$$

In other words, the future value with interest at 0% is $50,000. If interest is above 0%—as it usually is—the future value will be more than the $50,000. Therefore, the sum of the cash flows is a floor for the future value—the future value will not be less than the sum of the cash flows.

VALUING A PERPETUITY

Let's look at still another example. Suppose you are evaluating an investment that promises $10 every year forever. This type of cash flow stream is referred to as a *perpetuity*. The value of this investment is the present value of the stream of $10s to be received each year to infinity where each $10 is discounted the appropriate number of periods at some annual rate i:

$$\text{Present value of investment} = \frac{\$10}{(1+i)^1} + \frac{\$10}{(1+i)^2} + \frac{\$10}{(1+i)^3} + \cdots + \frac{\$10}{(1+i)^\infty},$$

which we can write in shorthand notation using summation notation as:

$$PV = \sum_{t=1}^{\infty} \frac{\$10}{(1+i)^t} = \$10 \sum_{t=1}^{\infty} \frac{1}{(1+i)^t}$$

As the number of discounting periods approaches infinity, the summation approaches $1 \div i$. To see why, consider the present value annuity factor for an interest rate of 10%, as the number of payments goes from 1 to 200:

Number of Payments in the Annuity	Present Value Annuity Discount Factor
1	0.0909
10	6.1446
50	9.9148
100	9.9993
1000	10.0000

That is,

$$\sum_{t=1}^{\infty} \frac{1}{(1+i)^t} \Rightarrow \frac{1}{i}$$

If the interest rate is 10%, as the number of payments increases, the factor approaches 10, or $1 \div 0.10$. Therefore, the present value of a perpetual annuity is very close to $1 \div i$.

We can rewrite the present value of the perpetual stream of $10 as

$$PV = \frac{CF}{i} = \$10 \left(\frac{1}{i}\right) = \frac{\$10}{i}$$

If the discount rate to translate this future stream into a present value is 10%, the value of the investment is $100:

$$PV = \frac{\$10}{0.10} = \$100$$

The 10% is the discount rate, also referred to as the *capitalization rate,* for the future cash flows comprising this stream. Looking at this investment from another angle, if you consider the investment to be worth $100 today, you are capitalizing—translating future flows into a present value—the future cash flows at 10% per year. As you see from these examples, the value of an investment depends on:

- The amount and timing of the future cash flows.
- The discount rate used to translate these future cash flows into a value today.

This discount rate represents how much an investor is willing to pay today for the right to receive a future cash flow. Or, to put it another way, the discount rate is the rate of return the investor requires on an investment, given the price he or she is willing to pay for its expected future cash flow.

Let's consider another example. Suppose you are considering an investment that promises to pay $100 each period forever, and the interest rate you can earn on alternative investments of similar risk is 5% per period. What are you willing to pay today for this investment?

$$PV = \$100 \div 0.05 = \$2,000$$

Therefore, you would be willing to pay $2,000 today for this investment to receive, in return, the promise of $100 each period forever.

FINANCIAL MATH IN ACTION

The government of the United Kingdom has had bonds outstanding that never mature. These bonds are referred to as *consolidated stock*, or *consols*, that are part of the government debt. The bonds currently pay interest at a rate of 2.5% per year, paid four times a year. What is the value of one Consolidated Stock if the appropriate discount rate is 4%? For £100 face value consol, the periodic cash flow is £2.5 ÷ 4 = £0.625 every four months. The discount rate per period is 4% ÷ 4 = 1%. The value of a 100 face value consol is £0.625 ÷ 0.01 = £62.5.

Let's look at the value of a perpetuity from a different angle. Suppose that you have the opportunity to purchase an investment for $5,000 that promises to pay $50 at the end of every period forever. What is the periodic interest per period (that is, the return) on this investment?

We know that the present value is PV = $5,000 and the periodic, perpetual payment is CF = $50. Inserting these values into the formula for the present value of a perpetuity:

$$PV = \$5,000 = \$50 \div i$$

Solving for i, $i = \$50 \div \$5,000 = 0.01$ or 1% per period.

Therefore, an investment of $5,000 that generates $50 per period provides 1% compound interest per period.

Example 3.3

Suppose you buy a share of stock that has a $2 dividend, paid at the end of each year. If you expect the dividend to be constant and paid each year, forever, what are you willing to pay for this share of stock if the opportunity cost of funds considering the risk of the stock, is 8%? Answer: **$25**.

$$PV = \frac{\$2}{0.08} = \$25$$

Example 3.4

You observe that a share of stock is currently selling for $30 per share. If this stock has a constant dividend of $3 per year, paid at the end of each year, forever, what is the required rate of return on this stock? Answer: **10%**.

$$i = \frac{\$3}{\$30} = 10\%$$

ANNUITIES

An *annuity* is a series of even cash flows. Because the cash flows are the same amount, the math is simpler. Suppose you have a series of three cash flows, each of $1,000. The first cash flow occurs one year from today, the second occurs two years from today, and the third occurs three years from today. The present value of this series is

$$PV = \frac{\$1,000}{(1+i)^1} + \frac{\$1,000}{(1+i)^2} + \frac{\$1,000}{(1+i)^3} = \sum_{t=1}^{3} \frac{\$1,000}{(1+i)^t} = \$1,000 \sum_{t=1}^{3} \frac{1}{(1+i)^t}$$

Using the notation CF to represent the periodic cash flow, we can represent this as

$$PV = \sum_{t=1}^{N} \frac{CF}{(1+i)^t} = CF \sum_{t=1}^{N} \frac{1}{(1+i)^t}$$

The term $\sum_{t=1}^{N} \frac{1}{(1+i)^t}$ is the annuity discount factor.

There are different types of annuities in financial transactions, which differ in terms of the timing of the first cash flow:

- An *ordinary annuity* is an annuity in which the first cash flow is one period in the future.
- An *annuity due* is an annuity in which the first cash flow occurs today.
- A *deferred annuity* is an annuity in which the first cash flow occurs beyond one period from today.

The example that we just completed is an example of an ordinary annuity. You can see the timing issue when comparing the time lines associated with each. Consider the following three-cash-flow annuities: the ordinary annuity, an annuity due, and a deferred annuity with a deferral of three periods.

	End of Period					
	Today	1	2	3	4	5
Ordinary annuity	*PV*	CF	CF	CF *FV*		
Annuity due	CF *PV*	CF	CF	*FV*		
Deferred annuity	*PV*			CF	CF	CF *FV*

CF represents the periodic cash flow amount. In the case of an annuity, this amount is the same each period. Because of the time value of money, the valuation of these annuities, whether we are referring to the present value or the future value, will be different.

Valuing an Ordinary Annuity

The ordinary annuity is the most common annuity that we encounter, although deferred annuities and annuities due do occur with some frequency as well. The future value of an ordinary annuity is simply the sum of the future values of the individual cash flows. Consider a three-payment ordinary annuity that has payments of $1,000 each and a 5% interest rate.

The future value of this annuity is

Today	1	2	3
	|	|	|
	$1,000	$1,000	$1,000.0
	↘	↘	1,102.5
			1,050.0
			FV = $\overline{3,152.5}$

The present value of this annuity is

Today	1	2	3
	|	|	|
$952.381	$1,000	$1,000	$1,000
907.029	↙	↙	↙
863.838			
PV = $2,723.248			

We can represent the value of the annuity in more general terms. Let t indicate a time period, CF represent the individual cash flow, and let n indicate the number of cash flows. The future value is the sum of the future values of the cash flows:

$$FV = CF(1+i)^{N-1} + CF(1+i)^{N-2} + \ldots + CF(1+i)^0 = CF \left(\sum_{t=0}^{N-1} (1+i)^t \right)$$

We can represent the present value of an ordinary annuity in mathematical terms as

$$PV = \sum_{t=1}^{N} \frac{CF}{(1+i)^t} = CF \sum_{t=1}^{N} \frac{1}{(1+i)^t} = CF \left(1 - \frac{(1+i)^N}{i} \right)$$

We used the notation CF to indicate a cash flow. In the case of an annuity, this cash flow is the same each period. The term

$$\left(\sum_{t=0}^{N-1} (1+i)^t\right)$$

is referred to as the *future value annuity factor* and the term, whereas

$$\sum_{t=1}^{N} \frac{1}{(1+i)^t}$$

is referred to as the *present value annuity factor*. In financial calculator applications, we refer to the cash flow associated with an annuity as a payment, or PMT.[5]

Consider another example. Suppose you wish to calculate the present value of a four-payment ordinary annuity that has annual payments of $5,000 each. If the interest rate is 5%, the present value is $17,729.75. Using a calculator, we input the known values (i.e., *n*, *i*, PMT) and solve for PV.[6]

TI-83/84 Using TVM Solver	HP10B	Microsoft Excel
N = 4	4 N	=PV(0.05,4,5000,0)* −1
I% = 5	5 I/YR	
FV = 0	5000 PMT	
PMT = 5000	PV	
PV = *Solve*		

Referring to the timeline above, you can see that the value you calculated occurs one period before the first cash flow (i.e., today).

Now suppose you wish to calculate the future value. You use the same inputs, but simply solve for the future value instead of the present value, resulting in a value of $21,550.63. Referring to the previous timeline, you can see that the value you calculated occurs at the same time as the last cash flow, which in this example is at the end of the fourth year.

---

[5]If we can use financial calculators or spreadsheets to solve these problems, why worry about the math? Because by laying the foundation of what consists of these mathematical relationships, you may be able to approach a problem that doesn't fit in to the simple, conventional type of problem if you understand the math behind it.
[6]Be sure that your calculator is set for one payment per period and in the END mode.

TI-83/84 Using TVM Solver	HP10B	Microsoft Excel
N = 4	4 N	=FV(0.05,4,5000,0)* −1
I% = 5	5 I/YR	
PV = 0	5000 PMT	
PMT = 5000	FV	
FV = *Solve*		

Example 3.5

What is the value of an investment that provides cash flows of $2,000 at the end of each year for the next four years if you have determined that the appropriate discount rate on this investment is 6%? Answer: **$6.930.21**

Because these cash flows are the same amount and occur at regular intervals of time, we can solve this using an ordinary annuity, which means we can use the calculator or spreadsheet shortcut involving the PMT—the periodic, even cash flow. We are given the following data inputs:

$$PMT = \$2,000$$
$$N = 4$$
$$i = 6\%$$

Solving for the present value of an annuity, the value of this investment is $6,930.21.

 TRY IT! 3.2 BACK AND FORTH WITH ANNUITIES

Consider a four-payment annuity in which the payment is $2,500 and the interest rate is 6%.

- What is the present value of this annuity?
- What is the future value of this annuity?

Valuing an Annuity Due

An annuity due is like an ordinary annuity, yet the *first cash flow occurs immediately*, instead of one period from today. This means that each cash flow is discounted one period less than each cash flow in a similar payment ordinary annuity:

$$FV = CF(1+i)^1 + CF(1+i)^2 + \ldots + CF(1+i)^{N+1} = CF\left(\sum_{t=0}^{N}(1+i)^{t+1}\right)$$

$$PV = \sum_{t=1}^{N}\frac{CF}{(1+i)^{t-1}} = CF\sum_{t=1}^{N}\frac{1}{(1+i)^{t-1}}$$

Consider the example of a three-payment annuity due with payments of $1,000 each and the interest rate is 5%. The future value of this annuity due is $3,310.125:

Today	1	2	3
|	|	|	|
$1,000	$1,000	$1,000	$1,157.625
			1,102.500
			1,050.000
			FV= $3,310.125

The present value of this three-payment annuity due is

Today	1	2	3
|	|	|	|
$1,000.000	$1,000	$1,000	
$952.381			
907.029			
PV = $2,859.410			

Comparing the values of the ordinary annuity with those of the annuity due, you'll see that the values differ by a factor of $(1+i)$:

	Value of Ordinary Annuity	Value of Annuity Due	Value of Annuity Due / Value of Ordinary Annuity
Present value	$2,723.248	$2,859.410	1.05
Future value	$3,152.500	$3,310.125	1.05

This factor represents the difference in the timing of the cash flows: the cash flows of the annuity due occur one period prior to the cash flows for a similar-payment ordinary annuity.

CALCULATION TIP

Using a financial calculator to value an annuity due requires changing the mode from END to BEG or BEGIN. Once in the BEG or BEGIN mode, you can input the values as you did with the ordinary annuity. A common mistake is to leave the calculator in the annuity due mode when calculating other, nondue problems.

Consider a five-payment annuity due with an annual payment of $3,000 and an interest rate of 6%. The present value of this annuity due is $13,395.317.

TI-83/84 Using TVM Solver	HP10B	Microsoft Excel
Set BEGIN	Set BEG	=PV(0.06,5,3000,0,1)* −1
N = 5	5 N	
I% = 6	6 I/YR	
FV = 0	3000 PMT	
PMT = 3000	PV	
PV = *Solve*		

The future value of this annuity due is $17,925.956:

TI-83/84 Using TVM Solver	HP10B	Microsoft Excel
Set BEGIN	Set BEG	=FV(0.06,5,3000,0,1)* −1
N = 5	5 N	
I% = 6	6 I/YR	
PV = 0	3000 PMT	
PMT = 3000	FV	
FV = *Solve*		

Example 3.6

Suppose you have just won a $1 million lottery. When you win the lottery, you generally receive payments of the lottery jackpot over 20 years, with the first payment immediately. Therefore, your $1 million lottery winnings consist of 20 annual payments of $50,000 each, beginning when you claim your prize.[7] But wait! Don't forget about taxes. The IRS will take 28% of each check, so you are left with $36,000 each year.

So what is the $1 million lottery jackpot worth to you today? If you can invest your funds to produce a return of 3%, that $1 million jackpot, valuing the winnings as an annuity due, is worth $551,656.77 today:[8]

$$PMT = \$36,3000$$
$$n = 20$$
$$i = 3\%$$

Solve for the present value of the annuity due, $PV = \$551,656.77$.

So, if someone offered you a lump-sum of $500,000 for your lottery winnings, would you take it? No. If someone offered you $600,000 for your lottery winnings, would you take it? Yes.

 ## TRY IT! 3.3 WHAT WOULD YOU TAKE?

Suppose you win a lawsuit and the lawsuit settlement will be paid in 10 annual installments of $400,000 each, with the first payment today. If you can earn 6% on your investments and if someone offers you $3 million in exchange for your settlement, would you take it? Why?

SUMMARY

Valuing an investment requires first identifying the type, amount, and timing of the cash flows associated with the investment. Once we estimate the amount and timing of the security's cash flows, the valuation of these cash flows requires the application of the time value of money mathematics to determine the present value of these future cash flows.

---

[7]This is an annuity due pattern of cash flows. It would be lousy public relations for a lottery commission to say, "Congratulations, you'll get your first check in one year," so most lotteries begin payments immediately.

[8]In mathematical terms, this is $PV = CF \left(\sum_{t=1}^{N} \frac{1}{(1+i)^{t-1}} \right) = \$36,000 \left(\sum_{t=1}^{N} \frac{1}{(1+i)^{t-1}} \right) = \$551,656.77$

We can use a financial calculator or spreadsheet's built-in functions to calculate the present value of a series, the present value of uneven cash flows, or the present value a series of even cash flows forever. When we want to calculate the value of a series of uneven cash flows out into the future, we must first determine the future value of each cash flow and then sum.

"TRY IT" SOLUTIONS

3.1. What's It Worth?
We are given the following data inputs:

$CF_1 = \$3,000$
$CF_2 = \$0$
$CF_3 = \$2,500$
$i = 5\%$

Solving for the net present value, the value of this investment is $5,016.7369.

3.2. Back and Forth with Annuities
The present value is $8,662.76, whereas the future value is $10,936.54.
a. Inputs: PMT = $2,500; $n = 4$; $i = 6\%$.
Solve for the present value. PV = $8,662.76
b. Inputs: PMT = $2,500; $n = 4$; $i = 6\%$.
Solve for the future value. FV = $10,936.54

3.3. What Would You Take?
No, because the value of the settlement annuity is $3,120,677:

Annuity due: PMT = $400,000; $n = 10$; $i = 6\%$. Solve for the present value.

PROBLEMS

3.1. What is the value at the end of 2009 of the following series of cash flows if the discount rate is 5%?
3.2. What is the value at the end of 2012 of the following series of cash flows if the interest rate is 5%?
3.3. What is the value today of a promised series of cash flows of $6,000 at the end of each of the next five years? Use a 10% discount rate.

Year	Cash Flow
2010	$1,000
2011	$0
2012	$3,000

Year	Cash Flow
2010	$1,000
2011	$0
2012	$3,000

3.4. What is the value today of the following series of cash flows if the discount rate is 10%?

Years from Now	Cash Flow
1	£0
2	£0
3	£10,000
4	£10,000

3.5. Suppose you deposit $1,000 in an account at the end of each year for three years. If the account earns 5% interest per year, what is the balance in the account at the end of three years?

3.6. Calculate the present value of a four-payment $1,000 ordinary annuity if the interest rate is 5%.

3.7. Suppose you deposit $1,000 each year for three years in an account that pays 5% interest, compounded annually. If you make the deposits at the beginning of the year, what is the balance in the account at the *end* of three years?

3.8. Suppose you win $7 million Powerball lottery. You receive your lottery winnings in 20 equal annual installments, with the first installment paid immediately. If you could invest the funds to yield 5% per year, what is the *smallest* lump sum that you would be willing to take today in exchange for your 20 installments?

3.9. Consider an annuity consisting of three payments of $4,000 each. If the interest rate is 5% per year, what is the present value of this as:
    a. An ordinary annuity?
    b. An annuity due?
    c. A deferred annuity, deferred two periods?
3.10. Your broker has proposed that you pay $50,000 today for an annuity of $5,000 per year for fifteen years. If your opportunity cost of funds is 6% and the returns from this investment are tax-free, is this a good deal?

For solutions to these problems, see Appendix E.

CHAPTER 4

Yielding for Yields

It has been my experience that competency in mathematics, both in numerical manipulations and in understanding its conceptual foundations, enhances a person's ability to handle the more ambiguous and qualitative relationships that dominate our day-to-day financial decision-making.

—Alan Greenspan

The basic concept underlying the time value of money is that when you invest, you are compensated for the time value of money and risk, and when you borrow, you must pay enough to compensate the lender for the time value of money and risk. Situations arise often in which we wish to determine the interest rate that is implied from an advertised or stated rate. There are also cases in which we wish to determine the rate of interest implied from a set of payments in a loan arrangement.

ANNUALIZED RATES OF INTEREST

A common problem in finance is comparing alternative financing or investment opportunities when the interest rates are stated in a way that makes it difficult to compare terms. One lending source may offer terms that specify 9.25% annual percentage rate (APR), with interest compounding annually, whereas another lending source may offer terms of 9% APR with interest compounding continuously. How do you begin to compare these rates to determine which is a lower cost of borrowing? Ideally, we would like to translate these interest rates into some comparable form.

One obvious way to represent rates stated in various time intervals on a common basis is to express them in the same unit of time—so we annualize them. To annualize a rate is to put it on an annual basis. Supposedly, if you put all the terms on the same, annual basis, they should be comparable. Right? Wrong.

There are two approaches to annualizing rates: the simple way, resulting in an APR, and the more complex way, resulting in an *effective annual rate* (EAR). These are both annualized rates, but they provide different information.

Annual Percentage Rate

In Chapters 1 and 2, we showed you how we use the APR for compounding and discounting when interest compounds more frequently than annually. We look at the APR here to set the stage for determining the EAR, the effective annual rate.

Suppose a bank is willing to lend to you at the rate of 12% APR, with interest compounded monthly. What does this really mean in terms of what you end up paying? It means that you are paying $12\% \div 12 = 1\%$ each month and that interest compounds 12 times a year. Let's put this into an equation. Let i be the rate of interest per period and let n be the number of compounding periods in a year. The annualized rate, also referred to as the *nominal interest rate* or the APR, is

$$APR = i \times n$$
$$APR = 0.01 \times 12 = 12\%$$

A compound period may be a day, a week, a month, a three-month period, or any other portion of a year. The key to understanding interest rates, and in particular APRs, is to understand how frequently interest compounds within a year.

Example 4.1

Suppose a bank offers you lending rates at 6% APR, with interest compounded monthly.

- What is the compounding period? Answer: **A month.**
- What is the rate per compounding period? Answer: **6%.**

The APR is 6% and there are 12 compound periods in a year. Therefore,

$$6\% \div 12 = 0.5\%$$

To check our work, $0.5\% \times 12 = 6\%$.

Example 4.2

Suppose your credit card states that interest on unpaid balances is 24% APR, with interest compounded monthly. What is the interest rate per month for this credit card? Answer: **2%**.

The APR is 24% and there are 12 months in a year. Therefore, the rate per month is 24% ÷ 12 = 2%.

Suppose you borrow $10,000 with the terms of interest at 12% APR, compounded monthly. If you repay the loan at the end of the year, how much interest do you have to pay? It's a bit more than 12% of the $10,000:

$$FV = \$10{,}000 \times (1 + 0.01)^{12} = \$11{,}268.25$$

The interest that you pay is $11,268.25 − $10,000 = $1,268.25, which is more than 12% of $10,000 (which would be $1,200). That additional $68.25 is because interest compounds monthly, even though you don't end up paying for it until the end of the year. Effectively, you are paying $1,268.25 ÷ $10,000 = 12.6825% on the monthly compounding 12% APR loan.

So why do banks and other lenders report the APR? This is because the Federal Truth in Lending Act requires lenders to disclose the annual percentage rate on consumer loans.[1] But because the annual percentage rate ignores compounding and, therefore, understates the true cost of borrowing, savvy consumers need to take the extra step to figure out the effective rate. To make matters worse, the APR does not consider some other costs associated with lending transactions, as pointed out in the Report to Congress by the Board of Governors of the Federal Reserve System.[2]

To see how the APR works, let's consider the Lucky Break Loan Company. Lucky's loan terms are simple: Pay back the amount borrowed, plus 50%, in six months. Suppose you borrow $10,000 from Lucky. After six months, you must pay back the $10,000, plus $5,000. The annual percentage rate on financing with Lucky is the interest rate per period (50% for six months) multiplied by the number of compound periods in a year (two six-month periods in a year). For the Lucky Break financing arrangement,

$$APR = 0.50 \times 2 = 1.00 \text{ or } 100\% \text{ per year}$$

---

[1] 15 U.S.C. §§ 1601–1666j; and Federal Reserve System Regulation Z, 1968.
[2] Board of Governors of the Federal Reserve System, Report to Congress, *Finance Charges for Consumer Credit under the Truth in Lending Act*, April 1996.

But what if you cannot pay Lucky back after six months? Lucky will let you off this time, but you must pay back the following at the end of the next six months:

- The $10,000 borrowed.
- The $5,000 interest from the first six months.
- 50% interest on both the unpaid $10,000 and the unpaid $5,000 interest ($15,000 × 0.50 = $7,500).

So, at the end of the year, knowing what is good for you, you pay off Lucky:

Amount of original loan	$10,000
Interest from first six months	5,000
Interest on second six months	7,500
Total payment at end of year	$22,500

It is unreasonable to assume that, after six months, Lucky would let you forget about paying interest on the $5,000 interest from the first six months. If Lucky would forget about the interest on interest, you would pay $20,000 at the end of the year—$10,000 repayment of principal and $10,000 interest—which is a 100% interest rate.

But Lucky doesn't forget. Using the Lucky Break method of financing, you have to pay $12,500 interest to borrow $10,000 for one year's time—or else. Because you have to pay $12,500 interest to borrow $10,000 over one year's time, you pay not 100% interest, but rather 125% interest per year:

Annual interest rate on a Lucky Break loan = $12,500 ÷ $10,000 = 125%

What's going on here? It looks like the APR in the Lucky Break example ignores the compounding (interest on interest) that takes place after the first six months.

And that's the way it is with *all* APR's: the APR ignores the effect of compounding. The APR understates the true annual rate of interest if interest compounds at any time prior to the end of the year. Nevertheless, APR is viewed as an acceptable method of disclosing interest on many lending arrangements because it is easy to understand and simple to compute. However, because it ignores compounding, it is not the best way to evaluate financing terms.

TRY IT! 4.1: APR

Suppose you borrow $1,000 using a payday loan that has finance charges of 17.5% of the loan for a 10-day period. What is the APR on this loan?

Effective Annual Rate As we've demonstrated, the APR ignores any compounding within a year. As a result, a loan with an APR of 6% and compounding monthly looks no different than a loan with an APR of 6% and annual compounding. But these loans are different—we just would never know it by looking at the APR. Consider a simple example. Suppose you want to borrow $10,000 and have three choices of financing:

>   A: APR of 6%, with monthly compounding.
>
>   B: APR of 6%, with quarterly compounding.
>
>   C: APR of 6%, with annual compounding.

If you pay off the loan at the end of the year, how much must you pay under each set of terms?

$$A: \quad \$10,000 \times (1 + 0.005)^{12} = \$10,616.78$$
$$B: \quad \$10,000 \times (1 + 0.015)^{4} = \$10,613.64$$
$$C: \quad \$10,000 \times (1 + 0.06) = \$10,600.00$$

Instead of having to work through financing terms and amounts owed, we can convert a stated interest rate into an effective rate of interest rate, which considers compounding. We can then compare effective rates to figure out the best financing terms.

The effective annual rate is the *true* economic return for a given time period because it takes into account the compounding of interest. The EAR is sometimes referred to as the *effective rate of interest*. Using our Lucky Break example, we see that we must pay $12,500 interest on the loan of $10,000 for one year. Effectively, we are paying 125% annual interest. Thus, 125% is the effective annual rate of interest.

The Federal Truth in Savings Act requires institutions to provide the APY for savings accounts, which is a rate that considers the effects of compound interest.[3] The APY is simply another name for the EAR. As a result of this law, consumers can compare the yields on different savings arrangements. Unfortunately, this law does not apply beyond savings accounts and, therefore, consumers and businesses must be able to calculate this yield on their own.

In the Lucky Break example, we can easily work through the calculation of interest and interest on interest. But for situations where interest is compounded more frequently, we need a direct way to calculate the effective annual rate. We can calculate it by resorting once again to our basic valuation equation:

$$FV = PV(1 + i)^n$$

Next, we consider that a return is the change in the value of an investment over a period and an annual return is the change in value over a year.

Suppose you invest $100 today in an account, which pays 6% annual interest, but interest compounds every four months. This means that 2% is paid every four months.

- After four months, you have $100 × 1.2 = $102.
- After eight months you have $102 × 1.02 = $104.04.
- After one year you have $104.04 × 1.02 = 106.1208, or, $100 × 1.02^3 = $106.1208.

The effective annual rate of interest is $6.1208 paid on $100, or 6.1208%. We can arrive at that interest by rearranging the basic valuation formula based on a one-year period:

$$\$106.1208 = \$100 \times (1 + 0.02)^3$$
$$\$106.1208 \div \$100 = (1 + 0.02)^3$$
$$1.061208 = (1 + 0.02)^3$$
$$EAR = (1 + 0.02)^3 - 1 = 0.061208 \text{ or } 6.1208\%$$

In more general terms, the effective interest rate, EAR, is

$$EAR = (1 + i)^n\ 1$$

The effective rate of interest—the EAR—is therefore an annual rate that takes into consideration any compounding that occurs during the year.

---

[3]Federal Reserve System Regulation DD, 199.

Let's look at how the EAR is affected by the compounding. Suppose that the Safe Savings and Loan promises to pay 6% interest on accounts, compounded annually. Because interest is paid once, at the end of the year, the effective annual return, EAR, is 6%. If the 6% interest is paid on a semi-annual basis—3% every six months—the effective annual return is larger than 6% because interest is earned on the 3% interest earned at the end of the first six months. In this case, to calculate the EAR, the interest rate per compounding period—six months—is 0.03 (that is, 0.06 ÷ 2) and the number of compounding periods in an annual period is 2:

$$EAR = (1 + i)^n - 1$$

$$EAR = (1 + 0.03)^2 - 1 = 1.0609 - 1 = 0.0609 \text{ or } 6.09\%$$

Extending this example to the case of quarterly compounding with a nominal interest rate of 6% we first calculate the interest rate per period, i, and the number of compounding periods in a year, n:

$$i = 0.06 \div 4 = 0.015 \text{ per quarter}$$

$$n = 12 \text{ months} \div 3 \text{ months} = 4 \text{ quarters in a year}$$

The EAR is

$$EAR = (1 + 0.015)^4 - 1 = 1.0614 - 1 = 0.0614 \text{ or } 6.14\%$$

Let's see how this math will help you compare investments. Suppose there are two banks: Bank A, paying 12% interest compounded semiannually, and Bank B: paying 11.9% interest compounded monthly. Which bank offers you the best return on your money? Comparing APR's, Bank A provides the higher return. But what about compound interest? We calculate the EAR for each account as

Bank A:

$$EAR = (1 + (0.12 \div 2))^2 - 1$$
$$= (1 + 0.06)^2 = 1.1236 - 1$$
$$= 0.1236 \text{ or } 12.36\%$$

Bank B:

$$EAR = (1 + (0.119 \div 12))^{12} - 1$$
$$= (1 + 0.0099)^{12} - 1 = 1.1257 - 1$$
$$= 0.1257 \text{ or } 12.57\%$$

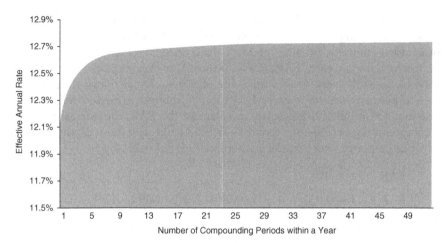

EXHIBIT 4.1   Effective Interest Rates for 12% APR with Different Frequencies of Compounding

Bank B offers the better return on your money, even though it advertises a lower APR. If you deposit $1,000 in Bank A for one year, you will have $1,123.60 at the end of the year. If you deposit $1,000 in Bank B for one year, you will have $1,125.70 at the end of the year, providing the better return on your savings.

You can see the effect on the EAR of the frequency of compounding within the year in Exhibit 4.1. In this exhibit, we graph the EAR that is equivalent to an APR of 12% for different frequencies of compounding, ranging from one compounding period a year (and, therefore, APR is equal to EAR), to compounding 52 times in a year (in other words, weekly). With weekly compounding, the EAR is 12.734%.

Example 4.3

Suppose a bank offers you lending rates at 6% APR, with interest compounded monthly. What is the effective rate of interest on this lending? The EAR is 6.168%: $EAR = (1 + 0.005)^{12} - 1 = \mathbf{6.168\%}$.

Example 4.4

Suppose your credit card states that interest on unpaid balances is 24% APR, with interest compounded monthly. What is the effective annual rate of interest on unpaid balances? The EAR is 26.824%: $EAR = (1 + 0.02)^{12} - 1 = \mathbf{26.824\%}$.

Example 4.5

The ABC Credit Card Company offers you a credit card with an APR of 19.5%. If interest compounds daily, what is the effective annual rate of interest on this credit card? You know the following: APR = 19.5%; n = 365 and $i = 0.195 \div 365 = 0.00534247$. The EAR is therefore 21.525%: EAR = $(1 + 0.00534247)^{365} - 1 = 0.21525$ or **21.525%**.

Example 4.6

A payday loan is a short-term loan with very high interest rates. In a typical payday loan, if you want to borrow $100 you write a check for $125. The lender holds on to your check during the loan period. At the end of the loan period, usually 10 to 14 days, the lender deposits your check. If you want to extend your loan, you pay the minimum of $25 cash and then enter into a new contract to pay. If you do not pay off the loan or pay the fee to roll over the loan, the lender will deposit your check and you risk being charged with writing bad checks.

What is the APR for this payday loan?

$$APR = 0.25\ (365/14) = \mathbf{651.79\%}.$$

What is the EAR for this payday loan?

$$EAR = (1 + 0.25)^{365/14} - 1 = \mathbf{3{,}351.86\%}.$$

The regulations pertaining to payday loans vary among states, but most states allow very generous lending terms—generous, that is, to the lenders.[4]

 TRY IT! 4.2 EFFECTIVE INTEREST RATES

A credit card offers a rate of 19.4% on unpaid balances. Interest compounds daily. What is the effective annual rate on this credit card?

Continuous Compounding   The extreme frequency of compounding is continuous compounding. Continuous compounding is when interest compounds at the smallest possible increment of time (that is, instantaneously,

---

[4]For a list of state limits on payday loans, see the Bankrate Monitor at *Bankrate.com*.

if you can imagine that). In continuous compounding, the rate per period becomes extremely small, which you can conclude if you divided the APR by infinity:

$$i = \text{APR} \div \infty$$

Along with this strange result, the number of compounding periods in a year, n, is infinite. As the rate of interest, i, gets smaller and the number of compounding periods approaches infinity, the EAR is

$$\text{EAR} = (1 + {^{\text{APR}}\!/\!_n})^n - 1$$

where APR is the annual percentage rate. What does all this mean? It means that the interest rate per period approaches 0 and the number of compounding periods approaches infinity—at the same time! In the 1730s, a mathematician, Leonhard Euler, who was working on a string of mathematical issues that originated in the 1600s, noticed that for a given nominal interest rate under continuous compounding, the relationship between the nominal interest rate and the effective rate hinges on e:

$$\text{EAR} = e^{\text{APR}} - 1$$

e is the mathematical representation for the base of the natural logarithm. While much of that is beyond what we need for our purposes, the use of e does help us figure out the effective rate.

FINANCIAL MATH IN ACTION

Euler's e, which we use when interest compounds continuously, came out of work on logarithms. So why is e so useful? Because, in addition to compound interest, we can use e to describe phenomena such as radioactive decay and astronomical functions.

Want to learn more about e? Check out *e: The Story of a Number* by Eli Maop (Princeton University Press, 1994).

For the stated 6% annual interest rate compounded continuously, the EAR is

$$\text{EAR} = e^{0.06} - 1 = 1.0618 - 1 \quad \text{EAR} = 0.0618 \text{ or } 6.18\%$$

The relation between the frequency of compounding, for a given stated rate, and the effective annual rate of interest for this example indicates that the greater the frequency of compounding, the greater the EAR.

Example 4.7

Which of the following terms represents the lowest cost of credit on an effective annual interest rate basis?

> A: 10% APR, interest compounded semiannually.
>
> B: 9.75% APR, interest compounded continuously.
>
> C: 10.5% APR, interest compounded annually.
>
> D: 9.8% APR, interest compounded quarterly.

Answer: **D.**

$$EAR = (1 + 0.05)^2 - 1 = 10.25\%$$
$$EAR = e^{0.0975} - 1 = 10.241\%$$
$$EAR = 10.5\%$$
$$EAR = (1 + 0.0245)^4 - 1 = 10.166\%$$

Calculator and Spreadsheet Applications   Financial calculators typically have a built-in program to help you go from APRs to EARs and vice versa. For example, using the financial calculator, we can calculate the EAR that corresponds to a 10% APR with quarterly compounding: [5] The result is an EAR of 10.3813%.

TI-83/84 Using TVM Solver	HP10B
EFF(10,4)	10 NOM%
ENTER	4 P/Y
	EFF%

In a similar manner, we can calculate the nominal (i.e., APR) rate that corresponds to a given EAR. Suppose we want to find the nominal rate with

---

[5]Because these calculations require changing the payments per period settings (i.e., P/YR) in some calculator models, be sure to change these back to one payment per period following the calculations—otherwise all subsequent financial calculations may be incorrect.

quarterly compounding that is equivalent to an effective rate of 10%. The equivalent APR is 9.6455%. In other words, if a lender charges 9.6455% APR, it will earn, effectively, 10% on the loan.

TI-83/84 Using TVM Solver	HP10B
NOM(10,4)	10 EFF%
ENTER	4 P/Y
	NOM%

Continuous compounding calculations cannot be done using the built in finance programs. However, most calculators—whether financial or not—have a program that allows you to perform calculations using e, the base of natural logarithms. The EAR corresponding to an APR with continuous compounding is 10.52%, which you can calculate as $e^{0.1} - 1$.

TI-83/84	HP10B
e^x(.1)-1 ENTER	.1
	$e^x - 1 =$

We can also use spreadsheet functions to calculate either the nominal rate or the effective rate. In Microsoft Excel, for example, you can calculate the effective rate that is equivalent to an APR of 10% with monthly compounding as

$$=EFFECT(.10,12)$$

which produces an answer of 10.471%.

Similarly, finding the nominal rate with monthly compounding that is equivalent to an EAR of 10%,

$$=NOMINAL(.10,12)$$

which produces an answer of 9.569%.

Suppose you have a loan of $100,000 that requires payments of $3,874.81 per month for 30 months. What is the effective annual rate? We can represent this problem in the mathematical relationship as

$$\$100,000 = \sum_{t=1}^{30} \frac{\$3,874.81}{(1 + i)^t}$$

The effective annual rate, EAR, is still calculated as

$$EAR = (1 + i)^{12} - 1$$

but we first have to determine the monthly rate. Using a financial calculator or spreadsheet to solve for the i, we have a monthly rate of 1%:

TI-83/84	HP10B	Microsoft Excel
N = 30	30 N	=RATE(30,3874.81,−100000,0)
PMT = 3874.81	3874.81 PMT	
PV = −100000	100000 +/− PV	
FV = 0	I/YR	
Solve for I		

Therefore, the EAR is $(1 + 0.01)^{12} -1 = 12.683\%$. The APR of this loan (that is, what is advertised) is 12%: APR = 1% × 12 = 12%.

The calculation of the effective annual rate depends on the information that the lender provides. Some lenders will quote the loan amount, the payments, and the number of payments. Other lenders simply provide the APR and the frequency of payments.

DETERMINING THE UNKNOWN INTEREST RATE

Let's say that you have $1,000 to invest today and in five years you would like the investment to be worth $2,000. What interest rate would satisfy your investment objective? We know the present value (PV = $1,000), the future value (FV = $2,000) and the number of compounding periods ($n = 5$). Using the basic valuation equation,

$$FV = PV(1 + i)^n$$

and substituting the known values of FV, PV, and n,

$$\$2,000 = \$1,000 \, (1 + i)^5$$

Rearranging, we see that the ratio of the future value to the present value is equal to the compound factor for five periods at some unknown rate:

$$\$2,000 \div \$1,000 = (1 + i)^5 \text{ or } 2.000 = (1 + i)^5$$

where 2.000 is the compound factor.

Therefore, we have one equation with one unknown, i. We can determine the unknown interest rate either mathematically or by using a financial calculator.

We can determine the interest rate more precisely, however, by solving for i mathematically:

$$2 = (1 + i)^5$$

Taking the fifth root of both sides, and representing this operation in several equivalent ways,

$$1 + i = 2^{1/5} = 20^{0.20}$$

You'll need a calculator to figure out the fifth root:

$$2^{0.20} = 1.1487 = (1 + i)$$
$$i = 1.1487 - 1 = 0.1487 \text{ or } 14.87\%$$

CALCULATION TIP

Want to take the root of a value that is not the square root? To take the nth root, you take the base to the power of $1/n$. Consider the following examples of taking roots of 100:

Root	Calculation	Value
3rd root	$\sqrt[3]{100} = 100^{1/3} = 100^{0.333}$	4.6416
4th root	$\sqrt[4]{100} = 100^{1/4} = 100^{0.25}$	3.1623
5th root	$\sqrt[5]{100} = 100^{1/5} = 100^{0.2}$	2.5119
10th root	$\sqrt[10]{100} = 100^{1/10} = 100^{0.1}$	1.5849

In the TI 83/84 calculator, use ^ for the power. In the HP 10B calculator, use y^x.

Therefore, if you invested $1,000 in an investment that pays 14.87% compounded interest per year, for five years, you would have $2,000 at the end of the fifth year. We can formalize an equation for finding the interest rate when we know PV, FV, and n from the valuation equation and notation: $FV = PV (1 + i)^n$. Thus, using algebra,

$$i = \left(\sqrt[n]{FV/PV} \right) - 1$$

As an example, suppose that the value of an investment today is $100 and we expect the value of the investment in five years is to be $150. What is the annual rate of appreciation in value of this investment over the five-year period?

We can use the math or financial programs in a calculator to solve for i, which is 8.447%.

TI-83/84 Using TVM Solver	HP10B	Microsoft Excel
N = 5	100 +/− PV	=RATE(5,0,−100,150,0,.10)
I% = Solve	5 N	
PV = −100	150 FV	
PMT = 0	I/YR	
FV = 150		

Example 4.8

Suppose you borrow $1,000, with terms that you will repay in a lump sum of $1,750 at the end of three years. What is the effective interest rate on this loan? The inputs are: PV = $1,000; FV = $1,750; and $n = 3$. Solving, $i = (\$1,750 \div \$1,000)^{1/3} - 1 = 20.51\%$.

Application: Time-Weighted Return There are many applications in which we need to determine the rate of change in values over time. To accomplish this, we calculate the time-weighted return. Examples include the growth in a savings account over time if interest rates change periodically and the growth in an investment portfolio over time. If values are changing over time, we refer to the rate of change as the *growth rate* if it is increasing over time, or the *rate of decline* or a *negative growth rate* if values are decreasing over time.

To make comparisons easier, we usually specify the growth rate as a rate per year. We can use the information about the starting value (the PV), the ending value (the FV), and the number of periods to determine the rate of growth of values over this time. To make comparisons among investments, we typically need to determine the average annual growth rate.

For example, consider an investment that has a value of $100 in year 0, a value of $150 at the end of the first year and a value of $200 at the end of two periods. What is this investment's annual growth rate?

$$PV = \$100$$

$$FV = \$200$$

$$n = 2$$

We know from the basic valuation equation that $FV = PV\,(1 + i)^n$. Rearranging and solving for i, we can see that

$$i = \sqrt[n]{\frac{FV}{PV}} - 1$$

Inserting the known values into this equation to solve for i, we conclude that the growth was 41.42%:

$$i = (\$200 \div \$100)^{1/2} - 1 = 20.5 - 1 = 1.4142 - 1 = 41.42\%$$

We could have easily used our spreadsheet program or financial calculator to perform this calculation as well.[6] Checking our work,

$$\$100\,(1 + 0.4142) \times (1 + 0.4142) = \$200$$

Therefore, $100 grows to $200 at the rate of 41.42% per year.

This rate is the geometric average of the annual growth rates. To see this, consider the two annual growth rates for this example. The growth

---

[6]Remember, though the inputs are PV = 100, FV = 200, and $n = 22$, you need to actually enter the present value as a negative value to use the built-in programs for solving for I/YR or RATE, for your financial calculator or spreadsheet functions, respectively.

rate in the first year is ($150 − 100) ÷ \$100 = \$150 ÷ \$100 = 50%. The growth rate for the second year is ($200 − 150) ÷ \$150 = 33.3333%. We calculate the *geometric average return* (or *geometric mean return*) as

$$\text{Geometric average return} = [(1 + i_1) \times (1 + i_2) \times \cdots (1 + i_n)]^{1/n} - 1$$

where the subscript on *i* indicates the period. For this example is

$$\text{Geometric average return} = [(1 + 0.50) \times (1 + 0.3333)]^{1/2} - 1 = 41.42\%$$

This is different from the arithmetic average rate of $(0.50 + 0.3333) \div 2 = 41.67\%$. The arithmetic average is not appropriate because it does not consider the effects of compounding. When we are dealing with returns on investments, we often refer to the geometric average of returns as simply the time-weighted return.

We can apply this return calculation to investments. Consider the returns on the S&P 500 Index for the following years:[7]

Year	Return
2001	−11.89%
2002	−11.20%
2003	28.69%
2004	10.88%
2005	4.91%
2006	15.79%
2007	5.49%

Over the years 2005 through 2007, the average annual return on the S&P 500 index was

$$\text{Return 2005–2007} = [(1 + 0.0491) \times (1 + 0.1579)$$
$$\times (1 + 0.0549)]^{1/3} - 1 = 8.6175\%$$

---

[7]We downloaded the total returns on the S&P 500 index from the Standard & Poor's web site, www2.standardandpoors/spf/xls/MONTHLY.xls. These returns include not only the change in the value of the index, but also the dividends paid on the index's stocks.

Over the years 2001 through 2007, the average annual return on the S&P 500 index was 5.2493%:

Year	1 + return
2001	0.8811
2002	× 0.8880
2003	× 1.2869
2004	× 1.1088
2005	× 1.0491
2006	× 1.1579
2007	× 1.0549
Product	1.052493
Less	1.000000
Return	0.052493

Example 4.9

Walt Disney Co. paid the following annual dividends from 2004 through 2008:

Year	Dividends Paid (in millions)	Dividends per Share
2004	$430	$0.21
2005	$490	$0.24
2006	$519	$0.27
2007	$637	$0.31
2008	$664	$0.35

1. What has been the growth in dividends paid between 2004 and 2008?
2. What has been the growth in dividends per share between 2004 and 2008?[8]

Answer:
1. PV = $430; FV = $664; $n = 4$; Solve for i. $i = 11.4743\%$.
2. PV = $0.21; FV = $0.35; $n = 4$; Solve for i. $i = 13.6219\%$.

---

[8]Dividends per share are dividends paid divided by the number of shares outstanding.

Why four periods, instead of five? Because we are looking at growth from 2004 through 2008, so therefore from 2004 to 2005 is one period, 2005 to 2006 is the second period, and so on.

The dividends per share grew at a faster rate than the total dollar of dividends paid because the company bought back some shares of stock, which reduces the number of shares outstanding.

FINANCE MATH IN ACTION

The Office of Federal Housing Enterprise and Oversight maintains an index of home values for the United States, regions, and metropolitan statistical areas (MSA).* We can use the financial math to determine the average annual growth in the value of homes, based on index values:

End of Year	Miami-Miami Beach, Florida MSA	Champaign-Urbana, Illinois MSA
1985	67.62	78.95
2000	127.97	127.58
2007	338.31	179.36

1985 through 2007

There are 22 years of growth from the end of 1985 to the end of 2007. The calculation for the Miami-Miami Beach MSA home price index indicates a growth of 7.583%:

$$\text{growth} = \sqrt[22]{\frac{338.31}{67.62}} - 1 = 7.583\% \text{ per year}$$

We could have also used a calculator or spreadsheet with the inputs of PV = 67.62; FV = 338.31, and $n = 22$.

The Champaign-Urbana MSA home price growth over the same period was 3.8%:

$$\text{growth} = \sqrt[22]{\frac{179.36}{78.95}} - 1 = 3800\% \text{ per year}$$

*You can find the value of the indexes for all MSA at the Office of Federal Housing Enterprise Oversight (OFHEO) web site, www.ofheo.gov.

(*Continued*)

FINANCE MATH IN ACTION (*Continued*)

2000 through 2007:

Miami-Miami Beach MSA: growth = $\sqrt[7]{\frac{338.31}{127.97}} - 1 = 14.899\%$ per year

Champaign-Urbana MSA: growth = $\sqrt[7]{\frac{179.36}{127.58}} - 1 = 4.987\%$ per year

Application: The Money-Weighted Return   The time-weighted return is useful in situations when you want to determine returns when there are no cash flows going in or out of the investment during its life. However, if you do have cash inflows or outflows during the investment's life, a better measure of return is the money-weighted return.

The *money-weighted return*, also known as the internal rate of return or the *dollar-weighted return*, considers the money flowing in and out of the investment. Suppose you have an investment with the following cash flows:

End of Year	Cash Flow
2011	−$100,000
2012	+20,000
2013	+30,000
2014	+40,000
2015	+50,000

The money-weighted return is the return that equates the present value of the cash inflows—the $20,000, $30000, $40,000 and $50,000—with the cash outflow—the $100,000.

Representing this in an equation,

$$CF_0 = \sum_{t=1}^{N} \frac{CF_t}{(1+IRR)^t}$$

and inserting the cash flows for the problem at hand:

$$-\$100,000 = \frac{\$10,000}{(1+IRR)^1} + \frac{\$20,000}{(1+IRR)^2} + \frac{\$30,000}{(1+IRR)^3} + \frac{\$40,000}{(1+IRR)^4}$$

We can solve this by using trial and error (which is usually no fun), the IRR function in a financial calculator, or the IRR function in a spreadsheet:

TI-83/84 Using TVM Solver	HP10B	Microsoft Excel
List: {20000,30000,40000,50000} STO L1 IRR(−100000,L1)	100000 +/− CFj 20000 CFj 30000 CFj 40000 CFj 50000 CFj IRR	

	A	B	
1	2011	−100000	
2	2012	20,000	
3	2013	30,000	
4	2014	40,000	
5	2015	50,000	
6			
7	IRR		← = IRR(B1:B5)

The internal rate of return for this series of cash flows is 12.826%.

Time- versus Money-Weighted Returns To see the difference between the time-weighted and money-weighted returns, let's compare these methods of calculation on the following investment. Suppose you buy the stock on January 1, 2010 and sell the stock on January 1, 2012, receiving dividends at the beginning of 2011 and 2012:

Date	Stock Value	Dividend
December 31, 2010	$20	
December 31, 2011	$25	$1
December 31, 2012	$20	$1

The time-weighted return requires you to calculate the return for each period. We refer to this return as the holding period return (HPR). For a given period, the HPR is

$$\text{HPR for one period} = \frac{\text{Ending value} + \text{dividend} - \text{beginning value}}{\text{Beginning value}}$$

In our example, we must calculate the HPR for two periods: the year ending December 31, 2011 and the year ending December 31, 2012:[9]

Date	Stock Value	Dividend	HPR for the Year
December 31, 2010	$20		
December 31, 2011	$22	$1	$\dfrac{\$25 - 20 + 1}{\$20} = 0.30$
December 31, 2012	$20	$1	$\dfrac{\$20 - 25 + 1}{\$25} = -0.16$

Using these HPR, the time-weighted return is

$$\text{Time-weighted return} = [(1 + 0.30) \times (1 - 0.16)]^{1/2} - 1 = 4.5\%$$

We have to first identify the cash inflows and outflows in order to calculate the money-weighted return:

Date	Cash Flow
December 31, 2010	−$20
December 31, 2011	$1
December 31, 2012	$21

The money-weighted return is 5%. So which return do you use? The money-weighted return is the true return on the investment and is therefore preferred.

When do you use the time-weighted return?

The time-weighted return on investment is useful when you want to determine a return from one point in time to another, such as when you want to check the return on your portfolio between specific years. However, if you invested additional money or withdrew funds from the portfolio within this time, the time-weighted return is not accurate.

When do you use the money-weighted return?

The money-weighted return on investment is useful when you want to compare investments that require different size investments. And

---

[9] So if this is the HPR, why don't we just calculate the return over the two years as the ratio of (1) the difference in the stock value (which is $0 in this example), plus the $2 of dividends, to (2) the beginning stock value? First, because there are two periods and we need to consider this fact, and second because we can't just add the two dividend payments because they are received at different points in time and, hence, have different time values.

money-weighted returns are useful in determining the return on an investment when there are deposits and/or withdrawals during the lifetime of the investment.

Mathematically, there is a problem when using the money-weighted return in certain circumstances. If the cash flows change sign—from positive to negative or negative to positive—more than once during the life of the investment, there is no unique, mathematical solution to the problem and therefore whatever return that the calculator or spreadsheet calculates is not useful.[10]

 ## TRY IT! 4.3: RETURN ON INVESTMENT

Suppose you bought a stock today for $45. If the stock does not pay dividends, but you expect this stock to increase by 5% in the first year and 7% in the second year, what is your anticipated annual return on investment?

FINANCIAL MATH IN ACTION

The Beardstown Business and Professional Women's Investment Club—more familiarly known as the Beardstown Ladies—was an investment group of women in Illinois who reported returns on their investments that were simply too good to be true.

Started in 1983, the Ladies pooled their funds and invested these funds. They reported returns that exceeded the return on the market for the same period, which led to television appearances and book deals.

What was the key to their success? As it turns out, their apparent success was from ignoring additional contributions to the investment funds. By calculating returns incorrectly—by looking at the growth in the total funds, while ignoring investors' additional contributions into the fund, they were able to report that they beat the market. Once the problem with return calculations was exposed in the press in 1998, the Ladies retreated from the limelight.*

Bottom line? If it looks too good to be true, it probably is.

*This was exposed by Shane Tritsch ["Bull Marketing," *Chicago magazine*, March 1998].

---

[10] In this last problem, there was only one sign change in the cash flows (from −$20 to $1), so there is no problem.

RULES

The Rule of 72

The *Rule of 72* is a quick and approximate method of determining the combination of interest rate and number of periods needed to double your money. For example, if the interest rate is 6%, the approximate number of periods is $72 \div 6 = 12$. Using a calculator or spreadsheet, it takes 11.8957 periods.[11]

We could also use this rule to determine the interest rate for a given number of periods. For example, what would the interest rate have to be for you to double your money in 12 years? According to the Rule of 72, the rate is 6%, and using a calculator the rate is 5.9463%.[12]

The Rule of 72 is a good approximation for the number of periods:

Interest Rate	Approximate Number of Periods	Accurate Number of Periods
3%	24.00	23.45
4%	18.00	17.67
5%	14.40	14.25
6%	12.00	11.90
7%	10.29	10.24
8%	9.00	9.01
9%	8.00	8.04
10%	7.20	7.27

Looking at this from the perspective of estimating the interest rate:

Number of Periods	Approximate Interest Rate	Accurate Interest Rate
3	24.00%	25.99%
4	18.00%	18.92%
5	14.40%	14.87%
6	12.00%	12.25%
7	10.29%	10.41%
8	9.00%	9.05%
9	8.00%	8.01%
10	7.20%	7.18%

---

[11] You can solve for the number of periods directly using the basic equation, $FV = PV (1 + i)^n$. To solve for n, you need to take logs, rearrange, and solve for n: $n = (\ln 2 - \ln 1) / \ln(1 + i)$; $n = 11.89566$.

[12] You can solve directly for the interest rate by rearranging the basic equation $FV = PV (1 + i)^n$, and considering that the ratio of the future value to the present value, $FV \div PV$ is 2: $i = \sqrt[12]{2} - 1 = 5.9463\%$.

The rule tends to be more accurate when solving for an interest rate when the number of periods is around ten periods, and more accurate when solving for the number of periods when the interest rate is around 7.85%, but it is a good rule-of-thumb no matter the rate or number of periods.

The Rule of 69

The *Rule of 69* is a quick and approximate method of determining the combination of interest rate and number of years needed to double your money if interest is continuously compounded. For example, if the interest rate is 6%, continuously compounded, the number of years needed to double your money is $69 \div 6 = 11.5$ years. Solving directly, the number of periods is 11.55245.[13]

Why do we refer to this rule as the Rule of 69? Because the natural logarithm of 2 is 0.693147, which, in percentage terms, is 69%. This rule is often "rounded up" and referred to as the *Rule of 70*, but as a Rule of 69, it's pretty accurate.

Other Rules

We can use other rules for simple approximations of interest rates and number of periods. The Rule of 114 is similar to the Rule of 72, but involves the tripling of values, whereas the Rule of 144 is the approximation for quadrupling values. You should note, however, that these are rules of thumb and that using a calculator or a spreadsheet will produce values that are more accurate.

SUMMARY

Understanding how to calculate effective interest rates and yields enables you to make better choices, whether you are involved in borrowing or in lending. One of the most useful mathematical tools in finance is the effective annual rate formula, which enables you to put different financing terms on a common, annual basis.

In addition to calculating effective annual rates, we also looked at calculating returns on investments. There are different types of returns that you can calculate to evaluate an investment, but the two most common are the time-weighted return and the money-weighted return. If you want to

---

[13] Solving this directly, $e^{\text{APR} \times n} = 2$; $\text{APR} \times n = \ln 2$; $0.06 \times n = 0.693147$; $n = 11.55245$.

evaluate the success of a particular investment over time, you can evaluate this using the time-weighted return, which is a geometric mean of the individual periods' returns. If the investment requires you to make additional investments or you intend to make withdrawals during the life of the investment, you will want to use the money-weighted return on investment to get the best reading of the return on your investment.

"TRY IT" SOLUTIONS

4.1. APR

First, identify the compounding period and the number of these periods in a year.

The compounding period is 10 days.

In a year period, there are 36.5 of these 10-day periods, so n is 36.5.

Second, identify the rate period compounding period. The interest per period, i, is 0.175.

The APR is therefore: APR $= i \times n = 0.175 \times 36.5 = 6.3875$ or **638.75%**

4.2. Effective Annual Rate of Interest

$$\text{EAR} = \left(1 + \frac{0.194}{365}\right)^{365} - 1 = 21.4034\%$$

4.3. Return on Investment

The average annual return on investment is $[(1 + 0.05) \times (1 + 0.07)]^{1/2} - 1 = 5.995\%$

Another way of looking at this is that you are anticipating that the stock will be worth $\$45 \times (1 + 0.05) \times (1 + 0.07) = \$50.5575$ two years from now. Solving for i,

$$i = \sqrt[2]{\frac{\$50.5575}{\$45}} - 1 = 5.995\%$$

PROBLEMS

4.1. Under what conditions does the effective annual rate of interest (EAR) differ from the annual percentage rate (APR)?

4.2. As the frequency of compounding increases within the annual period, what happens to the relation between the EAR and the APR?

4.3. If interest is paid at a rate of 5% per year, compounded quarterly, what is the:
   a. annual percentage rate?
   b. effective annual rate?

4.4. L. Shark is willing to lend you $10,000 for three months. At the end of six months, L. Shark requires you to repay the $10,000, plus 50%.
   a. What is the length of the compounding period?
   b. What is the rate of interest per compounding period?
   c. What is the annual percentage rate associated with L. Shark's lending activities?
   d. What is the effective annual rate of interest associated with L. Shark's lending activities?

4.5. The Consistent Savings and Loan is designing a new account that pays interest quarterly. They wish to pay, effectively, 16% per year on this account. Consistent S & L wants to advertise the annual percentage rate on this new account. What is the APR that corresponds to an effective rate of 16% for this new account?

4.6. If the annual percentage rate is 9.5% and interest compounds continuously, what is the effective annual rate of interest?

4.7. If the annual percentage rate is 10% and interest compounds quarterly, what is the effective annual rate of interest?

4.8. Consider an investment that earns 5% in the first year, 6% in the second year, and 7% in the third year. What is the time-weighted return on this investment?

4.9. Consider an investment that requires $5,000 today, but promises $4,000 one year from today and $2,000 two years from today. What is the money-weighted return on this investment?

4.10. If a mortgage requiring monthly payments is advertised as having a 6% APR, what is the effective annual rate on this mortgage?

For solutions to these problems, see Appendix E.

A Few Applications

Loans

To Amortize or Not to Amortize

Creditors have better memories than debtors.
—Benjamin Franklin,
Poor Richard's Almanac (1758)

In previous chapters, you learned how to value an annuity and how to calculate the yields and interest rates on different types of financial arrangements. Using these tools will help you learn how to apply these calculations to analyze a loan in this chapter.

LOAN AMORTIZATION

Suppose you borrow $100,000 and must repay this loan and interest at the end of two years. If interest is 5% per year, compounded monthly, how much must you pay at the end of two years? We need to solve for the future value:

$$FV = \$100,000 \times \left(1 + \frac{0.05}{12}\right)^{24} - 1 = \$110,494.13$$

Effectively, you are paying $(1 + \frac{0.05}{12})^{12} - 1 = 5.1162\%$ on this loan.

If you pay off the loan in monthly installments, you will end up paying some of the amount borrowed—the principal or $100,000—with each loan payment. If you pay off a loan in periodic payments, we say that we are amortizing the loan. Therefore, *loan amortization* is the process of paying off a loan over time.

A common type of amortized loan is the home mortgage. A *mortgage* is an agreement attached to a debt obligation that specifies the property or other collateral that the borrower gives up an interest in if he or she fails to make payments when promised. The lender then has a lien on the collateral specified in the mortgage. A *home mortgage* is an agreement that gives the lender a claim on the borrower's home in the event of a default on the loan.

With loan amortization, we can figure out how much of each payment consists of principal and interest. If we know the amount borrowed, the number of payments, and the APR, we can determine the amount of the loan payments. With this information, we can also break down each payment into its interest and principal repayment. This is useful, for example, when we need to figure out how much interest we paid on a loan for a given year—say, for tax purposes.

Calculating the Payment Amount

Consider a loan of $100,000 in which you repay the loan in 24 installments. If the interest rate is 5% per year, we can calculate the amount of each payment by applying the relationship:

$$\text{PV} = \text{CF (present value annuity factor for } N = 24 \text{ and } I = 0.05 \div 12 = 0.0042)$$

We are given the following:	And then determine the inputs:
Amount borrowed is $100,000	PV = $100,000
Annual rate is 5%, with monthly payments	$i = 5\% \div 12 = 0.4167\%$
The loan is for two years	$N = 2 \times 12 = 24$ months

Our goal is to solve for the payment. In mathematical terms, this is

$$\text{PV} = \sum_{t=1}^{N} \frac{\text{PMT}}{\left(1 + \dfrac{\text{APR}}{12}\right)^t}$$

$$\$100{,}000 = \sum_{t=1}^{24} \frac{\text{PMT}}{\left(1 + \dfrac{0.05}{12}\right)^t} = \sum_{t=1}^{24} \frac{\text{PMT}}{(1 + 0.004167)^t}$$

Using a financial calculator, we solve for the payment, PMT:

TI-83/84 Using TVM Solver	HP10B
N = 24	2 N
I% = 5/12	5/12
PV = −100000	−100000 PV
PMT = *Solve*	PMT

We can also use a spreadsheet to perform this calculation. In Microsoft's Excel, we can solve for the monthly payment using the PMT function:

$$= \text{PMT (rate, number of payments, amount of loan,}$$
$$\text{future value, timing indicator)}$$

where the timing indicator is 1 for beginning of the period flows (i.e., annuity due) and 0 for end of period flows (i.e., ordinary annuity).

$$= \text{PMT } (.05/12, 24, - 100000, 0, 0)$$

Using a spreadsheet or a calculator, the monthly payment, PMT, is $4,378.19. In other words, if payments of $4,378.19 are made each month for 24 months, the $100,000 loan will be repaid and the lender earns a return that is equivalent to a 5% APR on this loan.

Example 5.1

Suppose you borrow $30,000 today and pay off this loan in quarterly payments over four years, with each payment made at the end of a quarter. If the APR is 6%, what is the amount of the payment that will pay off this loan? Answer: **$4,992.41** per quarter. You are given the following data inputs:

$$\text{PV} = \$100,000$$
$$N = 24$$
$$i = 6\% \div 4 = 1.5\%$$

Solving for the payment, the payment is $4,992.41.

Example 5.2

Suppose a bank is offering you two different types of loans. Loan A is an amortized loan over five years, with annual payments. Loan B is not amortized, but rather requires payment of the interest end of the loan when you repay the principal. The interest rate on both loans is 8%.

1. In which loan arrangement do you pay the most interest, in terms of the present value of the interest? Answer: **Loan B.**
2. In which loan arrangement do you pay the most principal, in terms of the present value of the principal repayments? Answer: **Loan A.**
3. Why do the present value of the interest and principal differ between these two loan arrangements? Answer: **Because of the timing.**

Loan A

Year	Beginning Balance	Payment	Interest	Principal Repayment	Ending Principal
1	$10,000.00	$2,504.56	$800.00	$1,704.56	$8,295.44
2	$8,295.44	$2,504.56	$663.63	$1,840.93	$6,454.51
3	$6,454.51	$2,504.56	$516.36	$1,988.20	$4,466.30
4	$4,466.30	$2,504.56	$357.30	$2,147.26	$2,319.04
5	$2,319.04	$2,504.56	$185.52	$2,319.04	$0.00

The present value of the interest is $2,108.50, and the present value of the principal repayment is $7,891.50:[1]

Year	PV of Interest	PV of Principal
1	$740.74	$1,578.30
2	568.96	1,578.30
3	409.90	1,578.30
4	262.63	1,578.30
5	126.26	1,578.30
Total PV	$2,108.50	$7,891.50

---

[1]The present value of the interest on Loan A is the sum of the present value of $800 discounted one period at 8%, $663.63 discounted two periods at 8%, and so on.

Loan B   The payment required at the end of five years is

$$FV = \$10,000 \times (1 + 0.08)^5 = \$14,693.28$$

This future value is comprised of \$10,000 of loan repayment and \$4,693.28 of interest.

The present value of the interest portion is

$$\$4,693.28 \div (1 + 0.08)^5 = \$3,194.17$$

and the present value of the principal repayment is

$$\$10,000 \div (1 + 0.08)^5 = \$6,805.83$$

Summarizing

	Loan A	Loan B
Present value of interest	\$2,108.50	\$4,693.28
Present value of principal repayment	7,891.50	6,805.83
Total present value	\$10,000.00	\$10,000.00

You end up paying the same amount for both loans, but in Loan A you pay less interest because the interest is based on a declining, amortizing principal. In Loan B you pay more interest because the interest is based on the full amount of the loan, the \$10,000, but you pay less principal (in a present value sense) because you put off repaying it until the end of the loan period.

 TRY IT! 5.1: LOAN PAYMENT

Suppose you borrow \$54,000 and pay this loan back in quarterly installments over five years, with an annual percentage rate (APR) of 6%. How much are your quarterly payments if these payments are due at the end of each quarter?

EXHIBIT 5.1 Loan Amortization on a $100,000 Loan for 24 Months and an Interest Rate of 5% per Year

A	B	C	D	E	F
Payment = 0.05/12 x B	Beginning Principal	Loan Payment	Interest on the Loan	Principal Paid Off = C − D	Remaining Principal = B − E
Today		$0.00	$0.00	$0.00	$100,000.00
1	$100,000.00	$4,387.14	$416.67	$3,970.47	$96,029.53
2	$96,029.53	$4,387.14	$400.12	$3,987.02	$92,042.51
3	$92,042.51	$4,387.14	$383.51	$4,003.63	$88,038.88
4	$88,038.88	$4,387.14	$366.83	$4,020.31	$84,018.57
5	$84,018.57	$4,387.14	$350.08	$4,037.06	$79,981.51
6	$79,981.51	$4,387.14	$333.26	$4,053.88	$75,927.63
7	$75,927.63	$4,387.14	$316.37	$4,070.77	$71,856.85
8	$71,856.85	$4,387.14	$299.40	$4,087.74	$67,769.12
9	$67,769.12	$4,387.14	$282.37	$4,104.77	$63,664.35
10	$63,664.35	$4,387.14	$265.27	$4,121.87	$59,542.48
11	$59,542.48	$4,387.14	$248.09	$4,139.05	$55,403.44
12	$55,403.44	$4,387.14	$230.85	$4,156.29	$51,247.14
13	$51,247.14	$4,387.14	$213.53	$4,173.61	$47,073.54
14	$47,073.54	$4,387.14	$196.14	$4,191.00	$42,882.54
15	$42,882.54	$4,387.14	$178.68	$4,208.46	$38,674.07
16	$38,674.07	$4,387.14	$161.14	$4,226.00	$34,448.08
17	$34,448.08	$4,387.14	$143.53	$4,243.61	$30,204.47
18	$30,204.47	$4,387.14	$125.85	$4,261.29	$25,943.18
19	$25,943.18	$4,387.14	$108.10	$4,279.04	$21,664.14
20	$21,664.14	$4,387.14	$90.27	$4,296.87	$17,367.27
21	$17,367.27	$4,387.14	$72.36	$4,314.78	$13,052.50
22	$13,052.50	$4,387.14	$54.39	$4,332.75	$8,719.74
23	$8,719.74	$4,387.14	$36.33	$4,350.81	$4,368.94
24	$4,368.94	$4,387.14	$18.20	$4,368.94	$0.00

Determining the Amount of Principal Repayment and Interest

Once we know the amount of each payment, we calculate the amount of interest and principal repayment associated with each loan payment. We report in the *loan amortization schedule* in Exhibit 5.1 the amortization of a $100,000 loan over 24 months with an APR of 5%:

- *Column B.* This is the amount of the loan that is still outstanding. This is the same as the ending balance from the prior period.
- *Column C.* The loan payment in each period is the same, $4,378.19.
- *Column D.* You calculate interest by multiplying the interest of $0.05 \div 12 = 0.004167$ or 0.4167%, by the beginning amount of the principal for the period.
- *Column E.* You calculate the principal repayment for the period as the difference between the loan payment, $4,378.19, and the interest.
- *Column F.* You calculate the principal remaining by subtracting the principal repayment for the period from the beginning principal amount.

As you can see in Exhibit 5.1, (1) the principal amount of the loan declines as payments are made, and (2) the proportion of each loan payment devoted to the repayment of the principal increases throughout the loan period from $3,970.47 for the first payment to $4,368.94 for the last payment.

We show the decline in the loan's principal graphically in Exhibit 5.2. You'll notice that the decline in the remaining principal is not linear, but is *curvilinear* due to the compounding of interest.

If the payments are due at the beginning of the month, the calculations are similar, but we need to adjust for the difference in timing. If the same

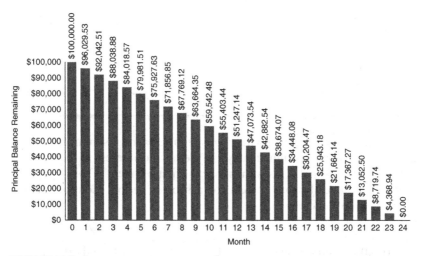

EXHIBIT 5.2 Loan Amortization of a $100,000 Loan for 24 Payments and an APR of 5%

$100,000 loan requires payments at the beginning of each month, the payments are $4,368.94 each month. Why are these payments less than when we make the payments at the end of each month? Because by making the payment sooner, you are paying off the principal sooner, and hence lowering your interest cost each period.

 TRY IT! 5.2: LOAN AMORTIZATION

Suppose you borrow $50,000 and will pay it back in semiannual installments over three years, and the APR on this loan is 8%. Complete the amortization schedule:

Year	Period	Beginning Balance	Payment	Interest	Principal Repayment	Ending Principal
1	1st six months	$50,000.00				
	2nd six months					
2	1st six months					
	2nd six months					
3	1st six months					
	2nd six months					

Here's a source of confusion when loans require payments immediately: The first payment is made immediately, so there is no interest in that first payment—it's all principal. This means that the first payment is solely principal and that you really have a loan for a shorter period. Consider the mathematical equivalency:

Scenario:

Loan of $100,000 paid off over 24 months, with a 5% APR. First payment made immediately.

Scenario:

Loan of $95,631.06 paid off over 23 months, with a 5% APR. First payment made at the end of the month.

Type of calculation: Type of calculation: Ordinary
  Annuity due   annuity

Inputs: Inputs:

$$PV = \$100,000$$
$$N = 24$$
$$i = 5\% \div 12$$

$$PV = \$95,631.06$$
$$N = 23$$
$$i = 5 \div 12$$

Solve for PMT   Solve for PMT
Payment = \$4,368.94   Payment = \$4,368.94

FINANCIAL MATH IN ACTION

Automobile dealers—once they get you in the office to talk to their
"finance" person—will provide you with the details of your payments
if you choose to finance the car. For example, the dealer often displays
a couple of financing options, quoting the APR, the monthly payment,
and the total interest paid over the life of the car.

Consider two financing options for buying a car for which you
need \$20,000 of financing.

	Option A	Option B
Amount borrowed	\$20,000	\$20,000
Loan period	36 months	12 quarters
Payment	\$626.73 per month	\$1,894.10 per quarter
Total interest paid	\$2,562.18	\$2,723.64

You will notice that you end up paying more interest over the life
of the loan in Option B, but does that matter? Not really, because this
is simply the sum of all the interest you pay over the three years—and
it doesn't consider that you'll be paying the interest sooner with the
monthly payments, as compared to the quarterly payments.

(Continued)

FINANCIAL MATH IN ACTION (*Continued*)

The effective annual rate on each loan lets us know that Option B is a better deal for the borrower:

	Option A	Option B
APR	8.000%	8.000%
EAR	8.300%	8.243%

In fact, the total interest paid over the life of the loan is actually a worthless piece of information because, with the time value of money, we know that you cannot sum values that occur in different periods of time without adjusting for the time value of money. But perhaps this helps steer consumers toward certain financing arrangements.

Bottom line? Don't worry about the sum total of interest paid over the life of the loan. Instead, focus on what you effectively pay on the loan.

INTEREST RATES ON LOANS

Loan arrangements often specify the amount of the loan, the payment amount, and the number of payments. However, what we really need in most cases, in order to compare borrowing opportunities, is to determine what it really costs us in terms of an interest rate. From basic loan information, you can calculate both the annual percentage rate and the effective annual rate of interest on the loan. We typically use an annualized rate of interest so that we can compare loans with different terms on some common basis.

Annual Payments

When a loan requires annual payment, solving for the interest rate on the loan is straightforward: Given the amount of the loan, the number of payments, and the amount of the payment, we can solve for the interest rate.

Consider a loan of $200,000 that is paid off with 10 annual payments of $25,000 each. We have the following data inputs:

$$PV = \$200,000$$

$$N = 10$$

$$PMT = \$25,000$$

We then have to solve for *i*, the interest rate.

TI 83/84 Using TVM Solver	HP10B	Excel
N =10	10 N	=RATE(10,25000, −200000,0)
PV = −200000	−200000 PV	
PMT = $25,000	25000 PMT	
Solve for I	*Solve for I*	

The rate is 4.2775%.[2] This means that the first payment of $25,000 represents $200,000 × 0.042775 = $8,555 of interest and $25,000 − $8,555 = $16,445 of principal repayment.

Payments More Frequent Than Annually

When comparing loan arrangements that have different terms, you need to be aware of two methods of stating interest: the annual percentage rate (APR) and the effective annual rate (EAR). By law, loan arrangements must report the APR. However, if compounding is more frequent than once per year, the APR will not be the true cost of the loan. Instead, for true comparability among loans, we need to use the EAR, which considers the frequency of compounding.

If the payments are annual payments, the interest APR and EAR are equivalent. If, however, the payments are more frequent than once per year we need to calculate the EAR, which will be greater than the APR.

Consider a loan for a Mustang convertible, with financing from Ford Motor Credit. The estimated selling price of the vehicle is $32,045. If you

---

[2]Using the mathematical representation of this problem, we could solve for the interest rate by using trial and error. However, the calculators and spreadsheets can perform this calculation a heck of a lot faster than we could using trial and error.

make no down payment, have no trade-in vehicle, and finance this over 60 months, your monthly payment will be $618.

So how do we translate this information into an APR or an EAR? First, we determine the basic information from the payment plan:

$$N = 60$$

$$PMT = \$618$$

$$PV = 32,045$$

Therefore,

$$PV = PMT \times \text{Present value annuity factor}$$

$$\$32,045 = \$618 \times \text{Present value annuity factor}$$

In this example, FV is zero and the type is 0, indicating payments made at the end of the month.

Using a calculator or spreadsheet, we first solve for the rate per compounding period, i:

TI-83/84	HP10B	Microsoft Excel
PV = −32045	PV = +/− 32045	=RATE(60,618, −32045,0,0)
N = 60	N = 60	
PMT = 618	PMT = 618	
I = Solve	I	

This generates the rate per month of $i = 0.4915\%$. We can then translate this rate into an APR by multiplying this rate by 12, and then translate this rate into an EAR by using compounding:[3]

$$APR = 0.4915\% \times 12 \qquad = 5.8979\%$$

$$EAR = (1 + 0.004915)^{12} - 1 \quad = 6.0601\%$$

---

[3]Why does this not work if you change the payments per year (P/Y)? Because compounding is *ignored* in the P/Y program. The following will produce the APR, not the EAR for i: PV = −32045; n = 60; PMT = 618; P/Y = 12; Solve for i. This will result in 5.8979%, not 6.0601%.

The key to solving for the effective annual rate is to find the rate per compounding period. If the compounding period is less than one year, we can then use the relation above, inserting the rate per compounding period and the number of compounding periods in a year to determine the effective annual rate.

Example 5.3

Consider a loan of $10,000 that is paid back in 24 monthly installments of $470.74 each, with the first installment due at the end of the first month. Calculating the EAR corresponding to this loan requires us to first calculate the monthly rate and then translate this rate into the EAR.

We are given the following data inputs:

$$PV = \$10,000$$
$$CF = \$470.74$$
$$N = 24$$

Using the ordinary annuity relation,

$$PV = CF \text{ (present value annuity factor, } N = 24, i =?)$$

and substituting the known values,

$$\$10,000 = \$470.74 \text{ (present value annuity factor, } N = 24, i =?)$$

we find that the present value annuity factor is 21.2431. Using a financial calculator, we find that the monthly rate, i, is 1%:

TI-83/84 Using TVM Solver	HP10B	Microsoft Excel
N = 24	10000 +/− PV	=RATE(24,470.74,−10000,0,0)
PV = −10000	24 N	
PMT = 470.74	470.74 PMT	
FV = 0	I/YR	
I% = Solve		

Therefore, the APR on this loan is $1\% \times 12 = 12\%$ and the effective annual rate on this loan is

$$\text{EAR} = (1 + 0.01)^{12} - 1 = 12.68\%$$

Example 5.4

Suppose you receive a loan of $10,000 that requires you to repay the loan in 60 monthly installments of $200 each. What is the effective annual rate of interest on this loan?

$$\text{Inputs: PV} = \$10,000; \ \text{CF} = \$200; \ N = 60$$

Using a calculator or spreadsheet function, $i = 0.61834\%$

$$\text{EAR} = (1 + 0.0061834)^{12} - 1 = 7.6778\%$$

 ## TRY IT! 5.3 INTEREST RATES ON LOANS

Consider a loan of $100,000, repaid in 30 semiannual payments of $5,783.01 each.

- What is the APR on this loan?
- What is the EAR on this loan?

DETERMINING THE NUMBER OF PERIODS

What if you want to make payments to pay off a loan, but you don't know how long it will take? As long as you know the APR, you can use an approach similar to what we did with the interest rate to solve for the number of payments.

Suppose you want to borrow $10,000. If the interest is 6% APR and payments are made quarterly, how long will it take to pay off this loan if you pay $1,000 each quarter? First, identify the given information: PV = $10,000; $i = 6\% \div 4 = 1.5\%$; PMT = $1,000.

The answer is 10.91565 periods. Because we are using discrete payments (that is, payments are made at the end of the period), it will take 11 quarterly payments—that is, two years and three quarters—to pay off this loan.

TI-83/84 Using TVM Solver	HP10B	Microsoft Excel
I% = 1.5	1.5 I/YR	=NPER(0.015,1000, −10000,0,0)
PV = −10000	10000 +/− PV	
PMT = 1000	1000 PMT	
FV = 0	N	
N = Solve		

VARIATIONS ON THE THEME

Using this basic information, you can determine the APR and effective rate for most any payment plan. Some of the variations that you may encounter are:

- *A down payment.* To adjust for a down payment, reduce the present value of the loan by the amount of the down payment so that the loan amount reflects only what is borrowed.
- *A balloon payment.* Add a future value to calculation in the amount of the balloon payment.
- *Additional payments.* How this affects your loan payment depends on the financing terms.
- *Interest-only adjustable rate loan.* This is a form of amortization in which the initial payments made on the loan are comprised solely of interest, and payments will pay down principal only after a specified period of time.

Balloon Payments

For example, in the Mustang financing example, if you also have a balloon payment of $1,000 at the end of the loan, you would include FV = 1,000 in the inputs to the calculator, and the monthly rate becomes 0.5695%, the APR is 6.8343% and the EAR is 7.2874%.

Example 5.5

Suppose you have the choice between two mortgages that require 360 monthly payments to retire the $400,000 borrowed. Mortgage A requires monthly payments of $2,528.27. Mortgage B requires monthly payments of $2,551.34 and a balloon payment of $50,000 at the end of 360 months.

Which mortgage has the lower cost? Mortgage A has a lower effective annual rate.

Input	Mortgage A	Mortgage B
PV	$400,000	$400,000
N	360	360
PMT	$2,528.38	$2,551.34
FV	$0	$50,000
i	0.5417%	0.5625%
APR	6.5004%	6.7500%
EAR	6.6976%	6.9628%

You'll notice that Mortgage B has higher payment than Mortgage A, even through it has a balloon payment at the end. Why? Because there is more interest paid earlier with Mortgage B because the principal is not amortized as fast as it is with Mortgage A; in other words, Mortgage B's payments have more interest and less principal, relative to Mortgage A.

You can see this when we graph the remaining principal for each mortgage, shown in Exhibit 5.3.

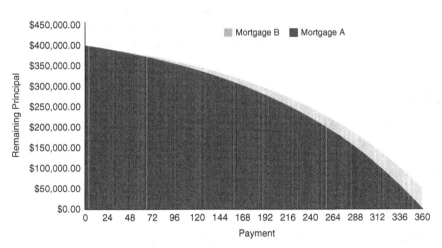

EXHIBIT 5.3 Remaining Principal for Mortgage A and Mortgage B. Both mortgages are loans of $400,000, but Mortgage B has a balloon payment of $50,000 at the end of 360 months.

Additional Payments

In some financing arrangements, you can pay more than your scheduled payment. We refer to these additional payments as *prepayments*. In most financing transactions, your periodic payment does not change. Instead, the remaining term of the loan changes, with the number of payments reduced accordingly.

Consider three financial arrangements:

	Loan C	Loan D	Loan E
Amount borrowed	−$100,000	−$100,000	−$100,000
APR	5%	5%	5%
Monthly payment	$536.82	$536.82	$536.82
Additional payment	$0	$10,000 at the end of the first 12 payments	$50 every payment
Original term of the loan	360 months	360 months	360 months

In the case of Loan D, the amortization proceeds as scheduled until you make the additional payment. At that point, the payments remain the same, but we adjust the number of payments. Consider the amortization of Loan D through the end of the first year:

Payment	Beginning Balance	Payment	Interest Paid	Principal Payment	Number of Payments Remaining
1	$100,000.00	$536.82	$416.67	$120.15	359.00
2	99,879.85	536.82	416.17	120.66	358.00
3	99,759.19	536.82	415.66	121.16	357.00
4	99,638.03	536.82	415.16	121.66	356.00
5	99,516.37	536.82	414.65	122.17	355.00
6	99,394.20	536.82	414.14	122.68	354.00
7	99,271.52	536.82	413.63	123.19	353.00
8	99,148.33	536.82	413.12	123.70	352.00
9	99,024.62	536.82	412.60	124.22	351.00
10	98,900.41	536.82	412.09	124.74	350.00
11	98,775.67	536.82	411.57	125.26	349.00
12	98,650.41	10,536.82	411.04	10,125.78	

The principal remaining after the twelfth payment is $98,650.41 − $10,125.78 = $88,524.63. If we amortize this remaining principal with payments of $536.82 each, how many payments are left? We know that PV = 88,524.63; PMT = 536.82; and $i = 5\% \div 12 = 0.4167\%$. Solving for N, we arrive at 279.43. In other words, there are 279 payments of $536.82 remaining, plus one payment of less than $536.82.

In the case of Loan E, we have to recalculate the number of remaining payments after each payment.

Payment	Beginning Balance	Payment	Interest Paid	Principal Payment	Number of Payments Remaining
1	$100,000.00	$586.82	$416.67	$170.15	296.74
2	99,829.85	586.82	415.96	170.86	295.74
3	99,658.98	586.82	415.25	171.58	294.74
4	99,487.41	586.82	414.53	172.29	293.74
5	99,315.11	586.82	413.81	173.01	292.74
6	99,142.11	586.82	413.09	173.73	291.74
7	98,968.38	586.82	412.37	174.45	290.74
8	98,793.92	586.82	411.64	175.18	289.74
9	98,618.74	586.82	410.91	175.91	288.74
10	98,442.83	586.82	410.18	176.64	287.74
11	98,266.19	586.82	409.44	177.38	286.74
12	98,088.81	586.82	408.70	178.12	285.74

Therefore, the payment of $10,000 at the end of the first year reduced the length of the loan more than the extra $50 per month:

	Loan C	Loan D	Loan E
Original term of the loan	360 months	360 months	360 months
Revised term of the loan	not revised	292 months	297 months

Interest-Only Adjustable Rate Mortgages

Interest-only (IO) *mortgages* are loans secured by a home, in which the payments in the early part of the loan period consist solely of interest. But after a specified period, the payments include both interest and principal. IO mortgages are typically a form of adjustable rate mortgages. Even if the interest rate on the loan remains the same, the payments on the loan will increase once the payments provide both interest and principal repayment.

Let's see how this type of amortization works by looking at a $200,000 loan for 30 years, repaid in monthly installments. If this is an IO mortgage, with a five-year IO payment period, and an initial interest rate of 5%, the monthly payments in the first five years is $(6\% \div 12) \times \$200,000 = \$1,000$. This monthly payment is solely interest, so the principal balance remaining at the end of five years is the $200,000. Therefore, when the first five years has passed, the payment will jump up to the monthly payment necessary to pay off the $200,000 mortgage in 25 years.

For the five-year IO with a rate of 6% for the life of the loan, the payment adjusts from $1,000 each period to $1,288.60:

Payment	Beginning Balance	Payment	Interest Paid	Principal Payment
60	$200,000.00	$1,000.00	$1,000.00	$0.00
61	$200,000.00	$1,288.60	$1,000.00	$288.60
62	$199,711.40	$1,288.60	$998.56	$290.05

We calculate the $1,288.60 payment with the inputs:

$$PV = \$200,000$$
$$N = 300$$
$$i = 6\% \div 12 = 0.5\%$$

If this were a traditional mortgage with a 6% rate paid over 360 months, the mortgage payment would be $1,199.10 each month.

The challenge that many homeowners faced with some of the adjustable rate mortgages in the early 2000s, is that the adjustment was at a rate different from the initial rate. For example, if the initial interest rate is 1% for the first three years of the 30-year $200,000 mortgage, and then adjusts to 8% after three years, the increase in the monthly payment is substantial.

For this adjustable rate mortgage, the initial monthly payments are $1\% \div 12 = 0.0833\% = \$166.67$. After three years, we calculate the monthly payments based on $PV = \$200,000$; $N = 324$; $i = 8\% \div 12 = 0.667\%$, which results in a payment of $1,508.56:

Payment	Beginning Balance	Payment	Interest Paid	Principal Payment
36	$200,000.00	$166.67	$166.67	$0.00
37	$200,000.00	$1,508.56	$1,333.33	$175.23
38	$199,824.77	$1,508.56	$1,332.17	$176.39

The cost of this mortgage, if the rate does not change after the third year adjustment to 8%, is effectively 6.477%. The problem that many homeowners face is the substantially larger mortgage payments (say, from $166.67 to $1,508.56), that they could not or would not want to pay.[4]

SUMMARY

Loans that require payments over time are very common borrowing arrangements. We can apply the basic financial math to calculate the amount of the payment, to determine the amount of interest and principal in each payment, or to figure out the cost of the financing. The ability to perform these calculations gives you the ability to compare different loan arrangements to determine the lowest cost.

"TRY IT" SOLUTIONS

5.1. Loan Payment

Inputs: $PV = \$54,000$; $N = 5 \times 4 = 20$; $i = 6\% \div 12 = 0.5\%$

Solve for PMT. PMT $= \$2,843.99$

5.2. Loan Amortization

Given: $i = 4\%$; $N = 6$; $PV = \$50,000$

Payment is $9,538.10

---

[4]Many homeowners had planned to either sell the home or refinance the mortgage prior to the adjustment, but credit and housing market conditions precluded that.

Amortization schedule:

Year	Period	Beginning Balance	Payment	Interest	Principal Repayment	Ending Principal
1	1st 6 months	$50,000.00	$9,538.10	$2,000.00	$7,538.10	$42,461.90
1	2nd 6 months	$42,461.90	$9,538.10	$1,698.48	$7,839.62	$34,622.29
2	1st 6 months	$34,622.29	$9,538.10	$1,384.89	$8,153.20	$26,469.08
2	2nd 6 months	$26,469.08	$9,538.10	$1,058.76	$8,479.33	$17,989.75
3	1st 6 months	$17,989.75	$9,538.10	$719.59	$8,818.51	$9,171.25
3	2nd 6 months	$9,171.25	$9,538.10	$366.85	$9,171.25	$0.00

5.3. Interest Rate on Loans

PMT = $5,783.01$; $N = 30$; PV = $100,000$. Solving for i, $i = 4\%$.

The APR is $4\% \times 2 = 8\%$.

The EAR is $(1 + 0.04)^2 - 1 = 8.16\%$.

PROBLEMS

5.1. What is the amount of periodic payment needed to repay a loan of $50,000 in 30 monthly payments if the APR on this loan is 6%?

5.2. Consider the terms for two loans for a loan of $100,000:

Loan A. Paid back in 24 end-of-month payments of $4,707.35 each

Loan B. Paid back in eight end-of-quarterly payments of $19,779.90 each

Which loan has the best deal in terms of the lowest effective annual cost?

5.3. Complete the following table for a loan of $15,000 that is repaid with three annual payments of $6,000 each:

Period	Beginning Balance	Payment	Interest	Principal Repayment	Ending Balance
Today	—	—	—	—	$15,000
1	$15,000	$6,000			
2		$6,000			
3		$6,000			$0

5.4. Suppose a car dealership is advertising a car loan with a 3% APR, and monthly payments over three years.

   a. If you buy a car and finance $30,000 with this loan, what is the amount of your monthly payment each month?

   b. What is the effective annual rate of interest on this loan?

5.5. Consider a loan of $100,000 that requires four annual installments of $28,201 each. Amortize this loan using the following table:

Period	Beginning Balance	Payment	Interest	Principal Repayment	Ending Balance
Today	—	—	—	—	$100,000
1	$100,000	$28,201.18			
2		$28,201.18			
3		$28,201.18			
4		$28,201.18			$0

5.6. Suppose you borrow $10,000 and are required to pay this back in three annual installments. And suppose the interest rate on this loan is 10%. What is the required payment each year?

5.7. Suppose you borrow $2,000 today and expect to pay $150 at the end of each year. If the interest rate is 6%, how long will it take to pay off the $2,000 loan?

5.8. Suppose you borrow $150,000 and pay it back over 20 years in annual payments. If the interest rate is 5%, complete the following information corresponding to the second year's payment:

Loan Payment	Interest	Repayment of Principal	End of Year Loan Balance

5.9. The Car Company will lend you $10,000 for your new car purchase. The Car Company requires that you pay the loan back in monthly payments of $332.14 each, for 36 monthly payments. What is the annual percentage rate (APR) and the effective annual rate (EAR) that The Car Company charges on this loan?

5.10. Suppose you can choose between two loans for $50,000, each with an APR of 6%:

	Loan 1	Loan 2
Term	36 months	36 months
Balloon payment at the end of the loan	$0	$10,000

What is the amount of monthly payment that is required for each loan?

For solutions to these problems, see Appendix E.

CHAPTER 6

Saving to Spend

You can be young without money, but you can't be old without it.
—Tennessee Williams

s you read in previous chapters, we can value any series of cash flows, whether we are valuing these cash flows today or in the future, and whether these cash flows are all the same or different. We build on the foundation of financial mathematics to solve common problems related to saving for later spending. We refer to these problems as deferred annuities because something—either withdrawals or deposits—is deferred to a later point in time.

We start with simple problems involving saving up for a series of cash flows, and then we will work our way to more complex retirement problems.

VALUING A DEFERRED ANNUITY

A *deferred annuity* is an annuity in which the first cash flow occurs beyond the end of the first period. The key to solving for the value of this annuity today is to break down the analysis into manageable steps. For example, if you are solving for a present value of a series of cash flows in the future, you can use these two steps:

Step 1. Solve for value of the series at a future point in time.

Step 2. Discount this value to the present.

Sound easy enough? Yes, but it is very easy to get tangled up in time, trying to figure out where values fall in the time continuum. We recommend that you diagram the problem, drawing a time line that depicts when the cash flows and values occur.

Ready to get tangled up in time? Consider a deferred annuity that consists of three payments of $1,000 and an interest rate of 5%, with the first cash flow three years from today. A few notes to sort out the flows and values:

- The annuity is deferred three periods: The first cash flow occurs at the end of the third period, the second cash flow occurs at the end of the fourth period, and so on.
- The series of future cash flows is an annuity—that is, the cash flows are even and periodic—so we can solve Step 1 as an ordinary annuity.
- A simple way of solving this problem is to first calculate the present value at the end of the second period, treating this as an ordinary annuity, and then discounting this present value (PV_2) two periods to the today (PV_0).

Step 1. Calculate the present value of a three-payment ordinary annuity

Today	1	2	3	4	5
		$952.381	$1,000	$1,000	$1,000
		907.029			
		863.838			
		$PV_2 = \$2,723.248$			

TI-83/84 Using TVM Solver	HP10B	Microsoft Excel
N = 3	3 N	=PV(0.05,3,1000,0) * −1
I% = 5	5 I/YR	
FV = 0	1000 PMT	
PMT =1000	PV	
PV = *Solve*	× −1	
× −1		

Step 2. Calculate the present value of a lump sum amount

Today	1	2	3	4	5
		$952.381	$1,000	$1,000	$1,000
		907.029	↩	↩	↩
		863.838			
		$PV_2 = \$2{,}723.248$			
$PV_0 = \$2{,}470.066$		↩			

Using a financial calculator or a spreadsheet:

TI-83/84 Using TVM Solver	HP10B	Microsoft Excel
N = 2	2 N	=PV(.05,2,0,2723.248,0)* −1
I% = 5	5 I/YR	
FV = 2723.248	2723.248 FV	
PMT = 0	PV	
PV = *Solve*	× −1	
× −1		

The present value of this deferred annuity is $2,470.07.[1] What does this mean? It means that if you deposit $2,470.07 in an account today that pays 5% interest, you will be able to make three withdrawals of $1,000 each from the account, staring in three years, leaving nothing in the account at the end.

After you deposit the $2,470.07 today, it earns interest at the rate of 5% per year. Even when withdrawals begin in the third year, what remains in the account still earns interest at the rate of 5% per year. We show the balance in the account at the end of each year in Exhibit 6.1. The balance in the account at the end of the third year would have been $2,859.41 if no withdrawal is made.

---

[1]When you calculate this problem using a financial calculator or a spreadsheet, you will get a negative value of the present value. Because we are using the present value as the input to the second step (the present value becomes a future value), we've multiplied the present value by negative one.

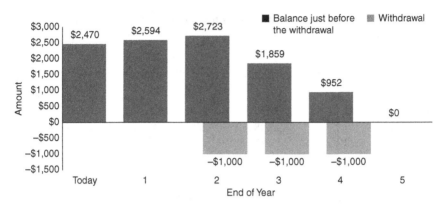

EXHIBIT 6.1   Balance in the Account Paying 5% Interest, if You Deposit $2,470.07 Today and Make Three Withdrawals of $1,000 Each, Starting in Three Years

Another version of this problem is to say that if you borrow $2,470.07 today, and invest it at 5%, you can repay the loan in three payments of $1,000 each, starting in three years. The math is the same—it's just a different application.

There is no built-in function for deferred annuities on your financial calculator or spreadsheet, so when faced with a deferred annuity you need to break it down into steps and execute each step using your calculator's functions.

You can perform this calculation in one step in Microsoft Excel, using a nesting of functions, but this gets pretty messy pretty quick:

$$= PV(0.05, 2, 0, PV(0.05, 3, 1000, 0))$$

You could also use a list in the TI-83/84 calculators or the spreadsheet to solve this. For example, in the TI-83/84 you could create a list that consists of {0,0,1000,1000,1000} and then use the NPV function, a function we have explained in previous chapters. However, once we get into more realistic problems, such as saving for retirement, this gets very messy to do—and breaking the calculation into steps will reduce the chance of error.

Another approach to this same problem is to view the problem as comprised of two parts, an annuity due and then a lump sum discounted to the present. So how is this different from what we just did? It changes the number of periods slightly, but we arrive at the same answer. Again, let's consider the three payments of $1,000 and an interest rate of 5%. What lump sum today is equivalent in value to this three-payment cash flow stream?

Step 1. Calculate the present value of a three-payment annuity due

Today	1	2	3	4	5
			$1,000.000	$1,000	$1,000
			952.381	↵	↵
			907.029		
			$PV_3 = \$2,859.410$		

Using a calculator or spreadsheet:

TI-83/84 Using TVM Solver	HP10B	Microsoft Excel
BEGIN	BEG	=PV(.05,3,1000,0,1) * −1
N = 3	3 N	
I% = 5	5 I/YR	
FV = 0	1000 PMT	
PMT =1000	PV	
PV = *Solve*	× −1	
× −1		

Therefore, if you intend to make these withdrawals, you will need to have $2,859.41 in the account at the end of the third year. If you have less than this, you won't be able to make three full withdrawals of $1,000 each. If you have more than this amount, you will have something left over in the account by the time you make your third withdrawal.

Step 2. Calculate the present value of a lump sum amount

Today	1	2	3	4	5
			$1,000.000	$1,000	$1,000
			952.381	↵	↵
			907.029		
			$PV_3 = \$2,859.410$		
$PV_0 = \$2,470.066$			↵		

Using a financial calculator or a spreadsheet, we can calculate this present value:

TI-83/84 Using TVM Solver	HP10B	Microsoft Excel
N = 2	2 N	=PV(0.05,2,0,2723.248)* −1
I% = 5	5 I/YR	
FV = 2723.248	2723.248 FV	
PMT = 0	PV	
PV = *Solve*	× −1	
× −1		

Instead of discounting the present value of the annuity two periods, as we did previously, we discount this value three periods. Why? Because when we calculate the present value of an annuity due, the present value of the series coincides in time with the first cash flows—which is three periods in the future in this example.

You may encounter many types of deferred annuities in financial situations, and each one is unique. Solving these depends on what information is given. Like all time value of money problems, we are given a number of known values and there is one unknown element that we want to solve for. In a deferred annuity, this unknown may be the amount of savings that lead up to withdrawals, the amount of withdrawals given a savings program, the number of savings deposits to make to satisfy planned withdrawals, or the number of withdrawals possible given a savings program. No matter the problem, it can usually be broken into two or three manageable pieces.

Example 6.1

Suppose that you wish to have a balance in your savings account when you retire at 65 years of age such that you can make withdrawals of $10,000 each year for 20 years, starting with your 66th birthday. How much must you deposit on your 35th birthday in an account paying 5% interest, compounded annually, so that you can meet your goal?

Step 1. Solve for the present value of the withdrawals
Given information: PMT = $10,000; $i = 5\%$; $N = 20$.

This is the balance required at the time of your 65th birthday (that is, at the end of 30 periods). Why the 65th birthday and not the 66th birthday?

Because we used an ordinary annuity approach to solving this, which means that the PV of the series occurs one period prior to the first cash flow—in other words, by using the ordinary annuity short-cut the PV is on your 65th birthday, not on your 66th birthday.[2]

Step 2. Solve for the present value of your 65th birthday balance
Given: PV = \$124,622; $N = 30$; $i = 5\%$.

$$PV = \$124,622/(1+0.05)^{30} = \$28,834.72$$

Check it out:

$$PV = \$28,834.72(1+0.05)^{30} = \$124,622$$

In other words, if you deposit \$124,622 on your 35th birthday, you will be able to withdraw \$10,000 each year for 20 years, beginning on your 66th birthday.

Example 6.2

Suppose you have \$200,000 put aside in an investment account that earns 4% per year. If you intend to retire 20 years from today and use these funds for your living expenses, how much could you withdraw from the account each year, with the first withdrawal a year after you retire, so that you leave nothing in the account after 20 years of withdrawals? Answer: **\$32,245.34**

Step 1. Solve for the balance in the investment account at the date of your retirement

$$FV = \$200,000 \times (1+0.04)^{20} = \$438,224,63$$

Step 2. Solve for the annual withdrawals that this account provides

Given: PV = \$438,224.63; $i = 4\%$; $N = 20$.
Solve for the payment.
The annual withdrawal that will leave a zero balance in the account after 20 withdrawals is \$32,245.34.

---

[2]Note: From 35 to 36 is one period, 35 to 37 is two periods, ..., 35 to 65 is 30 periods).

ANNUITIES WITH ANNUITIES

In the previous section, we illustrated how you can deposit an amount today and generate enough funds to support a series of withdrawals. More realistically, we need to think about problems involving periodic savings that lead to withdrawals. This is important in any type of retirement situation because we generally don't have a windfall lump sum to invest for retirement, but rather put aside funds periodically. To address these more realistic problems, let's first look at meeting a specific monetary goal, and then see how all the pieces fit together for a periodic-savings ⇨ periodic-withdrawal problem.

Meeting a Goal

Assume that you know what you will need upon retirement at 70 years of age. Now let's see what we need to do to get there. Assume that you have determined that you need $2 million by the time of your 70th birthday in order to satisfy your retirement needs. If you are 30 years old today and can earn 5% on your savings, what would you have to set to meet your goal?

To examine this, we will solve for several different ways in which you can meet your goal:

- A lump sum today.
- Annual payments, starting at the end of this year, with the last payment on your 70th birthday.
- Annual payments, starting today, with the last payment on your 69th birthday.
- Annual payments, starting today, with the last payment on your 70th birthday.
- Monthly payments, starting at the end of this month, with the last payment on your 70th birthday.

1. As a Lump Sum Today   We solve this as a straightforward present value of a lump sum problem. The basic inputs are as follows:

FV = $2 million
$i = 5\%$
$N = 40$

The present value is $2,000,000 ÷ (1 + 0.04)^{40} = \$284,091.36$.
Using a spreadsheet or financial calculator:

TI-83/84 Using TVM Solver	HP10B	Microsoft Excel
N = 40	40 N	=PV(.05,40,0,2000000)
I% = 5	5 I/YR	
FV = 2000000	2000000 FV	
Solve for PV	PV	

If you deposit $284,091.36 today, you will have $2 million by the time you retire.

2. As Annual Payments, Starting at the End of this Year with the Last Payment on Your 70th Birthday We solve this as an ordinary annuity with 40 payments. The basic inputs are as follows:

FV = $2 million
$i = 5\%$
$N = 40$

Using a spreadsheet or financial calculator:

TI-83/84 Using TVM Solver	HP10B	Microsoft Excel
N = 40	40 N	=PMT(0.05,40,0,2000000)
I% = 5	5 I/YR	
FV = 2000000	2000000 FV	
PMT = *Solve*	PMT	

We then solve for the payment that gets us to this goal. The payment is $16,556.32 per year, with the first payment due before your 31st birthday.

3. As Annual Payments, Starting Today, with the Last Payment on your 69th Birthday We solve this as an annuity due. In this case, the first payment is today and the last payment is on your 69th birthday. The basic inputs are as follows:

FV = $2 million
$i = 5\%$
$N = 40$

TI-83/84 Using TVM Solver	HP10B	Microsoft Excel
BEG	BEG	=PMT(0.04,40,0,2000000,1)
N = 40	40 N	
I% = 5	5 I/YR	
FV = 2000000	2000000 FV	
PMT = *Solve*	PMT	

The annual payment required to meet your goal is $15,767.93.

4. As Annual Payments, Starting Today, with the Last Payment on Your 70th Birthday   In this case, the first payment is today and the last payment is on your 70th birthday, which means you make 41 payments. This is a tricky problem because you want 41 payments, starting today and ending on your 70th birthday:

- If we use an annuity due with 41 payments, the FV that we get is one period after the last cash flow—which is your 71st birthday.
- If we use an annuity due with 40 payments, the FV that we get coincides with your 70th birthday, but we are one payment short.
- If we use an ordinary annuity with 40 payments, we leave out the payment today.
- If we use an ordinary annuity with 41 payments, the FV coincides with the last payment on your 70th birthday. This works.[3] The basic inputs are as follows:

FV = $2 million
$i = 5\%$
$N = 41$

TI-83/84 Using TVM Solver	HP10B	Microsoft Excel
N = 41	41 N	=PMT(0.05,41,0,2000000,1)
I% = 5	5 I/YR	
FV = 2000000	2000000 FV	
PMT = *Solve*	PMT	

The annual payment required to meet your goal is $20,034.75.

---

[3]You might wonder how this works, but it's as if you planned this on your 29th birthday, with the first payment at the end of your 29th year—which happens to be the start of your 30th year.

5. As Monthly Payments, Starting at the End of This Month   We solve this as an ordinary annuity, with $12 \times 40 = 480$ payments. The basic inputs are as follows:

FV = $2 million
$N = 480$

However, we do have a slight problem of dealing with interest rates. We have assumed in the first four analyses in this savings problem that the rate of interest is, effectively, 5% per year. If we were to simply use $5\% \div 12 = 0.41667\%$, we would overstate the interest per month. If 5% is the effective annual rate of interest, then we solve for the monthly rate using:

$$\text{EAR} = (1 + i)^N - 1$$
$$0.05 = (1 + i)^{12} - 1$$

Then $i = 0.0040742$ or 0.40742% per month. Using the financial calculators or spreadsheets:

TI-83/84 Using TVM Solver	HP10B	Microsoft Excel
N = 480	480 N	=PMT(0.00407042,480,0,2000000)
I% = .407042	.407042 I/YR	or
FV = 2000000	2000000 FV	=PMT(nominal(0.05,12)/12),480,0,2000000)
PMT = *Solve*	PMT	

You can meet your goal of $2 million by the time you are 70 years old if you deposit $1,349.02 in an account at the end of each month.[4]

The bottom line of all this is that you can meet your savings goal in a number of ways—and there are many more than what we presented. In savings-for-retirement planning, each person would select the method that works best with their financial situation. Of course, the more money you set aside sooner, the more you'll have for retirement.

---

[4]For this option, if we had used the 5% per year as an APR, the monthly payment would be $1,310, which is understated.

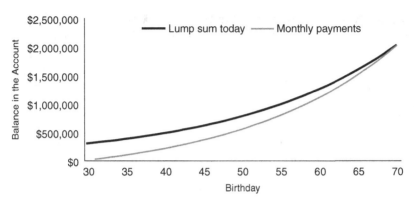

EXHIBIT 6.2 Comparison of the Build-Up in the Savings Account: Lump Sum Today versus Monthly Payments to Reach the Goal of $2 Million in 40 Years in the Account

TRY IT! 6.1 MEETING YOUR SAVINGS GOAL

Suppose you are currently 15 years from retirement. Your goal for your retirement is to have $1.5 million by the time you retire. If you already have $500,000 in investments earning 5% per year, how much must you deposit at the end of each year until your retirement so that you reach your goal?

Periodic Cash Flows to Satisfy Periodic Cash Flows

Most of us think of what cash flow we need to have periodically in retirement so that we can live comfortably. And most of us don't win the lottery or come into any other windfall that we can deposit at one time to meet our retirement goals. More realistically, we set aside funds periodically so that we can meet our cash flow needs upon retirement. We will address these situations, starting with a relatively simple example and then mucking it up with reality.

Suppose you have figured out that you need to have $40,000 per year after you retire so that you can live comfortably. And let's suppose that you are 25 years old today and plan to retire when you are 70 years old. Let's assume that you will need your first $40,000 at the end of the first year after your retirement. If you can earn 5% on your investments and you are guessing that you will live until you are 90 years old, how much do you have to put in to your investment account to meet this goal?

We need to break this problem into two pieces because to do otherwise would be too unwieldy. The first step is figuring out what you need to have in your investment account on the day of your retirement. The second step is figuring out what you need to deposit each year to meet this goal.

Step 1. What is needed in the retirement account on the day you retire According to our scenario, if you retire at 70, your first withdrawal will be on your 71st birthday. If you plan to live until you are 90, you will be making 20 withdrawals of $40,000 each. The basic inputs are as follows:

$$\text{PMT} = \$40,000$$
$$N = 20$$
$$i = 5\%$$

Using your financial calculator or spreadsheet to solve this ordinary annuity:

TI-83/84 Using TVM Solver	HP10B	Microsoft Excel
N = 20	20 N	=PV(0.05,20,40000,0,0)* -1
I% = 5	5 I/YR	
PMT = 40000	40000 PMT	
PV = *Solve*	PV	

You will need $498,488.41 in your investment account to make this work.

Step 2. What must be deposited in the investment account to meet your goal What was the present value in the first step becomes the future value (FV)—the goal—in the second step. If you are 25 years old today and make your first deposit into your investment account just before you turn 26, you will be making 45 deposits, including one on your 70th birthday. The basic inputs are as follows:

$$\text{FV} = \$498,488.41$$
$$N = 45$$
$$i = 5\%$$

Using your financial calculator or spreadsheet to solve this ordinary annuity:

TI-83/84 Using TVM Solver	HP10B	Microsoft Excel
N = 45	45 N	=PMT(0.05,45,0,498488.41,0)
I% = 5	5 I/YR	
FV = 498488.41	498488.41 FV	
PMT = *Solve*	PMT	

You will need to make annual deposits of $3,121.40 at the end of each year for 45 years to meet your retirement goal of making 20 withdrawals of $40,000 after retiring.

We show the balance in the account in Exhibit 6.3. As deposits are made and the balances earn interest, you'll notice that the balance in the account grows in a curvilinear fashion. This is the effect of the compounding of interest. You will also notice that when withdrawals begin, the account balance does not decline as a straight line, but rather as a curve because the balances that remain in the account earn interest.

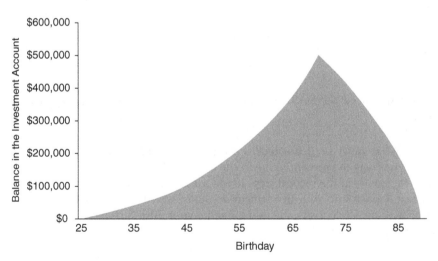

EXHIBIT 6.3 Saving for Retirement Problem, in which Deposits of $3,121.40 are Made Each Year for 45 Years and then Withdrawals of $40,000 are Made Each Year for 20 years

On your 90th birthday, you will have nothing left in your account. Variations that you can add to this analysis include:

- Leaving a lump sum for burial. Yes, this does sound depressing, but there most often are some costs when it's all over. To accomplish this in the financial math, vary Step 1 to include a FV for this amount. Then everything else in the calculation proceeds as above; it is just that the present value on your retirement will be slightly more. Or, even simpler, you could just leave these costs up to someone else or buy burial insurance. If you buy a burial policy, this is a cost that you must add somewhere along in your planning.
- Add a withdrawal on your retirement date. In many calculations, we assume that you earn funds up until retirement and don't need anything until you are well in to retirement. This is likely unrealistic and you can make an adjustment in our calculations by adding the amount needed for the first year of retirement to the present value at retirement.

Example 6.3

Suppose you deposit $1,000 in an account at the end of each year, starting next year, for 30 years (30 deposits). Your goal is to live off of the savings for 20 years, starting the year after your last deposit. If you can earn 6% on your deposits and your withdrawals in retirement are an even, annual amount, what is the amount you can withdraw once you retire?

Step 1. Determine the future value of the deposits   Solve for the future value of the deposits at the end of 30 years. The basic inputs are as follows:

$$\text{PMT} = \$1,000$$
$$N = 30$$
$$i = 6\%$$

$$\text{FV}_{30} \text{ of deposits} = \$79,058.129$$

Step 2. Determine the withdrawal   Solve for the payment that equates the present value of the withdrawal stream to the future value of the deposits. The future value of the deposits becomes the present value of the withdrawals in this step. The basic inputs are as follows:

$$\text{PV of withdrawals} = \$79,058.129$$
$$N = 20$$
$$i = 6\%$$

$$\text{Solving for the payment, PMT} = \$6,892.65$$

In other words, if you make the deposits as scheduled, and the funds earn the anticipated rate of return, you will be able to make 30 annual withdrawals of $6,892.65 each. By the time you make the last withdrawal, you will have nothing left in the account.

 TRY IT! 6.2 WHAT CAN YOU LIVE ON?

Suppose your 401K has a balance of $500,000 when you retire. Ignoring any tax effects, if you expect to live for 20 years after retiring, how much can you withdraw each year during retirement and leave $100,000 for your heirs if you can earn 4% per year on your invested funds?

FINANCIAL MATH IN ACTION

Suppose you are planning your finances and estimate that you will need $10,000 for burial expenses when you pass away. If your opportunity cost of capital is 5%, what would you be willing to pay for single-pay *burial insurance* (or *final expenses*) policy to cover this $10,000? It all depends on how old you are today and when you expect to pass away.

		Age when you pass away					
		65	70	75	80	85	90
Age today	25	$1,420	$1,113	$872	$683	$535	$419
	30	$1,813	$1,420	$1,113	$872	$683	$535
	35	$2,314	$1,813	$1,420	$1,113	$872	$683
	40	$2,953	$2,314	$1,813	$1,420	$1,113	$872
	45	$3,769	$2,953	$2,314	$1,813	$1,420	$1,113
	50	$4,810	$3,769	$2,953	$2,314	$1,813	$1,420
	55	$6,139	$4,810	$3,769	$2,953	$2,314	$1,813
	60	$7,835	$6,139	$4,810	$3,769	$2,953	$2,314
	65		$7,835	$6,139	$4,810	$3,769	$2,953
	70			$7,835	$6,139	$4,810	$3,769
	75				$7,835	$6,139	$4,810
	80					$7,835	$6,139

(Continued)

But as you hear in radio and television ads, most of these policies involve weekly payments of "as little as $3 a week." What would you be willing to pay each week?

		Age when you pass away					
		65	70	75	80	85	90
Age today	25	$1.51	$1.13	$0.86	$0.66	$0.50	$0.39
	30	$2.02	$1.51	$1.13	$0.86	$0.66	$0.50
	35	$2.76	$2.02	$1.51	$1.13	$0.86	$0.66
	40	$3.86	$2.76	$2.02	$1.51	$1.13	$0.86
	45	$5.60	$3.86	$2.76	$2.02	$1.51	$1.13
	50	$8.61	$5.60	$3.86	$2.76	$2.02	$1.51
	55	$14.83	$8.61	$5.60	$3.86	$2.76	$2.02
	60	$33.87	$14.83	$8.61	$5.60	$3.86	$2.76
	65		$33.87	$14.83	$8.61	$5.60	$3.86
	70			$33.87	$14.83	$8.61	$5.60
	75				$33.87	$14.83	$8.61
	80					$33.87	$14.83

As you can see, the "only $3 per week" advertised deal is only a good one for $10,000 of final expenses insurance if you don't plan on living more than 30 years from when you start the payments.* Otherwise, just set the $3 aside in your savings account each week.

*The precise break-even point for the $3 a week deal is 28 years, 39 weeks. We solved this by solving for N, with PMT = $3, FV = $10,000; $i = 5\% \div 52$.

A BIT OF REALISM

Now that you have the basics of solving for deposits and withdrawals, let's mix this up a bit to have a more realistic problem. We do not intend this problem to be a substitute for your personal financial planning, but rather it is intended to help you frame the problem and execute the financial mathematics to get you the answer you are looking for.

Let's consider a more complex, but more realistic scenario. Here are the assumptions that we will work with:

- You intend to retire on your 70th birthday.
- You expect to earn 8% APR, compounded monthly on your investments up until your 70th birthday, and then you will shift your investments to lower risk investments that earn 3% APR, compounded monthly.
- Your needs in retirement are twofold:
  1. Upon retirement, you plan to sell you home for $400,000 and move into an apartment. You expect that you will need enough funds so that you can live on $2,500 per month, in addition to anything you might get from Social Security.
  2. You expect to need to shift to assisted living eventually. For now, let's assume that you will be in assisted living once you turn 80, such that the first payment is at the end of the month in which you turn 80 years old. Your estimated cost of assisted living is $4,000 per month.
- You want to deposit funds in your investment account at the end of every month, starting at the end of this month, so that retirement account, plus your home proceeds, will fund your retirement needs.
- You expect to leave $10,000 upon your death to cover final expenses.
- You are 30 years old today and your life expectancy is 88 years old.

In this scenario, there are two phases, accumulation and use of funds, where you shift from one phase to another once you turn 70 years old. In the second phase, the need for funds shifts when you are 80.

We can treat this as a two step process: Step 1 is the determination of what is needed to fund your retirement and Step 2 is the determination of what deposits must be made to get you there.

Step 1. Retirement needs   In retirement, you have three cash flow streams to deal with:

- The final expenses lump sum at 88 years of age.
- The needed living expenses after 70, up until you are 80.
- The needed living expenses beyond your 80th birthday.

Let's deal with each separately, and then sum the needs.

1. The funds needed for final expenses   The final expenses are the easiest to deal with. We use the following inputs:

$FV = \$10,000$
$i = 3\% \div 12 = 0.25\%$
$N = 18 \times 12 = 216$

Solving for the present value, we find that we need $5,831.41.

2. The funds needed for assisted living The assisted living expenses are $4,000 a month from 80 years of age through your 88th birthday.

PMT = $4,000
$i = 3\% \div 12 = 0.25\%$
$N = 8 \times 12 = 96$

Solving for the value of these expenses as of your 80th birthday, we find the present value on your 80th birthday is $341,018.41.

We can then convert this to a value on your 70th birthday by discounting this lump sum 10 years:

FV = $341,018.14
$i = 3\% \div 12 = 0.25\%$
$N = 10 \times 12 = 120$

The present value of your assisted living expenses on your 70th birthday is $252,727.05.

3. The funds needed for apartment living Your living expenses between the ages of 70 and 80 are $2,500 per month. We use the following inputs to solve for the present value of these expenses:

PMT = $2,500
$i = 3\% \div 12 = 0.25\%$
$N = 10 \times 12 = 120$

The present value is $258,904.38.
Total needed:

Final expenses:	$5,831.41
Expenses 70 to 80 years old:	252,727.05
Expenses: 80 to 88 years old:	258,904.38
Total needed at 70 years of age:	$517,462.84
Proceeds on the sale of the home:	400,000.00
Total needed at 70 years of age in the retirement account:	$117,462.84

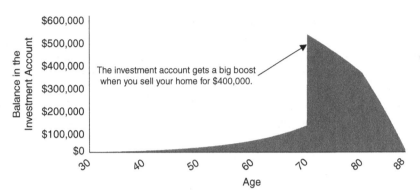

EXHIBIT 6.4   Balance in the investment account for a savings problem of $33.65 per month for 40 years, following by home sale proceeds of $400,000, 10 years of living expenses at $2,500 per month, and then 8 years of living expenses at $4,000. The account earns 8% APR until age 70, after which time it then earns 3% APR. The balance by your 88th birthday is $10,000.

Step 2. Funding requirements   You have 40 years of monthly deposits to make to meet your retirement goal of $205,754.20. Solving for the monthly deposit to meet your needs, the inputs are as follows:

$$FV = \$117,462.84$$
$$i = 8\% \div 12 = 0.6667\%$$
$$N = 40 \times 12 = 480$$

Solving for the payment, PMT = $33.65. In other words, if you deposit $33.65 in your investment account each month and these funds earn 8% APR, and if you can sell your home for $400,000, you will be able to retire and make the anticipated withdrawals.

As you can see in Exhibit 6.4, the sale of the home provides the largest contribution to your investment account. You can also see in this exhibit how the investment account balance declines more rapidly after you reach 80 years of age, once your expenses increase.

We've extracted from reality to present this problem because we've ignored taxes, Social Security income, and other items that affect your planning. However, with these tools, you can see how to analyze a problem, once you figure out your tax situation, other expenses, other income, and the like.

SUMMARY

Working with the savings-for-future-spending requires you to apply the financial mathematics that involves valuing a lump sum through time and valuing a series of cash flows. Though each retirement problem is different, once you understand how to break these complex problems into the simpler problems, you can understand how much you need in the future and how to save for it.

We use the retirement problem in our examples in this chapter, but these tools can be applied to any type of savings problem in which there is more than one withdrawal of funds in the future.

"TRY IT" SOLUTIONS

6.1. Your Present savings Will Provide Part of What You Need
FV of your savings: FV = $500,000 $(1 + 0.05)^{15}$ = $1,039,464.09.

This means that your deposits must have a future value of $1,500,000 – $1,039,464.09 = $460,535.91.

Next, we solve for the payments necessary to meet this amount using the following inputs:

FV = $460,535.91

$N = 15$

$i = 5\%$

Solving for the payment, PMT = $21,342.29

6.2. What can you live on?
Inputs: PV = $500,000; FV = $100,000; $i = 4\%$; $n = 20$.
Solve for PMT. PMT = $33,432.70.

PROBLEMS

6.1. If the discount rate is 5%, what is the present value of a series of four annual $5,000 cash flows, with the first cash flow occurring three periods from today?

6.2. If the discount rate is 5%, what is the present value of a series of 10 annual $5,000 cash flows, with the first cash flow occurring 20 periods from today?

6.3. If the discount rate is 5%, what is the present value of a series of four annual $5,000 cash flows, with the first cash flow occurring two years from today?

6.4. If you can earn 5% on your deposits, how much would you have to deposit in an account at the end of each year, starting at the end of this year, for 19 years, so that you can make 10 withdrawals of $5,000 each, starting 20 years from today.

6.5. Joe Investor is planning to retire in 20 years. He is guessing that he will live for 30 years past his retirement. He figures he needs $100,000 per year to live on, with his first withdrawal on his retirement date. He will make 30 withdrawals. What does he have to invest today to meet his retirement goal? His investments earn 15%.

6.6. Warren Wealthy wants to save for his retirement. His goal is to retire at 60 and have $60,000 per year to live on for 25 years, with the first withdrawal on his 61st birthday and the last withdrawal on his 85th birthday. Warren is 30 years old today and wants to begin making deposits to save for his retirement, starting next year, with the last deposit on his 60th birthday. What is the needed amount of the annual deposit if he can earn 5% on his investments?

6.7. Suppose you plan to retire on your 65th birthday and wish to begin withdrawing from your retirement savings beginning with your 66th birthday. And suppose that your savings earn 2% per year. If you intend on living a long life, requiring $20,000 per year through your 85th birthday, how much would you have to deposit as a lump sum on your 25th birthday to enable you to meet your retirement income goal?

6.8. Suppose you plan to retire on your 65th birthday and wish to begin withdrawing from your retirement savings beginning with your 66th birthday, but have $10,000 left over when you die to cover your final expenses. Your savings earn 5% per year. If you are 25 years old today and you intend on living a very long life, requiring $40,000 per year through your 95th birthday, how much would you have to deposit each year, at the end of each year including your 65th birthday, to enable you to meet your retirement income goal?

6.9. An insurance salesperson is offering to sell you an annuity. The terms of the annuity are that you purchase this annuity today, on your 50th birthday; the annuity of $20,000 for 20 years begins on your 66th birthday. The annuity will cost you only $100,000. Should you buy this annuity?

6.10. Suppose you buy an insurance policy today for $2 every week, starting next week that provides $10,000 for final expenses (burial insurance). How many years must you live for this to be a wise decision if your opportunity cost is 7%?

For solutions to these problems, see Appendix E.

CHAPTER **7**

Values Tied to Bonds

Promises make debt, and debt makes promises.

—Dutch proverb

When we value an investment, we need to know its expected future cash flows and the uncertainty of receiving them. To value securities, you must understand the nature of the cash flows, their timing, and the uncertainty associated with these future cash flows. In this chapter, we focus on one type of security: bonds.

A *bond* is a legal obligation to repay an amount borrowed—the principal—along with some compensation for the time value of money and risk. Corporations, municipalities, states, and the federal government issue bonds.

Most bonds represent obligations of the borrower to pay interest at regular intervals (usually every six months) and to repay the principal amount of the loan at the end of the loan period; that is, at maturity. We also use the terms *maturity value, face value, par value*, and *redemption value* to refer to this principal.

If you buy a bond, you are entering into a contract with the issuer of that debt security, the borrower. By owning the bond, you become a creditor of the issuer. Any interest and principal that the issuer promises to pay are legal obligations, and failure to pay as promised results in dire consequences for the issuer.

For a corporate issuer, bonds are senior to equity securities: The borrower must satisfy their obligations to the creditors before making payments to owners, the stockholders. Therefore, for a given corporation, the cash flows from bonds are more certain than the cash flows of either preferred stock or common stock.

BOND BASICS

A bond is a promise by the borrower to repay the principal amount. A bond may also require the borrower to pay interest periodically, typically semiannually or annually. We usually state interest as a percentage of the bond's maturity value, no matter the current price of the bond or its original offering price.

We refer to the interest payments as coupon payments or *coupons* and the percentage rate as the *coupon rate*. If these coupons are a constant amount, paid at regular intervals, we refer to the security paying them as having a *straight coupon*. A bond that does not have a promise to pay interest we refer to as a *zero-coupon* note or bond.

A bond typically has two types of cash flows:

- Interest, which is periodic
- Principal, which is a lump sum at maturity

The value of a bond today is the present value of the promised future cash flows; that is, the present value of the interest and the maturity value. Therefore, the present value of a debt is the sum of the present value of the interest payments and the present value of the maturity value:

$$\frac{\text{Present value}}{\text{of a bond}} = \frac{\text{Present value of}}{\text{interest payments}} + \frac{\text{Present value of}}{\text{maturity value}}$$

To calculate the value of a bond, we discount the future cash flows (that is, the interest and maturity value) at some rate that reflects both the time value of money and the uncertainty of receiving these future cash flows. We refer to this discount rate as the *yield*. The more uncertain the future cash flows, the greater the yield. It follows that the greater the yield, the lower the present value of the future cash flows—hence, the lower the value of the bond.

Most U.S. bonds pay interest semiannually, though European bonds often pay interest annually.[1] In Wall Street parlance, we use the term *yield-to-maturity* (YTM) to describe an annualized yield on a security if the security is held to maturity. For example, if a bond has a return of 5% over a six-month period, the annualized yield-to-maturity for a year is 2 × 5% or

---

[1]You should assume all bonds pay interest semiannually unless specified otherwise.

10%.[2] The yield-to-maturity, as commonly used on Wall Street, is the *bond equivalent yield*:

$$\text{Bond equivalent yield} = 6\text{-month yield} \times 2$$

When we use the term "yield" in the context of bond valuation without any qualification, the intent is that this is the bond equivalent yield.

The present value of the maturity value is the present value of a lump sum, a future amount. In the case of a straight-coupon security, the present value of the interest payments is the present value of an annuity. In the case of a zero-coupon security, the present value of the interest payments is zero, so the present value of the bond is the present value of the maturity value.

CALCULATION TIP

We use the coupon rates to determine the cash flows from interest. We use the yield to maturity to determine the discount rate.

We can rewrite the formula for the present value of a bond using some new notation and some familiar notation. Because there are two different cash flows—interest and maturity value—let PMT represent the coupon payment promised each period and M represent the maturity value. Also, let N indicate the number of periods until maturity, t indicate a specific period, and r_d indicate the six-month yield. The present value of a bond, V, is

$$V = \left[\sum_{t=1}^{N} \frac{\text{PMT}_t}{(1 + r_d)^t} \right] + \frac{M}{(1 + r_d)^N}$$

present value   present value
of an annuity   of a lump-sum

The discount rate, r_d, indicates the required rate of return on the bond; that is, r_d is what investors require when they invest in this particular bond. To see how the valuation of future cash flows from debt securities works,

---

[2]But is this the effective yield-to-maturity? Not quite. This annualized yield does not take into consideration the compounding within the year if the bond pays interest more than once per year.

let's look at the valuation of a straight-coupon bond and then a zero-coupon bond.

WHY DO THEY REFER TO INTEREST PAYMENTS AS COUPONS?

The interest payments are referred to as *coupons* because, in the days before electronic entries for bond ownership and the payment of interest, investors would need to clip a coupon from the bond itself and present it to receive their money. Each coupon had a date printed on it so the bond owner would know when it was time to clip it.

Valuing a Straight-Coupon Bond

Suppose you are considering investing in a straight coupon bond that:

- Promises interest of 10% each year.
- Promises to pay the principal amount of $1,000 at the end of 12 years.
- Has a yield of 5% per year.

What is this bond worth today? We have the following data:

Interest = $100 every year
Number of years to maturity = 12
Maturity value = $1,000
Yield to maturity = 5% per year

Most U.S. bonds pay interest twice a year. Therefore, we adjust the given information for the fact that interest is semiannual, producing the following:

$$PMT = \$100 \div 2 = \$50$$
$$N = 12 \times 2 = 24$$
$$M = \$1,000$$
$$r_d = 5\% \div 2 = 2.5\%$$

$$V = \left[\sum_{t=1}^{24} \frac{\$50}{(1+0.025)^t} \right] + \frac{\$1,000}{(1+0.025)^{24}} = \$1,447.1246$$

This value is the sum of the value of the interest payments (an ordinary annuity consisting of 24 $50 payments, discounted at 2.5%) and the value of the maturity value (a lump sum of $1,000, discounted 24 periods at 2.5%), as we depict in the time line:

Today	1	2	3	4	5	...	23	24	Period
	$50	$50	$50	$50	$50	...	$50	$50	Interest
$894.25 ↩	↩	↩	↩	↩	↩		↩	↩	
								$1,000	Principal
552.88								↩	
1447.13									

Using financial calculators or spreadsheets, we can perform this calculation in one step:

TI-83/84 Using TVM Solver	HP10B	Microsoft Excel
N = 24	1000 FV	=PV(0.025,24,50,1000)
I = 2.5	24 N	
PMT = 50	2.5 I/YR	
FV = 1000	50 PMT	
Solve for PV	PV	

Another way of representing the bond valuation is to state all the monetary inputs in terms of a percentage of the maturity value. Continuing this example, this requires the following:

$$PMT = 10 \div 2 = 5$$
$$N = 12 \times 2 = 24$$
$$M = 100$$
$$r_d = 5\% \div 2 = 2.5\%$$

$$V = \left[\sum_{t=1}^{24} \frac{5}{(1 + 0.025)^t} \right] + \frac{100}{(1 + 0.025)^{24}} = 144.71246$$

This produces a value that is in terms of a bond quote, which is a percentage of face value. For a $1,000 face value bond, this means that the present value is 144.71246% of the face value, or $1,447.1246.

Why bother with bond quotes? For two reasons: First, this is how you will see a bond's value quoted on any financial publication or web site; second, this is a more general approach to communicating a bond's value and can be used regardless of the bond's face value. For example, if the bond has a face value of $500 (i.e., it's a baby bond), a bond quote of 101 translates into a bond value of $500 × 101% = $505.

TI-83/84 Using TVM Solver	HP10B	Microsoft Excel
N = 24	100 FV	=PV(0.025,24,5,100)
I = 2.5	24 n	
PMT = 5	2.5 I/YR	
FV = 100	PV	
Solve for PV		

Premiums and Discounts

This bond has a present value greater than its maturity value, so we say that the bond is selling at a *premium* from its maturity value. Does this make sense? Yes: The bond pays interest of 10% of its face value every year. But what investors require on their investment—the capitalization rate considering the time value of money and the uncertainty of the future cash flows—is 5%.

So what happens? The bond paying 10% is attractive—so attractive that its price is bid upward to a price that gives investors the going rate, the 5%. In other words, an investor who buys the bond for $1,447.1246 will get a 5% return on it if it is held until maturity. We say that at $1,447.1246, the bond is priced to yield 5% per year.

Suppose that instead of priced to yield 5%, this bond is priced to yield 10%. What is the value of this bond?

$$C = \$100 \div 2 = \$50$$
$$N = 12 \times 2 = 24$$
$$M = \$1,000$$
$$r_d = 10\% \div 2 = 5\%$$

$$V = \left[\sum_{t=1}^{24} \frac{\$50}{(1+0.05)^t}\right] + \frac{\$1,000}{(1+0.05)^{24}} = \$1,000$$

TI-83/84 Using TVM Solver	HP10B	Microsoft Excel
N = 24	1000 FV	=PV(0.05,24,50,1000)
I = 5	24 n	
PMT = 50	5 I/YR	
FV = 1000	PV	
Solve for PV		

The bond's present value is equal to its face value and we say that the bond is selling "at par." Investors will pay face value for a bond that pays the going rate for bonds of similar risk. In other words, if you buy the 10% bond for $1,000.00, you will earn a 10% annual return on your investment if you hold it until maturity.

Suppose, instead, the interest on the bond is $20 every year—a 2% coupon rate. Now use the following data inputs:

$$PMT = \$20 \div 2 = \$10$$
$$N = 12 \times 2 = 24$$
$$M = \$1,000$$
$$r_d = 10\% \div 2 = 5\%$$

$$V = \left[\sum_{t=1}^{24} \frac{\$10}{(1 + 0.05)^t} \right] + \frac{\$1,000}{(1 + 0.05)^{24}} = \$448.0543$$

The bond sells at a *discount* from its face value. Why? Because investors are not going to pay face value for a bond that pays less than the going rate for bonds of similar risk. If an investor can buy other bonds that yield 5%, why pay the face value ($1,000 in this case) for a bond that pays only 2%? They wouldn't. Instead, the price of this bond would fall to a price that provides an investor earn a yield-to-maturity of 5%.

So when we look at the value of a bond, we see that its present value is dependent on the relation between the coupon rate and the yield. We can see this relation in our example: If the yield exceeds the bond's coupon rate, the bond sells at a discount from its maturity value and if the yield is less than the bond's coupon rate, the bond sells at a premium.

Example 7.1

Suppose a bond has a $1,000 face value, a 10% coupon (paid semiannually), five years remaining to maturity, and is priced to yield 8%. What is its value? Answer: **$1,081.14**

One approach is to value the pieces separately:

The present value of the interest is $405.54 [PMT=50; $N = 10$; $i = 4\%$].

The present value of the maturity value is $675.60 [FV = 1000; $N = 100$; $i = 4\%$]

Therefore, the value of the bond is $405.54 + 675.60 = $1,081.14.

Using a calculator, we can value this bond in one calculation with the following inputs:

$$i = 4\%$$
$$N = 10$$
$$PMT = \$50$$
$$FV = \$1,000$$

We use these inputs to solve for the present value. Using Microsoft Excel's spreadsheet function, we would specify the function: =PV(.04,10,50,1000,0) and then multiply by negative 1.

Example 7.2

As another example, consider a bond with five years remaining to maturity and is priced to yield 10%. If the coupon on this bond is 6% per year, the bond is priced at $845.57 (bond quote: 84.557). If the coupon on this bond is 14% per year, the bond is a premium bond, priced at **$1,154.43** (bond quote: 115.443).

We illustrate the relation between this bond's value and its coupon in Exhibit 7.1.

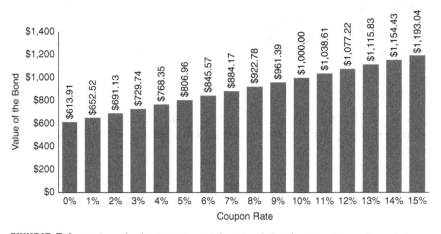

EXHIBIT 7.1 Value of a $1,000 Face-Value Bond that has Five Years Remaining to Maturity and is Priced to Yield 10% for Different Coupon Rates

TRY IT! 7.1 BOND QUOTES

Complete the following table, specifying the value of the bond based on the quote and face value.

Bond	Quote	Face Value	Value of the Bond
A	103.45	$1,000	
B	98.00	$1,000	
C	89.50	$500	
D	110.00	$100,000	
E	90.00	€1000	
F	120.25	¥10,000	
G	65.45	$10,000	

Different Value, Different Coupon Rate, but Same Yield?

The yield to maturity on a bond is the market's assessment of the time value and risk of the bond's cash flows. This yield will change constantly to reflect changes in interest rates in general, and it will also change as the market's perception of the debt issuer's risk changes.

At any point in time, a company may have several different bonds outstanding, each with a different coupon rate and bond quote. However, the yield on these bonds—at least those with similar other characteristics (e.g., seniority, security, indentures)—is usually the same or very close. This occurs because the bonds are issued at different times and with different coupons and maturity, but the yield on the bonds reflects the market's current perception of the risk of the bond and its time value.

Consider two bonds:

Bond A. A maturity value of $1,000, a coupon rate of 6%, 10 years remaining to maturity, and priced to yield 8%. Value = $864.0967.

Bond B. A maturity value of $1,000, a coupon rate of 12%, 10 years remaining to maturity, and priced to yield 8%. Value = $1,271.8065.

How can these bonds, one with a value of \$864.0967 and another with a value of \$1,271.8065, both give an investor a return of 8% per year if held to maturity? Bond B has a higher coupon rate than Bond A (12% versus 6%), yet it is possible for the bonds to provide the same return.

Bond B costs you more now, but also gets more interest each year (\$120 versus \$60). The extra \$60 a year for 10 years makes up for the extra you pay now to buy the bond, considering the time value of money.

Same Bond, Different Yields, Hence Different Values   As interest rates change, the value of bonds changes in the opposite direction; that is, there is an inverse relation between bond prices and bond yields.

Let's look at another example, this time keeping the coupon rate the same, but varying the yield. Suppose we have a \$1,000 face value bond with a 10% coupon rate that pays interest at the end of each year and matures in five years. If the yield is 5%, the value of the bond is

$$V = \$432.95 + \$783.53 = \$1,216.48$$

If the yield is 10%, the same as the coupon rate, the bond sells at face value:

$$V = \$379.08 + \$620.92 = \$1,000.00$$

If the yield is 15%, the bond's value is less than its face value:

$$V = \$335.21 + \$497.18 = \$832.39$$

When we hold the coupon rate constant and vary the yield, we see that there is a negative relation between a bond's yield and its value. We see a relation developing between the coupon rate, the yield, and the value of a bond:

- If the coupon rate is more than the yield, the security is worth more than its face value—it sells at a premium.
- If the coupon rate is less than the yield, the security is less that its face value—it sells at a discount.
- If the coupon rate is equal to the yield, the security is valued at its face value.

We can see the relation between the annualized yield-to-maturity and the value of the 8% coupon bond in Exhibit 7.2. The greater the yield, the

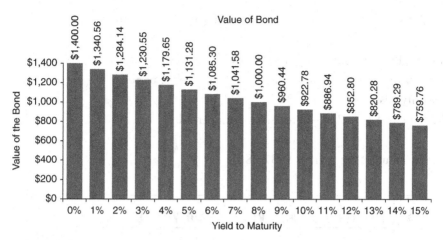

EXHIBIT 7.2 Value of a Five-Year, $1,000 Face Value Bond with an 8% Coupon for Different Yields to Maturity

lower the present value of the bond. This makes sense since an increasing yield means that we are discounting the future cash flows at higher rates.

For a given bond, if interest rates go up, its price goes down; if interest rates go down, its price goes up.

Example 7.3

Suppose we are interested in valuing a $1,000 face value bond that matures in five years and promises a coupon of 4% per year, with interest paid semiannually. This 4% coupon rate tells us that 2%, or $20, is paid every six months. What is the bond's value today if the annualized yield-to-maturity is 6%? 8%?

If the yield-to-maturity is 6%, the inputs to the calculation are:

Interest, PMT = $20 every six months

Number of periods, N = 5 times 2 = 10 six-month periods

Maturity value, M = $1,000

Yield, r_d = 6% ÷ 2 = 3% for six-month period

and the value of the bond is $914.69797.

If the yield-to-maturity is 8%, the inputs to the calculation are:

Interest, PMT = $20 every six months
Number of periods, N = 5 times 2 = 10 six-month periods
Maturity value, M = $1,000
Yield, r_d = 8% ÷ 2 = 4% for six-month period

and the value of the bond is **$837.7821.**

 TRY IT! 7.2 BOND VALUES AND YIELDS

Consider a bond that pays interest at the rate of 6% per year and has 10 years remaining to maturity. Calculate the value of the bond if its face value is $1,000 and the bond quote for the specific yields to maturity, completing this table:

Yield to Maturity	Value of Bond	Bond Quote
5%		
6%		
7%		
8%		

Valuing a Zero-Coupon Bond

A *zero-coupon bond* is a debt security issued without a coupon. Why would anyone ever buy a zero-coupon bond? Because they sell for deep discounts from the face value and you get your return from the increase in the value of the bond as it approaches maturity.

The value of a zero-coupon bond is easier to figure out than the value of a coupon bond. Let's see why. Suppose we are considering investing in a zero-coupon bond that matures in five years and has a face value of $1,000. If this bond does not pay interest—explicitly at least—no one will buy it at its face value. Instead, investors pay some amount less than the face value, with its return based on the difference between what they pay for it and, assuming they hold it to maturity, its maturity value.

If these bonds are priced to yield 10%, their present value is the present value of $1,000, discounted five years at 10%. We are given:[3]

$M = \$1,000$
$N = 10$
$r_d = 5\%$

Using financial calculators or a spreadsheet financial function:

TI-83/84 Using TVM Solver	HP10B	Microsoft Excel
N = 10	1000 FV	=PV(0.05,10,0,1000)
I = 5	10 N	
PMT = 0	5 I/YR	
FV = 1000	PV	
Solve for PV		

IF A ZERO-COUPON BOND DOES NOT PAY INTEREST, WHY USE TWO COMPOUNDING PERIODS A YEAR?

Perplexing, isn't it. If the zero-coupon bond does not pay interest, why do we use two compounding periods a year instead of one? That's because when we consider the available investments, we have a large number of coupon and zero-coupon bonds out there to invest in. If we want to evaluate these bonds based on what we can earn from them, we need to place their yields on a comparable basis. Convention has it—and likely because coupon bonds have been around longer and represent the vast majority of bonds—that we compare bonds on bond equivalent yield basis. Hence, if we start with a YTM on a zero coupon bond, it's going to be a bond equivalent yield.

Does it make a difference? Yes. In our example with a 10% YTM on a five-year zero-coupon bond, we calculate a value of $613.91 using the correct method, but $620.92 using the incorrect method.

---

[3]You will notice that we still convert the number of years into the number of six-month periods and we convert the yield to maturity to a six-month yield. This is because the convention for reporting yields on bonds, whether coupon or zero-coupon, is to assume an annualized yield that is the six-month yield multiplied by two.

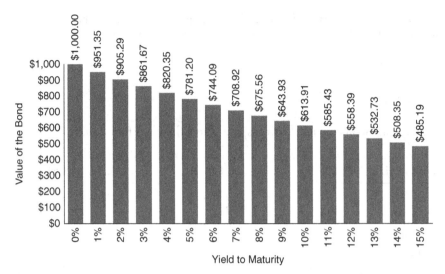

EXHIBIT 7.3   Value of a Five-Year Maturity Zero Coupon Bond for Different Yields to Maturity

The value of the bond is

$$V = \frac{\$1,000}{(1 + 0.05)^{10}} = \$613.91325$$

The price of the zero-coupon bond is sensitive to the yield: If the yield changes from 10% to 5%, the value of the bond increases from $613.91325 to $781.19840. We can see the sensitivity of the value of the bond's price over yields ranging from 1% to 15% in Exhibit 7.3.

CALCULATING THE YIELD TO MATURITY

In the previous section, we valued a bond, given a specific yield-to-maturity. But we are often concerned with the yield that is implied in a given bond's price. For example, what is the yield-to-maturity on a bond that has a current price of $900, has five years remaining to maturity, an 8% coupon rate, and a face value of $1,000? We have the following inputs:

$$N = 10$$
$$PMT = \$40$$
$$M = \$1,000$$
$$V = \$900$$

The six-month yield, r_d, is the discount rate that solves the following:

$$\$900 = \left[\sum_{t=1}^{10} \frac{\$40}{(1 + r_d)^t} \right] + \frac{\$1,000}{(1 + r_d)^{10}}$$

There is no direct solution, so we must use iteration.[4] In other words, without the help of a financial calculator or a spreadsheet, we would have to try different values of r_d until we cause the left- and right-hand sides of this equation to be equal. Fortunately, calculators and spreadsheets make calculations much easier. Using a financial calculator or spreadsheet:

TI-83/84 Using TVM Solver	HP10B	Microsoft Excel
N = 10	1000 FV	=RATE(10,40,−900,1000)
PV = −900	900 +/− PV	
PMT = 40	10 N	
FV = 1000	40 PMT	
Solve for I	I	

The six-month yield is 5.315%. Once we arrive at r_d, we multiply this by two to arrive at the yield-to-maturity: YTM = 5.315% × 2 = 10.63%.

Note that we can use either the dollar amounts (that is, $40, $1000, and $900 for PMT, FV, PV, respectively) or in bond quote terms (that is, 4, 100, and 90 for PMT, FV, and PV, respectively) to solve for the six-month yield, that we then annualize. For example, using the bond quote terms, we calculate the YTM:

TI-83/84 Using TVM Solver	HP10B	Microsoft Excel
N = 10	100 FV	=RATE(10,4,−90,100,0)*2
PV = −90	90 +/− PV	
PMT = 4	10 n	
FV = 100	4 PMT	
Solve for i	I	
X 2	X 2	

---

[4]That is, we cannot algebraically manipulate this equation to produce r_d on the left-hand side and the remainder on the right-hand side of the equation and solve.

The yield-to-maturity calculation is similar for a zero-coupon bond, with the exception that there is no interest: There is simply a present value, a future value, and a number of six-month periods. Again, we must multiply the rate from this calculation to produce the yield to maturity.

Example 7.4

BD, Inc. has a bond outstanding with eight years remaining to maturity, a $1,000 face value, and a coupon rate of 8% paid semiannually. If the current market price is $880, what is the yield to maturity (YTM) on the BD bonds?

Given the following data inputs:

$$FV = \$1,000$$
$$N = 16$$
$$PV = \$880$$
$$PMT = \$40$$

Solve for i:

$$i = 5.116434\%$$

$$YTM = 5.116434 \times 2 = \mathbf{10.232868\%}$$

Example 7.5

Suppose a zero-coupon bond with five years remaining to maturity and a face value of $1,000 has a price of $800. What is the yield to maturity on this bond?

Given the following data inputs:

$$FV = \$1,000$$
$$N = 10$$
$$PV = \$800$$
$$PMT = \$0$$

Solve for i:

$$i = 2.2565\%$$

$$YTM = 2.2565\% \times 2 = \mathbf{4.5130\%}$$

TRY IT! 9.3 YIELDS TO MATURITY

Consider a bond that pays interest at the rate of 6% per year, a face value of $1,000, and has 10 years remaining to maturity. Calculate the yield to maturity of the bond for the various bond values:

Bond Value	Yield to Maturity
$1,100	
$1,000	
$900	
$800	

ISSUES

Changes in Interest Rates

We have already seen that value of a bond changes as the yield changes: If the yield increases, the bond's price decreases; if the yield decreases, the bond's price increases. Just how much a bond's value changes for a given yield change depends on the cash flows of the bond and the starting point, in terms of yield.

Consider the 8% coupon bond with five years to maturity that we saw earlier. If the yield changes from 5% to 6%, the price of the bond goes from $1,131.28 to $1,085.30; in percentage terms, the price declines 4.064%. But if the yield changes from 10% to 11%, the price changes from $922.78 to $886.94, a decline of 3.884%. In other words, this bond's price is more sensitive to yield changes for lower yields.

We can also compare bonds and their price sensitivities. Consider two bonds with the following characteristics:

Bond C. A 5% coupon bond with six years remaining to maturity and a face value of $1,000.

Bond D. Zero-coupon bond with six years remaining to maturity and a face value of $1,000.

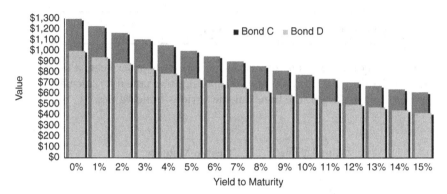

EXHIBIT 7.4 Value of Bonds with Six Years to Maturity: Bond C has a 5% Coupon and Bond D is a Zero-Coupon Bond

Bond C is more valuable because it has the additional cash flows from interest, relative to Bond D. But which bond's value is more sensitive to changes in yields? We graph the value of each bond in Exhibit 7.4 for yields from 0% to 15%. In percentage terms, the change in the price for a given yield change is greater for the zero-coupon bond, Bond D, than the coupon bond; for example:

	Percentage Change in the Bond's Value	
Change in Yield	Bond C	Bond D
From 5% to 6%	−4.98%	−5.67%
From 8% to 9%	−4.84%	−5.59%
From 14% to 15%	−4.57%	−5.44%

This is because the entire cash flow for the zero-coupon bond is 12 periods into the future, whereas the coupon bond has cash flows in the near periods as well, which are not as affected by the yield change as the maturity value.

Time Passage

We have seen examples in this chapter so far of bonds that trade at either a premium or a discount from their face values. This is usually the case: Borrowers often issue bonds at or near their face value, but as time passes,

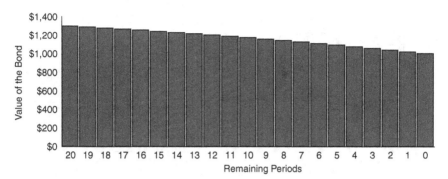

EXHIBIT 7.5 Value of a 10% Coupon, $1,000 Maturity Value Bond, with 10 Years to Maturity and Priced to Yield 6%

yields change and thus the value of the bond changes. Eventually, the value of the bond must be equal to the maturity value.[5] If the yield holds constant throughout the life the bond, the value of a bond approaches the maturity value as time passes. If the yield changes during the life of the bond, the value still approaches the maturity value as time passes, but perhaps not in a smooth path.

Consider a bond that has a 10% coupon, a maturity value of $1,000, 10 years (i.e., 20 periods) remaining to maturity, and is priced to yield 6%. If the yield does not change until the bond matures, the price of the bond will decline until it reaches $1,000, the maturity value, as shown in Exhibit 7.5. If this bond's yield changes, say to 4% with 10 periods remaining, the value adjusts appropriately (i.e., increasing) and the bond's value will decline towards $1,000 at maturity, as shown in Exhibit 7.6.

In a similar manner, a discount bond's value will increase over time, approaching the maturity value, as we show in Exhibit 7.7.

In Exhibit 7.8, We can see the convergence of the premium and discount bonds' values by comparing three bonds, each with a maturity of 20 years: a 4% coupon bond, a 6% coupon bond, and an 8% coupon bond.

Reinvestment Rate Issues

When we solve for the value of a bond for a given yield, or solve for a yield for a given bond's value, we are making an assumption about what we can

---

[5]Otherwise there would be a windfall gain or a large loss to someone owning the bond just prior to maturity.

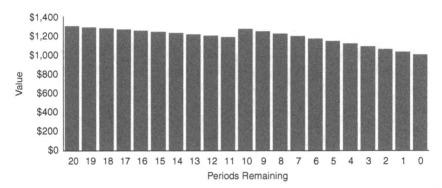

EXHIBIT 7.6 Value of a 10% Coupon, $1,000 Maturity Value Bond, with 10 Years to Maturity, and Priced to Yield 6% for the First Five Years and 4% for the Last Five Years

do with the interest when we get it. You didn't have to do anything special to make this assumption: It is built into the mathematics.

To see this, let's use the generic valuation equation for a series of cash flows:

$$P V = \sum_{t=1}^{N} \frac{\mathrm{CF}_t}{(1 + i)^t}$$

We used the same discount rate for each period's cash flow. We allowed the cash flows to be different each period, but we specified one and

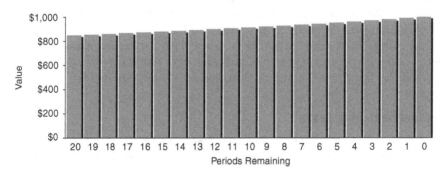

EXHIBIT 7.7 Value of a 4% Coupon, $1,000 Maturity Value Bond, with 10 Years to Maturity, and Priced to Yield 6%

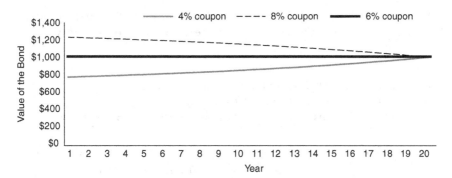

EXHIBIT 7.8 Comparison of Convergence of Values for Three 20-Year Bonds with Coupon Rates of 4%, 6%, and 8%, respectively, if the Yield to Maturity Remains at 6% throughout the Life of the Bonds

only one discount rate. The mathematics that we use assumes that each CF_t we receive is reinvested at the rate i. We did the same in the bond valuation:

$$V = \left[\sum_{t=1}^{N} \frac{PMT_t}{(1 + r_d)^t} \right] + \frac{M}{(1 + r_d)^N}$$

We specified one and only one discount rate, r_d. Let's see why this is so—and why it may be an issue. Consider a bond that has a face value of $1,000, a coupon rate of 4%, is priced to yield 6%, and has two years remaining to maturity. The value of this bond is $962.83.

Now let's see how the math works on the reinvestment:

	Cash Flow	Calculation	Value at the End of Two Years
1st six-month period	$20	$(1 + 0.03)^3$	$21.85
2nd six-month period	$20	$(1 + 0.03)^2$	21.22
3rd six-month period	$20	$(1 + 0.03)^1$	20.60
4th six-month period	$1,020		1,020.00
			$1,083.67

With FV = \$1,083.67; PV = \$962.83; N = 4; the r_d = 3% and the yield to maturity is 6%. In other words, you will earn a return of 6% on your investment if you:

- Buy the bond for \$962.83 and hold it for two years.
- Receive the coupon payments of \$20 each.
- Reinvest the coupons at 3% each six-month period, or 6% per year.

But what if you cannot earn 6% on your reinvested cash flows? What if returns on investments have changed and so have the reinvestment opportunities? In that case, your return will be something other than 6%.

What if the return that you can get on your reinvested cash flows is only 5% per year? In that case:

	Cash Flow	Calculation	Value at the End of Two Years
1st six-month period	\$20	$(1 + 0.02)^3$	21.22
2nd six-month period	\$20	$(1 + 0.02)^2$	20.81
3rd six-month period	\$20	$(1 + 0.02)^1$	20.40
4th six-month period	\$1,020		1,020.00
			\$1,082.43

With FV = \$1,082.43; PV = \$962.83; N = 4; the r_d = 2.97% and the yield to maturity is 5.94%.

We call the risk that you will earn less than what is expected *reinvestment risk*, because reinvested coupons earn a yield different from what was expected. An investor investing in zero-coupon bonds does not have an exposure to reinvestment risk because there are no cash flows other than the initial purchase price and the maturity value.

Bottom line? The return earned by holding a security depends on not only the cash flows of the security itself, but what you can earn on any reinvested cash flows.

Other Valuation Issues

A borrower could design a bond with any features that are necessary for the issuer's financial situation or creditors' demand. There are endless variations in debt securities' characteristics that may affect how we value the security. Consider a few of these characteristics:

Feature	Description	Valuation Considerations
Callable	At the discretion of the issuer, the bond may be bought back by the issuer at a specified price, according to a specified schedule.	The value of the security is the value of the straight bond, less the value of the option that the issuer possesses.
Convertible	At the discretion of the creditor, the bond may be exchanged for another security, such as a specified number of common shares.	The value of the security is the value of the straight bond, plus the value of the option to convert.
Deferred interest	Interest scheduled such that it is not paid in the first few years, but begins sometime in the future.	The value of the security is the present value of the interest (a deferred annuity) and the face value.
Step-up	The coupon rate of the bond changes from one rate to another, according to a pre-determined schedule.	The valuation requires valuing a coupon stream that is not constant, but rather changes at specific points in the security's life.

Other features include *security* (i.e., collateral), a *put option* (the investor's option to sell the security back to the issuer), a *sinking fund* (i.e., putting aside funds or periodically retiring the debt). A security issuer may combine these features, and others, in a given bond, making the valuation of the security quite challenging. Most of these features will affect the risk associated with the bond's future cash flows; for example, if the bond is secured, this reduces the risk of the bond's future cash flows because this collateral can be used to pay off the debt obligation.

INTEREST RATES

A casual examination of the financial news would be enough to convene the idea that nobody talks about an "interest rate." There are interest rates reported for borrowing money and for investing. These rates are not randomly determined; that is, there are factors that systematically affect how interest rates on different types of loans and debt instruments vary from each other.

The securities issued by the U.S. Department of the Treasury, popularly referred to as Treasury securities or simply Treasuries, are backed by the full faith and credit of the U.S. government.[6] Historically Treasury securities have served as the benchmark interest rates throughout the U.S. economy, as well as in international capital markets.[7]

Bonds that the U.S. Treasury do not back will have some risk of default, though for some bonds this is quite small. *Default risk* is the uncertainty that the issuer of the security is unable to make timely payments of interest and principal amount when promised. To get a better idea of what determines interest rate, let's ignore default risk for now and focus on the fundamentals.

We can think of interest rates providing compensation for the time value of money. The time value of money is compensation for not having use of the funds. Within this interest rate are two components: the real interest rate and the expected rate of inflation:

Interest rate = Real interest rate + Expected rate of inflation

The real interest rate is that that would exist in the economy in the absence of inflation. We generally look at interest rates with inflation expectations built into the rate.

Consider interest rates on two securities:

Security A: 5.4%

Security B: 6.5%

The difference between the yields, or *spread*, is 1.1%.

Rather than refer to this spread in percentage terms, such as 1.1%, market participants refer to the difference in terms of basis points. A *basis point* is equal to 0.01%. Consequently, 1% is equal to 100 basis points. In our example, the spread of 1.1% is equal to 110 basis points.

YIELD CURVES

One of the influences of a bond's yield is the yield curve. The *yield curve* is the relation between the time remaining to maturity and the yield. We

---

[6]At the time of this writing, most market participants view U.S. Treasuries as being free of default risk, although there is the possibility that unwise economic policy by the U.S. government may alter that perception.

[7]Yet there are other important benchmarks used by market participants, such as the London Interbank Offered Rate (LIBOR).

gauge the relation between yields and maturity by looking at the difference in yields for U.S. Treasuries. We do this so that we can look at interest rates for securities with different maturities, without having to worry about adjusting for differences in default risk. We refer to the difference in the yields at a point in time for U.S. Treasuries as the *maturity spread*.

Consider the yield curve that existed on three different dates:

Maturity	January 31, 2008	January 2, 2008	March 1, 2007	January 2, 2007
1 month	1.64%	3.09%	5.23%	4.79%
3 months	1.96%	3.26%	5.12%	5.07%
6 months	2.07%	3.32%	5.11%	5.11%
1 year	2.11%	3.17%	4.95%	5.00%
2 years	2.17%	2.88%	4.63%	4.80%
3 years	2.27%	2.89%	4.54%	4.71%
5 years	2.82%	3.28%	4.50%	4.68%
7 years	3.19%	3.54%	4.51%	4.68%
10 years	3.67%	3.91%	4.56%	4.68%
20 years	4.35%	4.39%	4.78%	4.87%
30 years	4.35%	4.35%	4.68%	4.79%

On January 2, 2007, the maturity spread for the 1-year and 30-year securities was 4.79% – 5% = –0.21% or –21 basis points, and the same spread on January 31, 2008 was 2.24% or 224 basic points.

We show the yield curves for two of these dates in a graph in Exhibit 7.9.

Yield curves may be upward sloping, downward sloping, flat, or even humped-shaped. The *normal yield curve* is upward sloping, with longer-maturity securities having higher yields than shorter-term securities. In other words, with the normal curve, the maturity spreads are positive. The January 31, 2008 curve resembles a normal curve. However, the January 2, 2007 curve is an inverted curve, which means that, in general, the shorter-term securities had higher yields than the longer-term securities. In other words, the maturity spread is negative. Inverted curves, while unusual, are often a precursor to a recessionary economic period. It is also possible for the yield curve to be flat, which means that the yields do not differ based upon maturity.

A number of factors affect the yield curve, with the largest influence being the general economy. As we show in Exhibit 7.9, yield curves can shift, though more likely in the shorter-term securities. Though we depict yield curves using U.S. Treasury securities so that we can compare yields

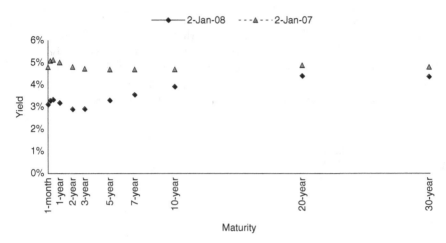

EXHIBIT 7.9   Yield curves on U.S. Treasury securities for two different dates

without having to worry about the effect of default risk on yields, corporate and municipal bond interest rates follow a similar pattern with respect to maturity: Longer-term securities generally have higher yields, though yields do change often.

Interest Rates and Credit Risk

Debt instruments not issued or backed by the full faith and credit of the U.S. government are available in the market at an interest rate or yield that is different from an otherwise comparable maturity Treasury security. We refer to the difference between the interest rate offered on a non-Treasury security and a comparable maturity Treasury security as the *credit spread*. The credit spread exists because an investor is exposed to the additional risks with a security not issued by the U.S. government.

Default risk refers to the risk that the issuer of a debt obligation may be unable to make timely payment of interest and/or the principal amount when it is due.

Most market participants gauge credit risk in terms of ratings assigned by the three major commercial rating companies:

- Moody's Investors Service
- Standard & Poor's Corporation
- Fitch Ratings

These companies, referred to as *rating agencies*, perform credit analyses of issuers and issues and express their conclusions by a system of ratings.

Let's see how credit risk affects spreads. For example, on August 5, 2008, the five-year Treasury yield was 3.29% and the same day the yield on five-year corporate bonds was as follows:[8]

Credit Rating	Yield
AAA	5.01%
AA	5.50%
A	5.78%

Therefore, the credit spreads were:

Credit Rating	Credit Spread
AAA	5.01% − 3.29% = 1.72% = 172 basis points
AA	5.50% − 3.29% = 2.21% = 221 basis points
A	5.78% − 3.29% = 2.49% = 249 basis points

Note that the lower the credit rating, the higher the credit spread.

Example 7.6

Consider the following two bonds, as of February 2006:[9]

- Verizon Communications: 5.55% coupon, with a yield of 5.492% and a bond rating of A.
- Boise Cascade Corporation: 7.35% coupon, with a yield of 7.284% and a bond rating of BB.

Both bonds mature at the same time and have similar features (in this case, both are noncallable and nonconvertible, fixed-rate bonds). A similar maturity U.S. Treasury bond has a yield of 4.653%.

What is the credit spread of each bond?

---

[8]The data is from finance.yahoo.com reported (based on information supplied by ValuBond).
[9]Source: *Yahoo!Finance*, February 13, 2006.

Answer:

- Verizon Communications: $5.55\% - 4.653\% = 0.847\%$ or **84.7 basis points.**
- Boise Cascade: $7.35\% - 4.653\% = 2.697\%$ or **269.7 basis points.**

BOND RATINGS AND YIELDS

Bond rating agencies, such as Standard & Poor's, Moody's, and Fitch, provide a rating of the creditworthiness of bonds. The more default risk, the lower the rating. The rating systems used by the three major ratings services are similar, but the ratings don't always agree.

As an example of ratings, consider Standard & Poor's system from AAA to D:*

	Rating	Description
Investment Grade	AAA	Capacity of issuer to meet obligations is extremely strong.
	AA	Capacity of issuer to meet obligations is very strong.
	A	Capacity of issuer to meet obligations is strong, but this capacity is susceptible to unfavorable economic conditions.
	BBB	Issuer has adequate capacity, but is vulnerable to adverse conditions.
Noninvestment-Grade (Junk) Bonds	BB	Debt is speculative, with ongoing uncertainties that may affect the ability of the issuer to meet its obligations.
	B	Debt is speculative and vulnerable to adverse conditions that may result in nonpayment of obligations.
	CCC	Debt is speculative and currently susceptible to adverse conditions.
	CC	Issuer is likely to be unable to meet obligations.
	C	Obligations are highly vulnerable to nonpayment, payments are currently not being made, or the issuer is in bankruptcy.
	D	Obligation is in default.

*For more information, check out the Standard & Poor's Ratings Definitions, available at *RatingsDirect.com* and *StandardandPoors.com*.

We can see the difference in the yields for different levels of risk by looking at a snapshot of yields on December 24, 2008:

Maturity	U.S. Treasury Bonds	Corporate AAA-Rated Bonds	Corporate A-Rated Bonds
5 years	1.54%	3.48%	4.97%
10 years	2.20%	4.82%	5.30%
20 years	2.94%	5.12%	5.73%

Other Influences on Interest Rates and Yields

We refer to the difference between a security's interest rate or yield and a Treasury security with the same maturity as the *risk premium*. The general factors that affect the risk premium between a non-Treasury security and a Treasury security with the same maturity, other than credit risk, include:

- Any features provided for in the non-Treasury security that make them attractive or unattractive to investors, such as a call or conversion feature.
- The tax treatment of the interest income from the non-Treasury security.
- The ability of the investor to sell the security close to its true value.[10]

Therefore, it is possible that you can observe, for example, two bonds with similar ratings and maturity that have different yields because one bond is callable and the other one is not.

SUMMARY

The valuation of bonds is an application of the time value of money mathematics. The key is to take the bond's characteristics (i.e., coupon, maturity value) and translate them into inputs for the financial mathematics.

---

[10]We refer to the ability to get a security's true value in the market as liquidity. The greater the chance of getting close to its true value when you sell the security, the better the liquidity.

Bond valuation can get more complicated than what we've discussed in this reading because issuers have a great deal of flexibility in designing these securities, but any feature that an issuer includes in the bond is usually just a simple extension of asset valuation principles and mathematics.

"TRY IT" SOLUTIONS

7.1. Bond Quotes

Bond	Quote	Face Value	Value of Bond[11]
A	103.45	$1,000	$1,034.50
B	98.00	$1,000	$980.00
C	89.50	$500	$447.50
D	110.00	$100,000	$110,000
E	90.00	€1000	€900,000
F	120.25	¥10000	¥12,025
G	65.45	$10,000	$6,545

7.2. Bond Values and Yields

Yield to Maturity	Value of Bond	Bond Quote
5%	$1,077.95	107.795
6%	$1,000.00	100.000
7%	$928.94	92.894
8%	$864.10	86.410

7.3. Yields to Maturity

Bond Value	Yield to Maturity
$1,100	4.733%
$1,000	6.000%
$900	7.435%
$800	9.087%

---

[11]Note that a comma is used in European math conventions, which is different than the U.S. convention of a decimal place.

PROBLEMS

7.1. Complete the following table, indicating whether the bond will be selling for a premium or a discount from its face value:

Bond	Coupon Rate	Yield to Maturity	Premium or Discount?
A	5%	4%	
B	6%	5%	
C	4%	5%	
D	8%	7%	

7.2. What is the value of a $1,000 face value bond that has five years remaining to maturity, a coupon rate of 8% (paid semiannually), and is priced to yield 10%?

7.3. What is the value of a $1,000 face value bond that has four years remaining to maturity, a coupon rate of 5% (paid semiannually), and is priced to yield 4%?

7.4. What is the current value of a five year, $1,000 face value bond that is priced to yield 6% and has a coupon rate of 10%?

7.5. ABC, Inc. has a bond outstanding with eight years remaining to maturity and a coupon rate of 8% paid semiannually. If the current market quote is 88, what is the yield to maturity (YTM) on the ABC bonds?

7.6. The DEF Company bonds have a face value of $1,000 and mature in five years. The bonds pay 4% interest in the first two years and 6% thereafter. Interest is paid semiannually. If you buy a DEF bond for $950 today and hold it to maturity, what is your return on this bond?

7.7. What is the current value of a $500 face value bond that is priced to yield 6%, has a coupon rate of 8%, and has four years remaining to maturity?

7.8. Suppose a $1,000 face value, zero-coupon bond has five years remaining to maturity. The bond is currently priced to yield 5%. What is the value of this bond?

7.9. Suppose a $1,000 face value, zero-coupon bond has five years remaining to maturity. The bond's current quote is 70. What is the yield to maturity on this bond?

7.10. Which of the following two bonds has the higher yield to maturity?

Bond 1. Five years remaining to maturity; coupon rate of 5%; the bond has a current quote of 94.

Bond 2. Seven years remaining to maturity; coupon rate of 6%; the bond has a current quote of 96.

For solutions to these problems, see Appendix E.

CHAPTER 8

Taking Stock

[A] stock is worth the present value of all the dividends ever to be paid upon it, no more, no less. The purchase of a stock represents the exchange of present goods for future goods...
—John Burr Williams
The Theory of Investment Value

If you invest in *common stock*, you are buying shares that represent an ownership interest in the firm. Shares of common stock are a perpetual security; there is no maturity. If you own shares of common stock, you have the right to receive a certain portion of any dividends, but dividends are not a sure thing.

Dividends are distributions of cash to shareholders in proportion to the ownership interest, and dividends may be in the form of cash or stock. *Cash dividends* are cash payments made directly to the shareholders from the company. *Stock dividends* are distributions of shares of stock and do not affect the total value of the stock of a company—just how many shares comprise that total value. What concerns us for valuing a stock are the cash dividends.

Whether a firm will pay dividends is up to its board of directors, who are the representatives of the common shareholders. Typically, we see some pattern in the dividends companies pay: Dividends are either constant or grow at a constant rate. However, there is no guarantee that dividends will be paid in the future and, if paid, what the monetary amount will be. In other words, dividends are uncertain.

A *preferred stock* is also an equity investment in the company. However, preferred shareholders have preference (i.e., seniority) over common shareholders with respect to both income and assets in the event of a liquidation of the company. In other words, a company must pay dividends to its preferred shareholders before it pays any dividends to common shareholders.

Preferred shareholders are in a similar situation as the common shareholders with respect to whether dividends will be paid. They expect to receive cash dividends in the future, but the payment of these dividends is up to the board of directors. However, there are three major differences between the dividends of preferred and common shares.

- First, the dividends on preferred stock usually specify a fixed rate or a floating rate determined by a formula, whereas the amount of dividends is not specified for common shares.
- Second, preferred shareholders have preference: The company must pay their dividends before any dividends are paid on common stock.
- Third, if the preferred stock usually has a cumulative feature, dividends not paid in one period accumulate and are carried over to the next period. Therefore, the dividends on preferred stock are more certain than those on common shares.

WHY DON'T WE WORRY ABOUT STOCK DIVIDENDS IN VALUATION?

Stock dividends are additional shares provided to current stockholders in proportion to existing holdings. These dividends do not involve cash and do not affect the value of a share of stock directly.

There is some evidence that stock dividends may provide a signal about the future prospects of the company. However, stock dividends should not affect the current value of the stock other than reducing the stock's value to reflect the additional shares outstanding (that is, the shareholder "pie" is sliced into more pieces after the stock dividend, though no cash has changed hands).

WHAT'S IN A VALUE? THE BASICS OF STOCK VALUATION

When you buy a share of common stock, it is reasonable to figure that what you pay for it should reflect what you expect to receive from it; that is, the return on your investment. What you receive are cash dividends in the future. How can we relate that return to what a share of common stock is worth?

The value of a share of stock should be equal to the present value of all the future cash flows you expect to receive from that share of stock:[1]

$$\text{Value of a share of stock} = \frac{\text{First period's dividend}}{(1 + \text{Discount rate})^1} + \frac{\text{Second period's dividend}}{(1 + \text{Discount rate})^2}$$

$$+ \frac{\text{Third period's dividend}}{(1 + \text{Discount rate})^3} + \cdots$$

When we discount future cash flows to the present, we can refer to this as *capitalizing*. The verb *capitalize* really means that we are calculating the value of some future cash flow.

Valuing Preferred Stock

If the share is preferred stock with a fixed, specified dividend, the valuation is quite straightforward: It is the present value of a perpetuity, calculated as the ratio of the perpetual cash flow (i.e., the dividend per share is the same each period) to the required rate of return for the preferred stock, r_p. The required rate of return is the return that investors in the stock expected to earn, which acts as a threshold of sorts—what the stock should earn.

If dividends are constant forever, the value of a share of stock is the present value of the dividends per share per period, in perpetuity. The summation of a constant amount (that is, if $D_1 = D_2 = \cdots = D_\infty = D$) discounted from perpetuity simplifies to:

$$P_0 = \frac{D}{r_p}$$

This is generally the case for a preferred stock and is the case for some common stocks. If the current dividend is \$2 per share and the required rate of return is 10%, the value of a share of stock is

$$P_0 = \frac{\$2}{0.10} = \$20$$

---

[1]The cash flows that are valued are the cash dividends.

Stated another way, if you pay $20 per share and dividends remain constant at $2 per share, you will earn a 10% return per year on your investment every year. A problem in valuing common stock, however, is that the amount of cash dividends often changes through time.

Example 8.1

If a preferred stock with a face value of $100 has a 5% dividend, the value of a share of this stock is the $5, divided by the required rate of return. If the required rate is 5%, the value of a share is $100; if the required rate is 6%, the value of a share is $83.33.

Example 8.2

If a preferred share has a $25 par value, a dividend rate of 10.25%, and a required rate of return of 8%, what is its value? The dividend is $25 × (1 + 0.1025) = $2.5625. The value per share of stock is $2.5625 ÷ 0.08 = $32.03.

Valuing Common Stock

Because common stock never matures, today's value is the present value of an infinite stream of cash flows. Another complication is that common stock dividends are not fixed, as in the case of preferred stock.[2] Not knowing the amount of the dividends, or even if there will be future dividends, makes it difficult to determine the value of common stock.

Let D_t represent the dividend per share of common stock expected next period, P_0 represent the value of a share of stock today, and r_e the required rate of return on common stock. The *required rate of return* is the return shareholders demand to compensate them for the time value of money tied up in their investment and the uncertainty of the future cash flows from these investments. The required rate of return is the opportunity cost of the owners' capital.

We can represent the current price of a share of common stock, P_0, as

$$P_0 = \frac{D_1}{(1+r_e)^1} + \frac{D_2}{(1+r_e)^2} + \frac{D_3}{(1+r_e)^3} + \cdots + \frac{D_\infty}{(1+r_e)^\infty}$$

---

[2]Though some preferred stock's dividends are fixed in amount, there remains uncertainty as to whether the dividends will be paid in the future because they are paid at the discretion of the company's board of directors.

which we can write using summation notation,

$$P_0 = \sum_{t=1}^{\infty} \frac{D_t}{(1+r_e)^t}$$

We refer to this as the *dividend valuation model*, or the *dividend discount model*. So what are we to do? Well, we can grapple with the valuation of common stock by looking at its current dividend and making assumptions about any future dividends it may pay.

A common assumption is that dividends grow at a constant rate forever. However, there are many different assumptions that we can use. For example, we could assume that dividends will grow at one rate for a specified number of years, and then this growth rate changes. This is what we commonly refer to as a *two-stage model*. Though we could develop assumptions of two, three, or any number of stages for a company's dividends, we will demonstrate the constant growth and the two-stage growth so that you can see how to apply the time value of money mathematics.

Valuing a Stock That Has Dividends That Grow at a Constant Rate If dividends grow at a constant rate, the value of a share of stock is the present value of a growing cash flow. Let D_0 indicate this period's dividend. If dividends grow at a constant rate, g, forever, the present value of the common stock is the present value of all future dividends.

$$P_0 = \frac{D_0(1+g)}{(1+r_e)^1} + \frac{D_0(1+g)^2}{(1+r_e)^2} + \frac{D_0(1+g)^3}{(1+r_e)^3} + \cdots + \frac{D_0(1+g)^{\infty}}{(1+r_e)^{\infty}}$$

Pulling today's dividend, D_0, from each term, the value of a share is equal to the current dividend, multiplied by a sum of factors that extend ad infinitum:

$$P_0 = D_0 \left[\frac{(1+g)}{(1+r_e)^1} + \frac{(1+g)^2}{(1+r_e)^2} + \frac{(1+g)^3}{(1+r_e)^3} + \cdots + \frac{(1+g)^{\infty}}{(1+r_e)^{\infty}} \right]$$

Using summation notation:

$$P_0 = D_0 \left[\sum_{t=1}^{\infty} \frac{(1+g)^t}{(1+r_e)^t} \right]$$

Using a math trick, we can know that $\left[\sum_{t=1}^{\infty} \frac{(1+g)^t}{(1+r_e)^t} \right]$ approaches $\left[\frac{(1+g)}{(r_e-g)} \right]$.

If we represent the next period's dividend, D_1, in terms of this period's dividend, D_0, compounded one period at the rate g,

$$P_0 = \frac{D_0(1+g)}{(r_e - g)} = \frac{D_1}{(r_e - g)}$$

$$= \frac{Next \text{ period's dividend}}{(\text{Required rate of return} - \text{Expected growth in dividends})}$$

We refer to this equation as the *Gordon model*.[3]

Consider a firm expected to pay a constant dividend of \$2 per share, forever. If we capitalize this dividend at 10%, the value of a share is \$20:

$$P_0 = \frac{\$2}{0.10} = \$20$$

If, on the other hand, we expect the dividends to be \$2 in the next period and grow at a rate of 6% per year, forever, the value of a share of stock is \$50:

$$P_0 = \frac{\$2}{(0.10 - 0.06)} = \$50$$

Does this make sense? Yes: if we expect dividends to grow in the future, the stock is worth more than if the dividends are expected to remain the same. The stock's price will actually grow at the same rate as the dividend.

If today's value of a share is \$50, what are we saying about the value of the stock next year? If we move everything up one period, D_1 is no longer \$2, but \$2 grown one period at 6%, or \$2.12. Therefore, we expect the price of the stock at the end of one year, P_1, to be \$53:

$$P_1 = \frac{\$2.12}{(0.10 - 0.06)} = \$53$$

At the end of two years, the price will be even larger:

$$P_2 = \frac{\$2.25}{(0.10 - 0.06)} = \$56.18$$

---

[3]The model was first presented by Myron J. Gordon, "Dividends, Earnings and Stock Prices," *Review of Economics and Statistics* 41 (May 1959): 99–105.

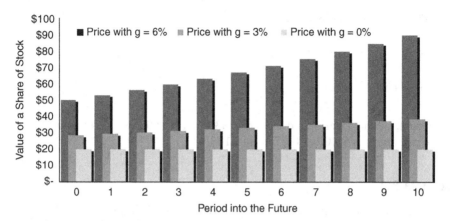

EXHIBIT 8.1   Price per Share Over Time Using Three Different Growth Rates, when the Required Rate of Return is 10% and Next Period's Dividend is $2 per Share

What is the growth in the price of this stock? From today to the end of one period, the price grew ($53 ÷ $50) – 1 = 6%.[4] From the end of the first period to the end of the second period, the price grew ($56.18 ÷ $53) – 1 = 6%.

Because we expect dividends to grow each period, we also are expecting the price of the stock to grow through time as well. In fact, the price will grow at the same rate as the dividends: 6%, per period. For a given required rate of return and dividend—in this case $r_e = 10\%$, and $D_1 = \$2$—we see that the price of a share of stock is expected to grow each period at the rate g.

We can see this in Exhibit 8.1, where the price of a stock with a dividend next period of $2 is plotted over time for three different growth rates: 0%, 3%, and 6%.

Example 8.3

The Pear Company has a current dividend of $3.00 per share. The dividends are expected to grow at a rate of 3% per year for the foreseeable future. If the current required rate of return on Pear Company stock is 10%, what is the price of a share of Pear common stock? Answer: **$44.143**.

---

[4]Where did this formula come from? Consider $FV = PV (1 + i)^n$. If $n = 1$, then $FV = PV (1+i)$ and therefore $i = (FV/PV) - 1$.

The basic inputs are as follows:

$D_0 = \$3.00$
$g = 3\%$
$r_e = 10\%$

Therefore, the next period's dividend is $\$3.00\,(1 + 0.03) = \$3.09$, and the value per shares is $\$3.09 \div 0.07 = \$44.143$.

Example 8.4

Suppose that a company has a current dividend of $2.50 per share. If investors expect the dividend to increase at a rate of 2% per year, and if the required rate of return on this stock is 8%, what is the value of a share of this stock? Answer: **$31.875**.

The basic inputs are as follows:

$D_0 = \$2.50$
$g = 2\%$
$r_e = 8\%$

The price per share is

$$P_0 = \frac{\$2.50(1 - 0.02)}{(0.10 - 0.02)} = \frac{\$2.55}{0.08} = \$31.875$$

What if we expect dividends to decline each year? That is, what if we expect a negative growth rate? We can still use the dividend valuation model, but each dividend in the future is expected to be less than the one before it. For example, suppose a stock has a current dividend of $5 per share and the required rate of return is 10%. If dividends are expected to decline 3% each year, what is the value of a share of stock today? We know that $D_0 = \$5$, $r_e = 10\%$, and $g = -3\%$. Therefore,

$$P_0 = \frac{\$5(1 - 0.03)}{(0.10 + 0.03)} = \frac{\$4.85}{0.13} = \$37.31$$

Next period's dividend, D_1, is expected to be $4.85. We capitalize this at 13%: 10% − 3%, or 10% + 3%. What do we expect the price of the stock to be next period?

$$P_0 = \frac{\$5(1 - 0.03)^2}{(0.10 + 0.03)} = \frac{\$4.70}{0.13} = \$36.19$$

The expected price goes the same way as the dividend: down 3% each year.

Example 8.5

The Sad Company has a current dividend of $3.00 per share. The dividends are expected to decline at a rate of 3% per year for the foreseeable future. If the current required rate of return on Sad Company stock is 10%, what is the price of a share of Sad common stock? Answer: **$22.385.**

The basic inputs are as follows:

$D_0 = \$3.00$
$g = -3\%$
$r_e = 10\%$

And the price per share is

$$P_0 = \frac{\$3(1 - 0.03)}{(0.10 - 0.03)} = \frac{\$2.91}{0.13} = \$22.385$$

 TRY IT! 8.1 VALUE A SHARE OF COMMON STOCK

Suppose the ABC Company pays $1 of dividends this year. If we expect dividends to grow at a rate of 6% per year and if shareholders' required rate of return is 10%, what is the value of a share of ABC stock today?

Valuing Common Stock if the Dividends Do Not Grow at a Constant rate
The dividend valuation model captures the valuation of stock whose dividends grow at a constant rate, as well as the valuation of stock whose dividends do not grow at all (that is, the perpetuity model, with $g = 0\%$). However, dividends may not follow a pattern of no growth or a steady growth. A corporation's Board of Directors declares dividends. There is no obligation on the part of the board to pay dividends of any amount or

periodicity. Dividends for a stock may simply not follow any discernable pattern and may not be paid at all.

We do observe that companies go through a life cycle, with fairly well defined stages: high growth at the outset, then maturity, and, perhaps, decline. Accompanying these growth stages, the dividends of some companies grow not at a constant rate forever, but rather in stages. Any number of different future growth rates may be appropriate, depending on the company's circumstances.

To see how to value a stock whose dividends are neither constant or of constant growth, consider a stock whose dividends grow at two distinct rates: high growth initially and then maturing. We can use a modification of the dividend valuation model to capture two stages. In this case, we need to value the dividends we expect in the first stage that grow at one rate, g_1, and then the value of the dividends that are expected in the second stage, that grow at rate g_2. If we assume that the second stage is the steady state forever, then the second stage is analogous to the dividend valuation model; that is, constant growth at g_2.

Consider a share of common stock whose dividend is currently $3 per share (that is, $D_0 = \$3$) and is expected to grow at a rate of 4% per year for three years (that is, $g_1 = 4\%$) and afterward at a rate of 2% per year after five years (that is, $g_2 = 2\%$).

This means that we expect dividends to be:

Period	Calculation	Expected Dividend
1	$\$3 \times (1 + 0.04)$	$3.1200
2	$\$3 \times (1 + 0.04)^2$	$3.2448
3	$\$3 \times (1 + 0.04)^3$	$3.3746
4	$\$3 \times (1 + 0.04)^3 \times (1 + 0.02)$	$3.4421
5	$\$3 \times (1 + 0.04)^3 \times (1 + 0.02)^2$	$3.5109
6	$\$3 \times (1 + 0.04)^3 \times (1 + 0.02)^3$	$3.5811
7	$\$3 \times (1 + 0.04)^3 \times (1 + 0.02)^4$	$3.6528

If the required rate of return is 10%, this becomes

$$P_0 = \frac{\$3(1+0.04)}{(1+0.10)^1} + \frac{\$3(1+0.04)^2}{(1+0.10)^2} + \frac{\$3(1+0.04)^3}{(1+0.10)^3}$$
$$+ \frac{\$3(1+0.04)^3(1+0.02)}{(1+0.10)^4} + \frac{\$3(1+0.04)^3(1+0.02)^2}{(1+0.10)^5} + \cdots$$

In other words,

$$P_0 = \frac{\$3.12}{(1+0.10)^1} + \frac{\$3.2448}{(1+0.10)^2} + \frac{\$3.3746}{(1+0.10)^3} + \frac{\$3.4421}{(1+0.10)^4}$$
$$+ \frac{\$3.5109}{(1+0.10)^5} + \cdots$$

The present value of dividends received after the third year—evaluated three years from today—is the expected price of the stock in three years, P_3, discounted to the present. The expected dividend in the fourth period, D_4, is $3.44208, so the price at the end of the third year is $43.0263:

$$P_3 = \frac{\$3.4421}{(0.10 - 0.02)} = \$43.0263$$

These calculations get pretty confusing pretty quick because we are trying to calculate a value today—but in order to do this, we have to estimate a value in the future. To see where this value of $43.026 comes from, let's put it in more familiar terms:

Suppose the next period's dividend is $3.4421. If we expect dividends to grow at a rate of 2% per year, forever, and if the required rate of return is 10%, the valuation based on the dividend valuation model is

$$\text{Value} = \frac{\$3.4421}{(0.10 - 0.02)} = \$43.0263$$

So, when we calculated the value at the end of the third year, we were calculating the value of the dividends beyond the third year—all as of the end of the third year.

In terms of a time line, we can see the cash flows as follows:

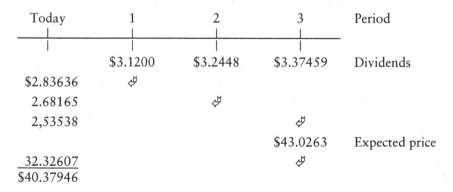

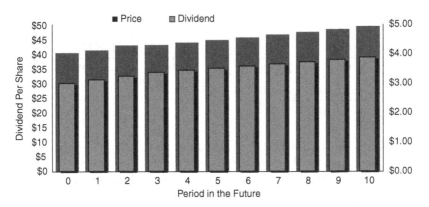

EXHIBIT 8.2 The Dividends and Price for a Share of Stock if Dividends Start at $3 per Share and then Grow at 4% per Year for Three Years, and then 2% per Year Thereafter

We can also represent this as discounted cash flows in a formula:

$$P_0 = \frac{\$3.12}{(1+0.10)^1} + \frac{\$3.2448}{(1+0.10)^2} + \frac{\$3.37459}{(1+0.10)^3} + \frac{\$3.44208/(0.10-0.02)}{(1+0.10)^3}$$

$$P_0 = \frac{\$3.12}{(1+0.10)^1} + \frac{\$3.2448}{(1+0.10)^2} + \frac{\$3.37459}{(1+0.10)^3} + \frac{\$43.026}{(1+0.10)^3}$$

$$P_0 = \$2.83636 + 2.68165 + \$2.53538 + \$32.32607 = \$40.37946$$

The value of a share of this stock today is $40.37946, which is comprised of the present value of the dividends in the first three years ($2.83636 + 2.68165 + 2.53538 = $8.05339) and the present value of the dividends beyond three years, worth $32.32607 today.

We show the price per share and dividends per share for the first 10 years in Exhibit 8.2.

In this example, we illustrate a two-stage dividend growth model. We can modify this calculation to accommodate three, four, or any other number of stages of growth. As you can see, the valuation problem for a two-stage growth model is simply an extension of the financial mathematics that we used to value a stock with a single growth rate. We can extend this approach further to cases in which there are three, four, or more different growth stages expected in a company's future.[5]

---

[5]If there is no discernable pattern in terms of future growth rates, we are left with simply discounted an uneven series of expected dividends.

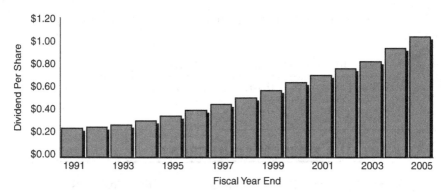

EXHIBIT 8.3 Dividends of Procter & Gamble, 1991 through 2005
Source: Procter & Gamble annual reports, various years.

The key is to forecast future dividends, and then estimate a future stock value at the beginning of the last growth phase. We refer to this future stock value as a terminal value because it is the estimated value of the investment if you terminated the investment at that point in time.

Consider the dividends of Procter & Gamble (P&G) as shown in Exhibit 8.3. Dividends per share grew at an annual rate around 12 to 13% in the years 1993 through 2000, and slowed to 8 to 9% in the years 2001–2004. The growth in dividends increased in 2005, which coincides with substantial restructuring of the company and the acquisition of Gillette (see Exhibit 8.3).

Example 8.6

A stock currently pays a dividend of $2 for the year. Expected dividend growth is 20% for the next three years and we then expect growth to revert to 7% thereafter for an indefinite amount of time. The appropriate required rate of return is 15%. What is the value of this stock?

First, we estimate the future cash flows:

Period	Calculation	Cash Flow
1	$D_1 = \$2\,(1.20)$	$2.40
2	$D_2 = \$2\,(1.20)^2$	2.88
3	$D_3 = \$2\,(1.20)^3 = \$3.456$ $P_3 = \$3.69792/(0.15 - 0.07) = \$46.224$	49.68

Second, we use the valuation equation to estimate the value of the stock:

$$P_0 = \frac{\$2.40}{(1+0.15)^1} + \frac{\$2.88}{(1+0.15)^2} + \frac{\$49.68}{(1+0.15)^3} = \$36.930057$$

TRY IT! 8.2 NONCONSTANT GROWTH

Suppose that the current dividend is $5.00 and that dividends are expected to grow at a 10% rate for the first two years and then at a rate of 5% thereafter. If the required rate of return is 8%, what is the value of a share of stock?

Stock Valuation and Financial Management Decisions

We can relate the company's dividend policy to its stock value using the price-earnings ratio in conjunction with the dividend valuation model.

Let's start with the dividend valuation model with constant growth in dividends, using the price of the stock as the current value:

$$P_0 = \frac{D_1}{r_e - g}$$

If we divide both sides of this equation by earnings per share, we can represent the dividend valuation model in terms of the price-earnings (P/E) ratio:

$$\frac{P_0}{EPS_1} = \frac{D_1/EPS_1}{r_e - g}$$

Because the ratio D_1/EPS_1 is the dividend payout, this tells us the P/E ratio is influenced by the dividend payout ratio, the required rate of return on equity, and the expected growth rate of dividends. For example, an increase in the growth rate of dividends increases the price-earnings ratio. As another example, an increase in the required rate of return decreases the price-earnings ratio.

Another way of using this information is to estimate the required rate of return implied in a stock's current price. If we rearrange the last equation to solve for r_e,

$$r_e = \frac{D_1/EPS_1}{P_0/EPS_1} + g = \frac{D_1}{P_0} + g$$

we see that the required rate of return is the sum of the dividend yield and the expected growth rate. In other words, what investors expect for a return has two components: the dividend yield and the capital gain yield.

RETURN ON STOCKS

One way to look at the return on stocks is to consider it as composed of two parts:

$$r_e = \frac{D_1}{P_0} + g$$

$$\text{Dividend} \quad \text{Capital}$$
$$\text{yield} \quad \text{yield}$$

The return has the two components: (1) the return in the form of dividends—the *dividend yield* and (2) the appreciation (or depreciation) in the market price of the stock—the *capital yield*.

If the stock does not pay dividends, then the entire return is the capital yield. If, on the other hand, both the change in the value of the stock and the cash flows from dividends affect a stock's return.

Example 8.7

Suppose a company has a current dividend of $2 per share. If this dividend is expected to grow at a rate of 5% per year, forever, and if the current stock price per share is $20, what is the required rate of return on this stock? Answer: **12.5%**.

Calculation:

$$r_e = \frac{D_1}{P_0} + g = \frac{\$2(1+0.05)}{\$20} + g = 0.105 + 0.02 = 0.125 \text{ or } 12.5\%$$

Example 8.8

What do investors expect from Procter & Gamble (P&G)? Using information as of December 2008, P&G has a current dividend of $1.45, an anticipated growth rate of 10.5%, and a stock price of $59.11, and using the equation:[6]

$$r_e = \frac{D_1}{P_0} + g,$$

the estimated return is 13.21%:

$$r_e = \frac{D_1}{P_0} + g = \frac{\$1.45(1 + 0.105)}{\$59.11} + g = 0.0271 + 0.105$$

$$= 0.1321 \text{ or } 13.21\%$$

Return with No Dividends

Let's first ignore dividends. The return on common stock over a single period of time (e.g., one year) where there are no dividends is the change in the stock's price $(P_1 - P_0)$, divided by the beginning share price, P_0:

$$\text{One period return} = \frac{\text{End of period price}}{\text{Beginning of period price}} = \frac{P_1 - P_0}{P_0} = \frac{FV - PV}{PV}$$

If the period of time which this spans is more than one year, we can determine the annual return using time value of money math with the following data inputs:

FV = Ending price
PV = Beginning price
$\quad n$ = number of years in the period

We calculate the annual return as

$$\text{Annual return on a share of stock} = i = \sqrt[n]{\frac{FV}{PV}} - 1$$

---

[6]These values and estimates are from Reuters.com.

Solving for I, you get the average annual return, which is the geometric average return.

Let's see how this works. At the end of 1996, Multiclops stock was $20 per share, and at the end of 2010 Multiclops stock was $40 a share. The average annual return on Multiclops was:

$$\text{Return on Multiclops stock, 1990--2005} = \sqrt[10]{\frac{\$40}{\$20}} - 1 = \sqrt[10]{2} - 1$$

$$= 2^{1/10} - 1 = 7.177\%$$

Multiclops stock has an average annual return of 7.599% per year.

TI-83/84 Using TVM Solver	HP10B	Microsoft Excel
N = 15	20 +/− PV	=RATE(10,0,−20,40)
PV = −20	40 FV	
PMT = 0	15 N	
FV = 40	I/YR	
Solve for I		

Example 8.9

Suppose you bought a share of stock in 1990 for $40 per share. If the stock does not pay dividends, but is worth $120 at the end of 2010, what is your average annual return on this stock? Answer: **5.647%**.

Calculation:

$$i = \sqrt[n]{\frac{FV}{PV}} - 1 = \sqrt[20]{\frac{\$120}{\$40}} - 1 = 5.647\%$$

Return with Dividends at the End of the Period

If there are no dividends, we simply compare the change in the price of the shares with the original investment to arrive at the return. However, if there are dividends, we need to consider them as cash inflows, as well as the change in the share's price, in determining the return. The simplest way to calculate the return is to assume that we receive dividends at the end of the period.

Consider an example, but first, to simplify our analysis, let's ignore our stock broker's commission. Suppose you bought 100 shares of Purple Computer common stock at the end of 2009 at $35.25 per share. You have invested $100 \times \$35.25 = \$3,525$ in Purple stock. During 2009, Purple Computer paid $0.45 per share in dividends, so we earned $45.00 in dividends. If you sold the Purple shares at the end of 2009 for 43 ($43.00 per share, or $4,300.00 for all 100 shares), what was the return on our investment? It depends on when we receive the dividends. If we assume that we receive the dividends at the end of 2009, we calculate the return by comparing the stock's appreciation and dividends to the amount of the investment:

- Return on Purple Computer stock $= (\$4,300.00 - 3,525.00 + 43.00)$ $\div \$3,525.00$.
- Return on Purple Computer stock $= 0.2321$ or 23.21% in 2009

We can break this return into its capital yield (that is, appreciation in the value of the stock) and dividend yield components:

$$\text{Return on Purple Computer stock} = \frac{\$4,300 - 3,525}{\$3,525} + \frac{\$43}{\$3,525}$$
$$= 21.99\% + 1.22\% = 23.21\%$$

Most of the return on Purple stock was from the capital yield, 21.99%—the appreciation in the stock's price.

In the preceding example, we assumed that you sold the investment at a specific point in time, realizing the capital appreciation or depreciation in the investment—that is, actually getting cash. But we can also think about a return without actually selling the investment.

What if you didn't sell the Purple stock at the end of 2009? You would receive the dividends for 2009 whether or not you sold the stock at the end of the year, so you would have the dividend yield of 1.2%. Your investment would still have increased in value during the year, even if you didn't sell it. If you don't sell the Purple stock, you still have a capital yield for the year, it's just not *realized*. A capital gain on a stock you haven't sold is what many refer to as a *paper gain*.

You can see that we can compute returns on investments whether or not we have sold them. In the cases where we do not sell the asset represented in the investment, we compute the capital yield (gain or loss) based on the market value of the asset at the point of time we are evaluating the investment.

It becomes important to consider whether we actually realize the capital yield only when we are dealing with taxes. We must pay taxes on the capital gain only when we realize it. As long we you don't sell the asset, we are not taxed on its capital appreciation.

Like most dividend-paying companies, however, Purple does not pay dividends in a lump sum at the end of the year. It pays dividends at the end of each quarter. If we want to be painfully accurate, we could calculate the return on a quarterly basis and then annualize.

Let's look at an example of how we solve for the return on a stock. Consider an investment in stock of $100 today, in which you get a dividend of $10 one year from today, $10 two years from today, and then expect to sell the stock for $115 three years from today. The return on this stock is the return, r, that solves the following:

$$\$100 = \frac{\$10}{(1+r)^1} + \frac{\$10}{(1+r)^2} + \frac{\$115}{(1+r)^3}$$

We can either solve this using trial and error, which is rather tedious, or we can use the financial calculator or spreadsheet internal rate of return function. Using either produces the IRR of 19.5547%.

TI-83/84 Using IRR	HP10B	Microsoft Excel
{10,10,115} STO 2nd L1	100 +/− CFj	=IRR(−100,10,10,115)
APPS	10 CFj	
FINANCE	10 CFj	
IRR	115 CFj	
IRR(−100,L1)	■ IRR	

The IRR of 19.5547% is the average annual return on the investment. This is also referred to as the money-weighted return because it considers the cash flows—both in and out—during the investment.

Example 8.10

Consider the case of the Green Computer company stock. Suppose you buy Green Computer stock at the end of 2002 for $40 per share. And suppose that Green paid dividends of $2 at the end of 2003, $3 at the end of 2004, no dividend in 2005, and $2.5 at the end of 2006. And suppose you sell the stock at the end of 2006 for $50. What is your return on Green Computer stock? To determine this, we first translate this information into cash flows and then determine the return, the internal rate of return. Be sure to combine the two cash flows that occur at the end of 2006: $2.50 + $50 = $52.50.

End of Period	Cash Flow
2005	−$40.00
2006	$2.00
2007	$3.00
2008	$0.00
2009	$52.50

The return is the internal rate of return on this set of cash flows, which is 10.11433%.

TI-83/84	HP10B	Microsoft Excel
{2,3,0,52.50} STO L1 IRR(−40, *listname*)	40 +/− CF$_j$ 2 CF$_j$ 3 CF$_j$ 0 CF$_j$ 52.5 CF$_j$ ■ IRR	=IRR(−40,2,3,0,52.5)

 TRY IT! 8.3 CALCULATING A RETURN

Suppose a stock had a value of $28.23 per share at the end of 2007. And suppose the stock paid $2 in dividends at the end of 2008 and $2.25 at the end of 2009. If the stock's value is $30 at the end of 2009, what was its annual return from 2007 to 2009?

SUMMARY

The valuation of common stocks is difficult because you must value a future cash flow stream that is uncertain with respect to both the amount and the timing. However, understanding that stock's dividends exhibit patterns helps us manage the valuation of these securities.

Investors are constantly valuing and revaluing common stocks as expectations about future cash flows change, whether this is the timing and amount or the uncertainty associated with these expected future cash flows. Though they may not each have the dividend valuation model, or some variation, in their head, we assume that they are rational and will value a stock according to the best estimates regarding the risks and rewards from investing in the stock.

"TRY IT" SOLUTIONS

8.1. Value a Share of Common Stock

Given:

$D_0 = \$1$

$g = 6\%$

$r = 10\%$

Solve for today's price:

$$P_0 = \frac{\$1(1 + 0.06)}{(0.10 - 0.06)} = \frac{\$1.06}{0.04} = \$26.50$$

8.2. Nonconstant Growth

Given:

$D_0 = \$5$

$g_1 = 10\%$

$g_2 = 5\%$

$r_e = 8\%$

Therefore, dividends in the first growth stage:

$D_1 = \$5 \ (1 + 0.10) = \$5.50$

$D_2 = \$5 \ (1 + 0.10)^2 = \$5.50 \ (1 + 0.10) = \$6.05$

$D_3 = \$5 \ (1 + 0.10)^2(1 + 0.05) = \$6.05 \ (1 + 0.05) = \$6.3525$

The price at the end of the first growth stage is the present value of dividends beyond the first growth stage:

$$P_2 = D_3/(r_e - g_2) = \$6.3525/(0.08 - 0.05) = \$211.75$$

Assembling all the pieces:

$$P_0 = \frac{D_1}{(1 + 0.08)^1} + \frac{D_2}{(1 + 0.08)^2} + \frac{P_2}{(1 + 0.08)^2}$$

$$P_0 = \frac{D_1}{(1 + 0.08)^1} + \frac{D_2}{(1 + 0.08)^2} + \frac{D_3/(r_e - g_2)}{(1 + 0.08)^2}$$

$$P_0 = \frac{\$5.50}{(1 + 0.08)^1} + \frac{\$6.05}{(1 + 0.08)^2} + \frac{\$211.75}{(1 + 0.08)^2}$$

$$P_0 = \$5.0926 + \$5.1869 + \$181.5415$$

$$P_0 = \$191.82$$

8.3. Calculating a Return

End of Period	Cash Flow
2007	−$28.23
2008	$2.00
2009	$32.25

HP 10B		TI-83/84	Microsoft Excel
28.23 +/−	CFj	{2,32.25} STO	=IRR(−28.23,2,32.25)
2	CFj	L1	
32.25	CFj	IRR(−28.23,L1)	
∎	IRR	Solve	

Solution: 10.48421%

PROBLEMS

8.1. Suppose the ABC stock has a current dividend of $10.00 per share. If dividends grow at a rate of 3% per year, forever, and if the required rate of return on ABC stock is 12%, what is the value of a share of ABC stock?

8.2. The DEF Company stock pays a dividend of $1.50 per share. If the growth rate of future dividends is expected to be 5% per year, for the foreseeable future and if the required rate of return is 10%, what is the value of a share of DEF Company stock?

8.3. Investors expect the GHI Company to pay $2.50 in dividends next year and the growth rate of future dividends to be 1%. If the required rate of return is 12%, what is the current value of a share of GHI Company stock?

8.4. The XYZ Company currently pays a dividend of $2.00 per share. Dividends are expected to decline at a rate of 5% per year for the foreseeable future. If the required rate of return is 12%, what is the value of a share of XYZ stock?

8.5. A stock currently pays a dividend of $2 for the year. Expected dividend growth is 20% for the next three years and 7% thereafter for an indefinite amount of time. The appropriate required rate of return is 15%. What is the value today of a share of this stock?

8.6. Suppose you buy a stock for $20 per share at the end of 2009. If you receive $3 of dividends at the end of 2010 and sell the stock for $25 at the end of 2011, what is your return on this stock?

8.7. Intermark, Inc. paid dividends of $0.055 per share in 2007. In 2011, Intermark paid dividends of $0.09 per share. What was the average annual growth rate of Intermark's dividends from 2007 to 2011?

8.8. Suppose a stock has a current value of $50 per share and a dividend of $2 per share this year, and investors expect its dividends to grow at a rate of 3% per year. What is the return that investors require on this stock?

8.9. Consider two stocks: Company A stock and Company B stock. Investors require a return of 10% for each stock. Company A has a current dividend of $2.5 per share and investors expect its dividends to grow at a rate of 5% per year, forever. Company B has a current dividend of $4 per share and investors expect these dividends to grow at a rate of 2% per year, forever. According to the dividend valuation model, which stock has the higher value?

8.10. Consider the following path of the stock price and dividends per share for the Comet stock:

End of Year	Price per Share	Dividend per Share
2010	$50	$2
2011	$60	$3
2012	$55	$3

Complete the following table:

End of Year	Dividend Yield	Capital Yield	Total Return
2011			
2012			

For solutions to these problems, see Appendix E.

CHAPTER 9

A Capital Idea

Our favorite holding period is forever.
—Warren Buffett

One of the most important tools in business and investing is evaluating an investment that provides cash flows over a long time period. We refer to these types of decisions as *capital budgeting* because we use *capital*—that is, long-term sources of funds—and are evaluating what we can spend now to get these future benefits—hence, the budgeting part. Capital budgeting decisions lean quite heavily on the time value of money skills. Whether the decision maker is an individual making a personal-finance decision or is a manager of a large corporation, the techniques for evaluating capital budgeting decisions are the same—it's just the scale of the problem that differs.

Consider two investment opportunities, which we call Thing One and Thing Two. We've estimated the cash flows associated with each investment:

	End of Period Cash Flows	
Year	Thing One	Thing Two
Today	−$1,000	−$1,000
1	$0	$325
2	$200	$325
3	$300	$325
4	$900	$325

Can you tell by looking at the cash flows for Thing One whether or not it is a good investment? Or can you tell by just looking at Thing One and Thing Two which one is better? Perhaps, with some investments, you may think you can pick out which one is better simply by gut feeling or eyeballing the cash flows. But why take chances with eyeballing when we can use the time value of money skills to give us a better idea of which is better?

WHAT CASH FLOWS DO WE USE?

The cash flows that we evaluate should be incremental cash flows. What we mean by that is that when we evaluate a decision, we are looking at the situation as having choices: We can either stay with the status quo, or we can make an investment. Therefore, when we focus on the investment, we want to see how your cash flows change once you make this investment—hence, the incremental part.

In this chapter, we look at three techniques that are commonly used to evaluate long-term investments:

- Net present value
- Profitability index
- Internal rate of return

Once we explain each one with a simple example, we apply each to evaluating Thing One and Thing Two.

Earlier in this book, you've come across the net present value and the internal rate of return. The profitability index is simply a rearrangement of the net present value information, so it is not entirely new.

THE NET PRESENT VALUE

Suppose you have an investment opportunity that costs $5,000 today, and that promises to pay you $7,000 two years from today. If your opportunity cost for investments of similar risk is 10%, would you make this investment? To determine whether or not this is a good investment you need to compare your $5,000 investment with the $7,000 cash flow you expect in two years. Because you determine that a discount rate of 10% reflects the degree of uncertainty associated with the $7,000 expected in two years, today it is worth:

$$\text{Present value of \$7,000 to be received in 2 years} = \frac{\$7,000}{(1+0.10)^2} = \$5,785.12$$

By investing $5,000, you are getting in return, a promise of a cash flow in the future that is worth $5,785.12 today. In other words, it a good deal because you increase your wealth by $785.12 when you make this investment.

Another way of stating this is that the present value of the $7,000 cash inflow is $5,785.12, which is more than the $5,000, today's cash outflow to make the investment. When we subtract today's cash outflow to make an investment from the present value of the cash inflow from the investment, we refer to this difference as the net present value.

The *net present value* (NPV) is the present value of all expected cash flows, that is

Net present value = Present value of all expected cash flows

The word "net" in this term indicates that we consider all cash flows— both positive and negative.

We can represent the net present value using summation notation, where t indicates any particular period, CF_t represents the cash flow at the end of period t, i represents the cost of capital, and n the number of periods comprising the economic life of the investment:

$$\text{NPV} = \begin{matrix} \text{Present value} \\ \text{of cash inflows} \end{matrix} - \begin{matrix} \text{Present value} \\ \text{of cash outflows} \end{matrix} = \sum_{t=1}^{N} \frac{CF_t}{(1+i)^t}$$

Cash inflows are positive values of CF_t and cash outflows are negative values of CF_t. For any given period t, we collect all the cash flows (positive and negative) and net them together. For example, if you are investing in rental property, you would net: the rental payments you receive, the taxes you pay on this rental income, and maintenance expenses. To make things a bit easier to track, let's just refer to cash flows as inflows or outflows, and not specifically identify them as operating or investment cash flows.

Take another look at Thing One. Using a 10% cost of capital, the present values of inflows are:

	Thing One	
Year	Cash Flow	Discounted Cash Flow
Today	−$1,000	−$1,000.00
1	$0	$0.00
2	$200	165.29
3	$300	225.39
4	$900	614.71
		NPV = +$53.96

Using a financial calculator or a spreadsheet:

TI-83/84	HP10B	Microsoft Excel		
{0,200,300,900}	1000+/−			
STO *listname*	CF_j		A	B
NPV(10,-	0 CF_j	1	0	−$1,000
1000, *listname*)	200 CF_j	2	1	$0
	300 CF_j	3	2	$200
	900 CF_j	4	3	$300
	10 i/YR	5	4	$900
	NPV	6	NPV	$53.96 ← =NPV(.10,B2:B5)+B1

This NPV tell us that if we invest in Thing One, we expect to increase the value of the firm by $53.96. Calculated in a similar manner, the net present value of Thing Two is $30.21.

Net Present Value Decision Rule

A positive net present value means that the investment provides a return better than the cost of the capital we invest. In other words, the return is more that sufficient to compensate for the required return of the investment. We say that investments with a return better than the cost of capital is profitable—in an economic sense.[1] A negative net present value means that the investment return is less than the cost of capital. A zero net present value means that the return just equals the required return. Therefore,

If . . .	this means that . . .	and you . . .
NPV > $0	The investment is expected to increase wealth.	Should invest.
NPV < $0	The investment is expected to decrease wealth.	Should not invest.
NPV = $0	The investment is expected not to change wealth.	Should be indifferent between investing and not investing.

---

[1]We are not saying that there is any relation between what is profitable in an economic sense and what is profitable in accounting terms. We don't care whether the investment results in our income statement looking better—rather, we care whether it enhances our wealth. An investment that enhances wealth is profitable for our purposes.

Based on this, we can conclude that both Thing One and Thing Two are profitable investments.

If these are independent investments—that is, you can invest in one, both, or none—then you should invest in both. If you can only invest in one investment, then the better investment is Thing Two because it is more profitable. Why might you only be able to invest in one investment?

Perhaps you have limited funds to invest today, so your choice is one investment or none. We refer to this situation as *capital rationing*: You have a limit on your investment budget. Or perhaps you have some other limitation—such as you can only keep track of one rental property at a time and both investments are rental properties. This is a situation in which the investments are *mutually exclusive*: that is, the investment in one precludes the investment in the other.

Consider an example on a larger scale. Suppose an airline needs one additional jet. It can choose between a jet manufactured by Airbus or Boeing. But since it needs only one jet, it must choose between the two jets—or simply not invest in either if both are not profitable.

THE PROFITABILITY INDEX

We use some of the same information from the net present value to create the profitability index. The *profitability index* (PI) is the ratio of the present value of the inflows to the outflows, and hence conveys the same information as the net present value, but in terms of an index.

Whereas the net present value is

$$\text{NPV} = \frac{\text{Present value}}{\text{of cash inflows}} - \frac{\text{Present value}}{\text{of cash outflows}} = \sum_{t=1}^{N} \frac{\text{CF}_t}{(1+i)^t}$$

The profitability index, PI is

$$\text{PI} = \frac{\dfrac{\text{Present value}}{\text{of cash inflows}}}{\dfrac{\text{Present value}}{\text{of cash outflows}}} = \frac{\sum_{t=1}^{N} \dfrac{\text{CIF}_t}{(1+i)^t}}{\sum_{t=1}^{N} \dfrac{\text{COF}_t}{(1+i)^t}}$$

where CIF and COF are cash inflows and cash outflows, respectively. We can calculate the PI of Thing One as:

	Thing One	
Year	Cash Flow	Discounted Cash Flow
1	$0	$0.00
2	$200	165.29
3	$300	225.39
4	$900	614.71
	$\sum_{t=1}^{N} \dfrac{CIF_t}{(1+r)^t} = +\$1,005.40$	

Therefore, the profitability index is

$$PI_{\text{Thing One}} = \frac{\$1,005.40}{\$1,000.00} = 1.0054$$

The index value is greater than one, which means that the investment produces more in terms of benefits than costs.

The decision rule for the profitability index therefore depends on the PI relative to 1.0:

If ...	this means that ...	and you ...
PI > 1.0	The investment is expected to increase wealth.	Should invest.
PI < 1.0	The investment is expected to decrease wealth.	Should not invest.
PI = 1.0	The investment is expected not to change wealth.	Should be indifferent to investing.

There is no direct solution for PI on your calculator; what you need to do is calculate the present value of all the cash inflows and then divide this value by the present value of the cash outflows. In the case of Thing One, there is only one cash outflow and it is already in present value terms (i.e., it occurs today). You'll notice that we use the present value of the outflows as a positive number in the PI.

FINANCIAL MATH IN ACTION

Some folks like to supplement their income by buying rental property and becoming landlords. This type of investment is often viewed as a long-term investment because the transaction costs of buying and selling real estate can be pretty steep. Many investors consider real estate as a long-term investment, but with some end in sight. For example, suppose you are considering buying rental property, and that you intend to sell the property when you retire to Florida. You'll sell it when you retire so that you don't have to worry about dealing with tenants, maintaining the property, and the like while playing golf.

Suppose this rental property would cost you $200,000 today, and you intend to retire in 20 years, expecting to sell the property for about what you paid for it. And suppose you can earn 8% per year on similar risk investments, on an after-tax basis. If you rent the property at $15,000 per year, after taxes and costs of maintaining the property, with the payment up front for the year, is this a profitable investment?

Why after tax? Because taxes are an important cash outflow (because the consequences are nasty if we don't pay taxes), so we put everything—rental income, expenses, and so on, on an after-tax basis. If we invest in the property, we also get to take depreciation on the property, reducing our tax bill. Therefore, when we consider the income from any investment that we want to analyze, we put it on an after-tax basis to better represent the cash flows of the investment. We also put the cost of capital on an after-tax basis, because some costs (such as borrowing to finance the investment) may be tax-deductible.

The cash flows would be a net cash outlay of $185,000 initially (that is, the $200,000 outlay, adjusted for the first rent), followed by nineteen cash flows of $15,000 each. Twenty years from now, you expect cash flows of $200,000.

The net present value of this investment is $1,963.63, or a return of 8.108%.

Using a financial calculator or a spreadsheet:

TI-83/84	HP10B	Microsoft Excel

TI-83/84	HP10B			
{0,200,300,900}	0 +/– CF$_j$		A	B
STO *listname*	0 CF$_j$	1	0	–$1,000
NPV(10,0,*listname*)	200 CF$_j$	2	1	$0
ENTER	300 CF$_j$	3	2	$200
÷ 1000 ENTER	900 CF$_j$	4	3	$300
	10 i/YR	5	4	$900
	NPV	6	PI	1.0054 ←=NPV(.10,B2:B5)/B1*–1)
	÷ 1000			

Using the same approach with Thing Two's cash flows, the profitability index for Thing Two is 1.0302.

 TRY IT! 9.1 NPV AND PI

Consider an investment that has the following expected cash flows:

Year	Cash Flows
Today	–€10,000
1	€1,000
2	€1,000
3	€9,000

What is the net present value and profitability index of this investment?

THE INTERNAL RATE OF RETURN

Suppose you have an investment opportunity that requires you to put up $50,000 and has expected cash inflows of $28,809.52 after one year and $28,809.52 after two years. We can evaluate this opportunity using a time line:

```
         0                1                  2
      ---|----------------|------------------|----------
      -$50,000    $28,809.52      $28,909.52
```

The return on this investment is the discount rate that causes the present values of the $28,809.52 cash inflows to equal the present value of the $50,000 cash outflow, calculated as

$$\$50,000 = \frac{\$28,809.52}{(1+\text{IRR})^1} + \frac{\$28,809.52}{(1+\text{IRR})^2}$$

We calculate this return by either tedious trial and error to solve for IRR, or we use financial calculators or spreadsheets to solve for IRR:

TI-83/84	HP10B	Microsoft Excel		
{28809.52,28809.52} STO	50,000 +/−			
listname	CF_j		A	B
IRR(−50000,*listname*)	0 CF_j	1	0	−50,000
	28,809.52 +/−	2	1	28,809.52
	CF_j	3	2	28,809.52
	28,809.52 +/−	4	IRR	$10.00% ← =IRR(B1:B5)
	CF_j			
	IRR			

The IRR is 10%.

Another way to look at this is to consider the investment's cash flows discounted at the IRR of 10%. The NPV of this investment if the discount rate is 10% (the IRR in this example), is zero:

$$\$50,000 = \frac{\$28,809.52}{(1+0.10)^1} + \frac{\$28,809.52}{(1+0.10)^2}$$

An investment's internal rate of return is the discount rate that makes the present value of all expected future cash flows equal to zero. We can represent the IRR as the rate that solves:

$$\$0 = \sum_{t=1}^{N} \frac{CF_t}{(1+\text{IRR})^t}$$

Now let's return to the investments in Thing One and Thing Two. The IRR for Thing One is the discount rate that solves the following:

$$-\$1,000 = \frac{\$0}{(1+\text{IRR})^1} + \frac{\$200}{(1+\text{IRR})^2} + \frac{\$300}{(1+\text{IRR})^3} + \frac{\$900}{(1+\text{IRR})^4}$$

Using a calculator or a computer, we get the more precise answer of 10.172% per year:

TI-83/84	HP10B	Microsoft Excel		
{0,200,300,900} STO	1000 +/–			
listname	CF$_j$		A	B
IRR(–1000,*listname*)	0 CF$_j$	1	0	–$1,000
	200 +/–	2	1	$0
	CF$_j$	3	2	$200
	300 +/–	4	3	$300
	CF$_j$	5	4	$900
	900 +/–	6		10.172% ← =IRR(B1:B5)
	CF$_j$			
	IRR			

Repeating this process for Thing Two's cash flows, you will see that the internal rate of return for Thing Two is 11.388%.

 TRY IT! 9.2 IRR

Consider an investment that has the following expected cash flows:

Year	Cash Flows
Today	–€10,000
1	€1,000
2	€1,000
3	€9,000

What is the internal rate of return on this investment?

Internal Rate of Return Decision Rule

The internal rate of return is a yield—what we earn, on average, per year.[2] How do we use it to decide which investment, if any, to choose? Let's

---

[2]In earlier chapters in this book, we referred to the internal rate of return as the *money-weighted return*.

revisit investments Thing One and Thing Two and the IRRs that we just calculated for each. If, for similar risk investments, owners earn 10% per year, then both Thing One and Thing Two are attractive investments. They both yield more than the rate owners require for the level of risk of these two investments:

Investment	IRR	Cost of Capital
Thing One	10.172%	10%
Thing Two	11.388%	10%

The decision rule for the internal rate of return is to invest in an investment if it provides a return greater than the cost of capital. The cost of capital, in the context of the IRR, is a hurdle rate—the minimum acceptable rate of return. For independent investments and situations in which there is no capital rationing, then:

If ...	this means that ...	and you ...
IRR > cost of capital	The investment is expected to increase wealth.	Should invest.
IRR < cost of capital	The investment is expected to decrease wealth.	Should not invest.
IRR = cost of capital	The investment is expected not to change wealth.	Should be indifferent to investing.

The IRR and Mutually Exclusive Investments

What if we were forced to choose between Thing One and Thing Two because they are mutually exclusive or there is a limit on how much we can invest? Thing Two has a higher IRR than Thing One—so at first glance we might want to accept Thing Two.

What about the NPV of these investments? What does the NPV tell us to do? If we use the higher IRR, it tells us to go with Thing Two. Choosing the investment with the higher net present value is consistent with maximizing wealth. Why? Because if the cost of capital is 10%, we would calculate different NPVs and come to a different conclusion.

When evaluating mutually exclusive investments, the one with the highest IRR may not be the one with the best NPV. The IRR may give a different decision than NPV when evaluating mutually exclusive investments because of the reinvestment assumption:

- NPV assumes cash flows reinvested at the cost of capital.
- IRR assumes cash flows reinvested at the internal rate of return.

This reinvestment assumption may cause different decisions in choosing among mutually exclusive investments when one or more of the following apply:

- The timing of the cash flows is different among the investments.
- There are scale differences (that is, very different cash flow amounts).
- The investments have different useful lives.

With respect to the role of the timing of cash flows in choosing between two investments: Thing Two's cash flows are received sooner than Thing One's. Part of the return on either is from the reinvestment of its cash inflows. And in the case of Thing Two, there is more return from the reinvestment of cash inflows. The question is "What do you do with the cash inflows when you get them?" We generally assume that if you receive cash inflows, you'll reinvest those cash flows in other assets.

With respect to the reinvestment rate assumption in choosing between these investments: Suppose we can reasonably expect to earn only the cost of capital on our investments. Then for investments with an IRR above the cost of capital we would be overstating the return on the investment using the IRR.

With respect to the NPV method: If the best we can do is reinvest cash flows at the cost of capital, the NPV assumes reinvestment at the more reasonable rate (the cost of capital). If the reinvestment rate is assumed to be the investment's cost of capital, we would evaluate investments on the basis of the NPV and select the one that is the most profitable.

Bottom line? If we evaluate investments on the basis of their IRR, it is possible that we may select one that does not maximize value.

Multiple Internal Rates of Return

The typical investment usually involves only one large negative cash flow initially, followed by a series of future positive flows. But that's not always the case. Suppose you invest in a business that uses environmentally sensitive chemicals, such as a dry cleaner. It may cost you a great deal to clean up the chemicals when you close the business. That will mean a negative cash flow at the end of the investment.

Suppose we are considering an investment that has cash flows as follows:

Period	End of Period Cash Flow
0	−$100
1	+260
2	+260
3	−490

What is this investment's IRR? One possible solution is IRR = 14.835%, yet another possible solution is IRR = 191.5%. We can see this graphically in Exhibit 9.1, where we show the NPV of these cash flows for discount rates from 0% to 250%.

Remember that the IRR is the discount rate that causes the NPV to be zero. In terms of this graph, this means that the IRR is the discount rate where the NPV is $0, the point at which the present value changes sign— from positive to negative or from negative to positive. In the case of this investment, the present value changes from negative to positive at 14.835% and from positive to negative at 250%.

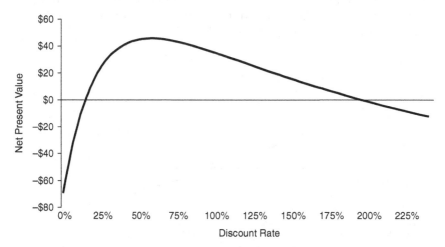

EXHIBIT 9.1   The IRR is not unique when you have an investment with more than one sign change in the cash flows.

TRY IT! 9.3 MULTIPLE IRRs

Consider an investment that requires an initial cash investment of $1,000, but promises a cash flow of $2,500 at the end of two years, and requires you to pay $1,500 at the end of three years. What is the internal rate of return for this investment?

Bottom line? We can't use the internal rate of return method if the sign of the cash flows changes more than once during the investment's life.

The Investment Profile

The cost of capital that we use in the analysis of an investment—whether as a discount rate in the NPV and PI or as a hurdle rate in the IRR—is an estimate of the return required for the investment's risk. As such, it is an estimate, a guess. We may want to see how sensitive our decision is to invest to changes in our cost of capital. We can see this sensitivity in how an investment's net present value changes as the discount rate changes by looking at an investment's *investment profile*, also referred to as the *net present value profile*.

The investment profile is a graphical depiction of the relation between the net present value of an investment and the discount rate: The profile shows the net present value of an investment for each discount rate, within some range. We illustrate this profile in Exhibit 9.2 for Thing One.

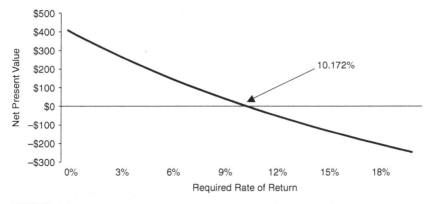

EXHIBIT 9.2   The Investment Profile of Thing One for Costs of Capital from 0% to 20%

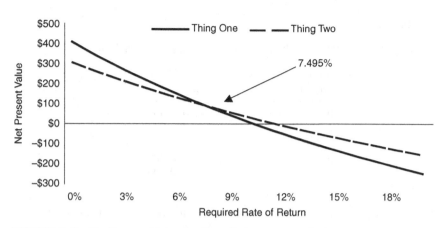

EXHIBIT 9.3 Net Present Value Profiles of Thing One and Thing Two

You should be able to see in Exhibit 9.2 that the NPV is positive for discount rates from 0% to 10.172%, and negative for discount rates higher than 10.172%. The 10.172% is the internal rate of return; that is, the discount rate at which the NPV is equal to $0. Therefore, Thing One is profitable if the cost of capital on this investment is less than 10.172%, and is not profitable if the cost of capital on this investment is greater than 10.172%.

Let's impose Thing One's NPV profile on the NPV profile of Thing Two, as we show in Exhibit 9.3. If Thing One and Thing Two are mutually exclusive investments—we invest in only one or neither investment—this graph clearly shows that the investment we invest in depends on the discount rate. For higher discount rates, Thing One's NPV falls faster than Thing Two's because the Thing One's larger cash flows are farther in time—so the discounting with higher rates will cause the NPV to fall faster.

If the discount rate is less than 7.495%, Thing One adds more values than Thing Two. If the discount rate is more than 7.495% but less than 11.338%, Thing Two is more profitable than Thing One. If the discount rate is greater than 11.338%, we should invest in neither investment because both would be unprofitable.

The 7.495% is the *crossover rate, or crossover discount rate,* which produces identical NPV's for the two investments. If the discount rate is 7.495%, the net present value of both investments is $88,660.[3]

---

[3]The precise crossover rate is 7.49475%, at which the NPV for both investments is $88,659.

Example 9.1

Consider an investment that has the following expected cash flows:

End of Year	Cash Flow
0	−$1,000,000
1	800,000
2	400,000
3	70,000
4	30,000

Draw this investment's investment profile for discount rates from 0% to 20%.

Step 1. Calculate the NPV if the discount rate = 0%. You calculate this by simply adding up all cash flows (both positive and negative). In this example, this is $300,000.

Step 2. Calculate the IRR. In this case, this is 19.95%.

Step 3. Calculate the NPV for some discount rate between 0% and the IRR.

Step 4. Mark the result from Steps 1, 2, and 3 on the graph and connect the points.

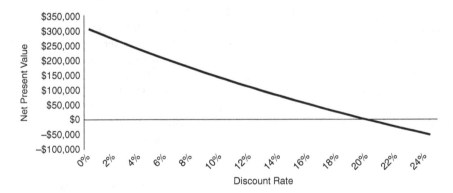

Solving for the Crossover Rate

For Thing One and Thing Two, the crossover rate is the rate that causes the net present value of the two investments to be equal. While that may sound daunting, there is a very simple approach to solving for this rate: Calculate the differences in the cash flows and then solve for the internal rate of return of these differences.

Year	Thing One	Thing Two	Difference
0	−$1,000	−$1,000	$0
1	$0	$325	−$325
2	$200	$325	−$125
3	$300	$325	−$25
4	$900	$325	$575

The internal rate of return of these differences is the crossover rate. Does it matter which investment's cash flows you deduct from the other? Not at all—just be consistent each period.

TI-83/84	HP10B	Microsoft Excel

TI-83/84	HP10B
{−325,−125,−25,575} STO	0 +/− CF$_j$
listname	325 +/− CF$_j$
IRR(0,listname)	125 +/− CF$_j$
	25 +/− CF$_j$
	575 CF$_j$
	IRR

	A	B	
1	0	0	
2	1	−325	
3	2	−125	
4	3	−25	
5	4	575	
6	IRR		← =IRR(B1:B5)

Bottom line? The crossover rate is the decision point between two mutually exclusive investments.

Example 9.2

Consider two investments with the following sets of cash flows:

End of Period	P	Q
0	−$10	−$20
1	4.2	0
2	4.2	0
3	4.2	26

What is the crossover rate for these two investments' investment profiles?

Calculation:

End of Period	P	Q	Difference
0	−$10	−$20	+$10
1	4.2	0	+4.2
2	4.2	0	+4.2
3	4.2	26	−21.8

The crossover rate is the IRR of the differences, or **7.52%**.

 TRY IT! 9.4 CAPITAL BUDGETING TECHNIQUES

Suppose an investment requires an initial outlay of $500,000 and has expected cash flows of $100,000, $350,000 and $200,000 for the first three years, respectively. What is this investment's:

- Net present value using a 10% required rate of return?
- Internal rate of return?

SUMMARY

The net present value method and the profitability index consider all of the cash flows from an investment and involve discounting, which incorporates the time value of money and risk. The net present value method produces an amount that is the expected added value from investing in an investment. The profitability index, on the other hand, produces an indexed value that is useful in ranking investments.

The internal rate of return is the yield on the investment. It is the discount rate that causes the net present value to be equal to zero. IRR is hazardous to use when selecting among mutually exclusive investments or when there is a limit on investment spending.

"TRY IT" SOLUTIONS

9.1. NPV and PI
The net present value is –€366.051. You would lose $366.051 if you invest in this investment.
The profitability index is €8,497.37 ÷ €10,000 = 0.8497. This PI is less than 1.0, so this is not a profitable investment.

9.2. IRR
The internal rate of return is 3.565%.
Note: We knew that this IRR was less than 5% from Try it! 9.1: The net present value at a cost of capital of 5% is negative. Hence, the investment's IRR must be less than 5%.

9.3. Multiple IRRs
We know that there are multiple internal rates of return for this set of cash flows because there is more than one sign change. In fact, there are two sign changes, which means that there will be two possible solutions to the equation involving the cash flows:

Period	Cash Flow	
0	−$1,000	
1	0	
2	$2,500	← Sign change negative to positive
3	0	
4	−$1,500	← Sign change positive to negative

The two possible IRRs are: **0%** and **22.47%**. Unfortunately, because the IRR are not unique, they are useless as far as decision making goes.
Note that when we use a spreadsheet, the spreadsheet will respond to the =IRR function with one of the possible IRRs. In most calculators, you will receive a message of either no solution or an error.

9.4. Capital Budgeting Techniques

$$\text{Present value of inflows} = \$530,430$$
$$\text{Present value of outflows} = \$500,000$$
$$\text{NPV} = \$5.3043 - 5 = \$30,430$$

We know that the IRR must be greater than 10% because the NPV is positive when the discount rate is 10%.

$$\text{IRR} = 13.13\%$$

PROBLEMS

9.1. Suppose you are evaluating an investment opportunity that requires a $1,000 investment today. Your return from this investment is $1,100 two years from today. What is the value of this investment today if your opportunity cost of capital for this type of investment is 10%?

9.2. Suppose you are evaluating an investment opportunity that requires a $1,000 investment today. Your return from this investment is $1,100 two years from today. What is the return on this investment?

9.3. Consider an investment CCC, which has the following expected cash flows:

Period	End of Period Cash Flow
0	−$100,000
1	35,027
2	35,027
3	35,027
4	35,027

What is CCC's net present value and profitability index if the cost of capital is 6%?

What is CCC's internal rate of return?

9.4. Suppose you are evaluating investment DDD that has the following expected cash flows:

Period	End of Period Cash Flow
0	−$100,000
1	43,798
2	43,798
3	43,798

What is DDD's net present value and profitability index if the cost of capital is 5%?

What is DDD's internal rate of return?

9.5. Suppose you are evaluating investment EEE, which has the following estimated cash flows:

Period	End of Period Cash Flow
0	−$200,000
1	65,000
2	65,000
3	65,000
4	65,000
5	65,000

What is EEE's net present value and profitability index if the cost of capital is 8%?

What is EEE's internal rate of return?

9.6. Suppose you are evaluating investment FFF, which has the following anticipated cash flows:

Period	End of Period Cash Flow
0	−$100,000
1	0
2	0
3	0
4	174,901

What is FFF's net present value and profitability index if the cost of capital is 10%?

What is FFF's internal rate of return?

9.7. Which investment, if any, would you choose if you are offered the following two investments?

Year	Cash Flows A	B
Today	−£100	−£100
1	£80	£0
2	£120	£210

The cost of capital for both investments is 10%.

9.8. Consider two investments, A and B:

	Cash Flows	
Year	A	B
Today	−£100	−£100
1	£80	£0
2	£120	£210

At what cost of capital does your preference for one investment change to prefer the other investment?

9.9. If the profitability index of an investment is equal to 1.25 and the initial cash flow is $1,000 what is the investment's net present value?

9.10. Consider two investments, C and D:

	Cash Flows	
Year	A	B
Today	−€100	−€100
1	€40	€0
2	€40	€0
3	€40	€130

Which investment is more profitable if the cost of capital of both investments is 8%?

For solutions to these problems, see Appendix E.

CHAPTER 10

Finance Fact or Fiction?

In mathematics you don't understand things. You just get used to them.

—Johann von Neumann

We encounter finance decisions in our daily lives, and we often rely on rules-of-thumb or financial lore to make decisions. The purpose of this chapter is to show that you can use the financial mathematics tools in this book to address such wisdom to determine whether it is fact or fiction. We've chosen a few "rules" to explore, but hopefully you will get the hang of this and be able to apply financial mathematics to any of the financial lore that you encounter.

FACT OR FICTION: IT PAYS TO GET AN MBA

The decision to get an advanced degree involves many cash flows that we need to sort out. Consider the simple problem:

- You are 30 years old and plan to work until you are 65.
- You currently make $60,000 per year.
- If you go for your MBA, you would leave your current employment, attending school full time for two years to earn your MBA.
- The cost of tuition, books, and fees is $20,000 per year. These expenses are paid at the beginning of the academic semester, with one half due immediately and the other half of the year's tuition due in six months.
- Once you complete your MBA, you believe that you can earn $24,000 more per year than if you did not have the advanced degree.
- You can earn 6% APR on your savings, compounded monthly.
- Your tax rate on income is 28%.

Is it worth it? Let's check out the math. To keep things simple, let's assume that you enter the MBA program on your 30th birthday and complete your degree on your 32nd.

We can classify the cash flows into two groups:

- Investment cash flows
- MBA-incremental cash flows

The investment cash flows consist of:

- Tuition, books, and fees for the two years.
- Foregone earnings. That is, what you could have earned instead of going to school.

The MBA-incremental cash flows consist of:i incremental earnings, after taxes, for each year until retirement. So, does it pay?

Investment Cash Flows

The present value of the investment cash flows required discounting two streams:

Tuition, Books, and Fees   We've assumed that the tuition, books, and fees are not tax deductible. If any of these are deductible, or are associated with a tax credit, as has been the case in some years in our tax history, we would reduce the present value appropriately.

Point in Time	Cash Flow	Calculation	Present Value
30th birthday	$10,000		$10,000.00
Six months later	$10,000	$10,000 \div (1 + 0.005)^6$	9705.28
31st birthday	$10,000	$10,000 \div (1 + 0.005)^{12}$	9419.05
Six months later	$10,000	$10,000 \div (1 + 0.005)^{18}$	9141.36
		Total present value	$38,265.69

Forgone Income   This is an ordinary annuity if we assume that you are paid at the end of each month. The annuity consists of the following:

$$PMT = \$60,000 \div 12 = \$5,000$$
$$n = 24$$
$$i = 6\% \div 12 = 0.5\%$$

Solving for the present value, the present value of the foregone income is \$112,814.33. After tax, this is \$112,814.33 × (1 − 0.28) = \$81,226.32.

Incremental Earnings

We need to view the incremental earnings as a deferred annuity because the additional earnings do not begin until after the completion of the degree. Therefore, we first calculate the present value of the incremental earnings, after tax, and then discount this value to the present.

We calculate the present value of the incremental earnings, as of the beginning of the month of graduation. We need to make two adjustments to the cash flows that we will be working with. First, we put the income on a monthly basis by dividing by 12. Second, we put the cash flows on an after-tax basis because we only get to use what is left over after paying taxes. The inputs are the following:

$$\text{PMT} = (\$24,000 / 12) \times (1 - 0.28) = \$2,000 \ (1 \times 0.28) = \$1,440$$
$$i = 6\% \div 12 = 0.5\%$$
$$n = 33 \text{ years} \times 12 = 396$$

The present value of the incremental earnings is \$248,039.40.

Assembling the Pieces   We need to assemble the pieces so that we can make a decision that considers both the benefits and the costs:

	Benefits	Costs
Present value of tuition, books, and fees		\$38,265.69
Present value of foregone income		81,226.32
Present value of incremental earnings	\$248,039.40	
Total	\$248,039.40	\$119,492.01

Therefore, there is a net benefit of \$248,039.40 − 119,492.01 = \$128,547.39 from getting the MBA degree, based on our assumptions.

Does this mean that it always pays to get your MBA? No. Much of this analysis depends on the assumptions regarding what you currently earn, what you potentially can earn with an MBA, the cost of the tuition, your tax situation, and your opportunity cost of funds.

Of course, we haven't included a lot of reality here. First, giving up a job to go back to school has risks because you have to go back into the job market once you complete your MBA. Second, there is uncertainty about the costs of tuition, books, and fees, which could increase once you enter the program. Third, there is no guarantee that you will earn more once you have the degree. The earnings available to graduates will depend on the work experience of the graduate, the quality of the MBA program, and your grades while in the MBA program, among many other things. We've applied the same discount rate to the expenses, the foregone income, and the incremental earnings. Because the risks are significantly higher for the anticipated incremental earnings, we may want to use a higher discount rate for these expected additional earnings than we do for the foregone earnings.

Consider what happens when we vary the assumptions.

- What if you were 40 years old instead of 30 when you begin your MBA program? This would mean that the estimated benefits are $215,295.81 instead of $248,039.40.
- What if the cost of tuition, books, and fees is $40,000 per year? The present value of the tuition, books, and fees would be $67,086.58, and the estimated costs would therefore be $148,312.90 and the net benefit from the MBA would shrink from $128,547.39 to $119,492.01.
- What if the incremental earnings are $12,000 per year instead of $24,000? The present value of the incremental earnings shrinks from $248,039.40 to $124,019.70, and the net benefit from the MBA is $4,527.69.

NPV OF THE MBA: WHAT'S THE EVIDENCE?

There are a few analyses out there that rely on typical earnings and costs of an MBA. For example, in a *BizEd* article, on average, an MBA degree is a positive net present value investment. However, not all MBAs are better off in terms of compensation, and there are a lot of factors to consider. (See Antony Davies and Thomas W. Cline, "The ROI on the MBA," *BizEd,* January–February 2005.)

FACT OR FICTION: LEASING A CAR COSTS LESS THAN BUYING A CAR

We can address the decision to lease versus buy a new car using financial mathematics. The lease versus buy decision may be complicated by a number of factors, such as differences in insurance and security deposits. Let's sweep these aside for now so that we can get a grip on the problem. Suppose you want a new car that costs $25,000, and face three choices:

Deal 1. Buy outright, in an all-cash deal.

Deal 2. Finance at 8% APR over 36 months, with a down payment of $2,500.

Deal 3. Lease over 36 months, with financing costs of 8% APR and a depreciation cost of 2% per month, with a down payment of $2,500.

Cars depreciate in value, so in this analysis we have to estimate what the value of the car will be at some point in time. If we estimate that the car depreciates in value such that it is worth only $7,000 at the end of 36 months, this means that the rate of depreciation is 3.6% per month (PV = $7,000; FV = $25,000; $n = 36$; Solve for i).

Let's assume that you can earn 3% on your money, so this will become the discount rate that we use to evaluate the cash flows of each deal.

The Cost of Deal 1

The cost of Deal 1 is easy: $25,000 right now, and then sell the car at the end of three years for its depreciated value of $7,000. The present value of this deal is:

$$\text{Present value} = -\$25,000 + \left[\$7,000 \div (1 + (0.03/12))^{36} \right] = -\$18,017.46$$

The Cost of Deal 2

The cost of Deal 2 is similar to what we did earlier in the book regarding mortgages. We calculate the monthly payment for this loan using the following:

$$PV = \$25,000 - 2,500 = \$22,500$$
$$i = 8\% \div 12 = 0.667\%$$
$$n = 36$$

The payment is $705.77 per month for 36 months. The cost of the car in this deal is:

Down payment	−$2,500
Present value of 36 payments of $705.77 each, discounted at 3% APR	−24,244.86
Present value of resale value of the car at the end of 36 months, discounted at 3% APR for 36 months	6,398.24
Total cost	−$20,346.62

The Cost of Deal 3

The leasing deal involves two parties, the *lessor*—who owns the car and accepts payments for its use—and the *lessee*—the party who makes the payments in exchange for using the car. The leasing deal requires payments that have both the financing cost (that is, the 8% APR), but also the depreciation charge, which is 3.6% per month. Therefore, the discount rate we use in determining the payments is $8 + 3.6 = 11.6\%$. The inputs we need to calculate the monthly lease payment are the following:

$$PV = \$25,000 - 2,500 = \$22,500$$
$$i = 11.6\% \div 12 = 0.967\%$$
$$n = 36$$

The monthly lease payment is $743.03. The total cost of the leasing deal, from the perspective of the *lessee*—the owner making payments for the car's use—is, therefore:

Down payment	−$2,500
Present value of 36 payments of $743.03 each, discounted at 3% APR	−25,550.18
Total cost	−$28,050.20

Summary

The costs of the three financing arrangements over the three-year period—all translated into values today—differ by quite a bit in our example:

Deal 1. Buy with cash	−$18,017.46
Deal 2. Finance	−$20,346.57
Deal 3. Lease	−$28,050.20

The attractiveness of these deals depends on a number of factors, including:

- *The discount rate that reflect your opportunity cost of funds* (that is, what you could earn with your funds). If this rate were different, the costs would still follow this same rank-order (that is, cash is the lowest cost), but would be different.
- *The amount of depreciation included in the lease payment.* We included the compound rate of 3.6% per month. If we had included say, 2%, the lease deal looks slightly better than the financing deal (but not as good as the cash deal).

■ *The holding period for the car.* How long you plan to own the vehicle makes a difference. Lease deals are for a period less than the car's life, but some car owners want to hold onto cars beyond a typical lease period. If you compare the deals with a six-year holding period for the car, you would have to factor in a second lease deal to follow the first in order to make the deals comparable.

■ *Differences in other costs.* In addition to the financing and depreciation that we considered, there may be some differences in other costs, such as maintenance and insurance. You would need to factor these into the analysis. Additionally, some leases charge additional fees for exceeding a specified mileage, and you would need to consider these fees in the costs of Deal 3. Still another consideration is that some lessors—the leasing companies—require compensation for any damages, even minor dings and dents, at a prescribed rate, or to be repaired at your expense at the body shop of their choice.

FACT OR FICTION: GOLD HAS ALWAYS BEEN A GOOD INVESTMENT

Gold has been a refuge for many investors when securities markets or world political affairs have been quite turbulent. But is it a good investment? You will hear hype about the price of gold increasing by 200%, or some other figure, and that it is a safe place to invest. But is it the treasure trove that the advertisements make it out to be? Maybe. Maybe not. The way to tackle this problem is to evaluate the return that you would get on this investment and compare it to other investments after adjusting for risk. Let's just work on the first part: What have been the returns on gold investments?

We could look at gold from as far back as the seventeenth century, but this is not really what we need because the price of gold had been fixed by law in many countries for many years. Instead, let's look at the price of gold since the United States let the market determine the price—that is, since July of 1968.

Consider the price of gold, as we show it in Exhibit 10.1. The price has risen over time, from a $43.5 per ounce at the end of 1968 to $833.2 at the end of 2007. Its price has increased over time, so it's a good deal. Right? We need to put things in perspective in order to draw any conclusions.

Using the time value of money principles related to the return, given a present value and a future value, we can calculate the annual return on gold for different intervals of time.

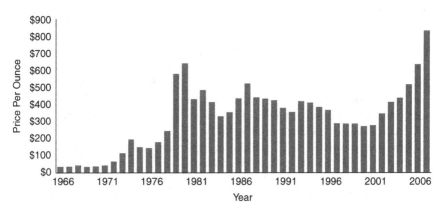

EXHIBIT 10.1 Closing Price Per Ounce of Gold, 1968–2007
Data on gold prices obtained from, "Modern and Ancient Spot Gold Prices,"
www.onlygold.com/TutorialPages/Prices200YrsFS.htm (accessed 19 March 2009).

EXHIBIT 10.2 The Price of an Ounce of Gold at the End of Each Year, 1967–2007

End of Year	Price of Gold per Ounce	End of Year	Price of Gold per Ounce
1967	$35.50	1988	$441.00
1968	$43.50	1989	$433.40
1969	$35.40	1990	$423.80
1970	$37.60	1991	$379.90
1971	$43.80	1992	$356.30
1972	$65.20	1993	$419.20
1973	$114.50	1994	$409.80
1974	$195.20	1995	$385.60
1975	$150.80	1996	$367.80
1976	$145.10	1997	$288.80
1977	$179.20	1998	$288.00
1978	$244.90	1999	$287.50
1979	$578.70	2000	$272.15
1980	$641.20	2001	$278.70
1981	$430.80	2002	$346.70
1982	$484.50	2003	$414.80
1983	$415.00	2004	$438.10
1984	$331.30	2005	$517.20
1985	$354.20	2006	$636.30
1986	$435.20	2007	$833.20
1987	$522.90		

Data on gold prices obtained from, "Modern and Ancient Spot Gold Prices,"
www.onlygold.com/TutorialPages/Prices200YrsFS.htm (accessed 19 March 2009).

So, what is the return on the investment in gold for different intervals of time? Consider the following intervals and the returns:

Period	Beginning of the Period	Starting Value	Ending Value	Years	Calculation	Return
A	End of December 1967	$35.50	$833.20	1968–2007	$\sqrt[40]{\dfrac{\$833.20}{\$35.50}} - 1$	8.209%
B	End of December 1977	$179.20	$833.20	1978–2007	$\sqrt[30]{\dfrac{\$833.20}{\$179.20}} - 1$	5.256%
C	End of December 1987	$522.90	$833.20	1988–2007	$\sqrt[20]{\dfrac{\$833.20}{\$522.90}} - 1$	2.357%
D	End of December 1997	$288.80	$833.20	1998–2007	$\sqrt[10]{\dfrac{\$833.20}{\$288.80}} - 1$	11.177%

You will notice, for example, that we use the ending value for 1967 as the beginning value of the 1968–2007 interval, and that this interval has a holding period of 40 years: 1968, 1969, 1970 and so on.

Does that mean that it was a good or bad investment? Not necessarily. We haven't considered three important factors:

- The volatility of the price of gold, which makes the returns on gold quite uncertain.
- The holding costs of owning gold.
- What you could have earned on a similar or lower risk investment.

There is a great deal of volatility—and hence risk—in a gold investment. Further, if you invest in gold directly, you will incur some costs of storing your investment because unless you invest in gold indirectly through stocks of gold mining companies, or through futures on gold, you will have to store it safely.

Comparing gold with other investments, you can see that the price of gold is more volatile than the stock market in general, as represented by the S&P 500 Index. For example, if, at the end of 1967, you had invested $1 in gold and $1 in the stocks that comprise the S&P 500, you would have had an investment worth $23.47 in gold and $9.28 in the S&P 500.

How did we determine this? We calculate the return for each investment in each period, and then use compounding to determine the value of the investment at different points in time. For example, the return on gold for 1968 is ($43.50 − 35.30) ÷ $35.50 = 22.535%. If you invested $1 at the end of 1967, you would have had an investment worth $1 × (1 + 0.22535) = $1.2254 at the end of 1968.

Continuing this calculation, you can see how the value of the investment grows with compounding:

End of Year	Price of Gold per Ounce	Return	Value of $1 Invested at the End of 1967
1967	$35.50		$1.0000
1968	$43.50	22.535%	$1.2254
1969	$35.40	−18.621%	$0.9972
1970	$37.60	6.215%	$1.0592
1971	$43.80	16.489%	$1.2338
1972	$65.20	75.613%	$1.8366

If we continue this process until 2007, we calculate that the value of that $1 grew to $23.4704 by the end of 2007.

We graph the value of $1 in gold and the value of $1 invested in the S&P 500 in Exhibits 9.3 and 9.4; we graph 1968–2007 in Exhibit 10.3,

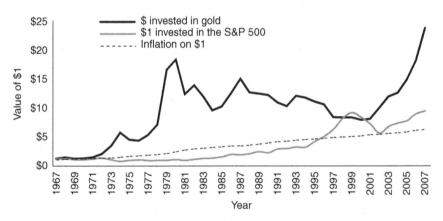

EXHIBIT 10.3 The Value of an Investment of $1 in Gold and the S&P 500 Index, 1968–2007
Data obtained from Standard & Poor's Index Services, www2.standardandpoors.com/spf/xls/index/MONTHLY.xls; and U.S. Bureau of Labor Statistics, Consumer Price Index, www.bls.gov (accessed 19 March 2009).

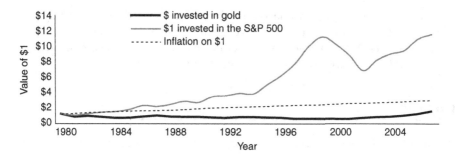

EXHIBIT 10.4 The Value of an Investment of $1 in Gold and the S&P 500 Index, 1980–2007
Data obtained from Only Gold, "Modern and Ancient Spot Gold Prices," www.onlygold.com/TutorialPages/Prices200YrsFS.htm; Standard & Poor's Index Services, www2.standardandpoors.com/spf/xls/index/MONTHLY.xls; and U.S. Bureau of Labor Statistics, Consumer Price Index, www.bls.gov (accessed 19 March 2009).

and 1980–2007 in Exhibit 10.4. If we focus on 1968–2007, we conclude that gold outperformed an investment in stocks over this period, though with more volatility. If we focus on 1980–2007, we conclude that gold underperformed the S&P 500.

Bottom line? It depends when you begin your evaluation of returns.

We can compare the returns on gold and the S&P 500 by calculating the average annual return based on what an investment would be worth at different points in time, as we did with gold prices earlier. We can calculate the return on gold over the 40 years using:

$$PV = \$1$$
$$FV = \$23.47$$
$$n = 40$$

Solving for i, $i = 8.209\%$.

Investment	Value at the End of 1967	Value at the End of 2007	Average Annual Return, 1968–2007	Average Annual Return, 1988–2007
Gold	$1	$23.47	8.209%	2.357%
S&P 500 Index	$1	$9.28	5.728%	8.788%
Inflation			4.646%	3.039%

You can use the basic valuation mathematics to calculate the average annual return on different types of investments to determine the return on the investments. What mathematics does not tell us is how much risk each investment has, but we will leave that for another book.

SUMMARY

In this book, we have covered a lot of ground in financial mathematics. Prepared with the basic time value of money mathematics, you can analyze most any financial transactions, evaluating the cash flows to determine values at different points in time or returns on investments. We show in this chapter that you can apply these financial mathematics tools to help evaluate career decisions, personal finance decisions, and investment decisions. Though all of these decisions are more complex than what we have demonstrated, armed with these financial mathematics tools, you can make a more informed decision—at least the financial part of these decisions.

Using Financial Calculators

Financial calculators can save you lots of time and trouble in performing the mathematics described in this book. However, there are some basics that you need to know before becoming reliant upon the calculators for financial transactions. In this appendix, we cover the basic set-up and use of the financial functions in several popular financial calculators, as well as a versatile scientific calculator. If we do not cover the particular calculator that you have, don't worry. Most financial calculators follow similar programming and keys to the ones we discuss, so you just need to find your closest match.

The financial calculators that we cover in this appendix are the following:

- Hewlett-Packard 10B (HP10B)
- Texas Instruments BAII Plus (TI-BAII)
- Hewlett-Packard 12C (HP12C)

The Hewlett-Packard 17B and 19B calculators (HP17B and HP19B, respectively) have similar functions to the HP10B, so we don't perform each calculation with these calculators. (Refer to the instructions for the HP10B as needed.) However, where there are some differences, we will note these briefly in this appendix.

In the book, we simplify our presentation by presenting the calculations for the HP10B. The HP10B is the simplest financial calculator to set up and use and its financial functions are very similar to those of the TI-BAII, HP12C, HP17B, and HP19B.

The scientific calculator that we cover is the Texas Instruments TI-83, whose financial calculations are identical to the more recent model, the TI-84. In referring to these calculators, we simply designate the calculator as TI-83/84.

PREPARING THE CALCULATOR

Your calculator may come from the factory with certain display and calculation settings. For example, the HP10B comes ready to perform calculations using two decimal places (a display setting) and 12 payments per year (a calculation setting). If you need more precision, you need to adjust the display. Also, if you require one payment per period, as in most of our calculations, you need to adjust the payments per year.

Adjust the Number of Digits Displayed

Because financial transactions often use interest rates and compounding, use at least four places to the right of the decimal place for all calculations. You can set your calculator's display program to display a specified number of decimal places. To change the setting to display four decimal places, for example:

HP10B ■ DISP 4

HP12C f 4

HP17B DSP FIX 4 INPUT

You can adjust the number of decimal places that your calculator displays, but this adjustment does not affect the precision of the calculation within the calculator. As long as you perform the calculation within the calculator, the model determines the precision of the calculation. You may be displaying only four decimal places, but the calculation may use 14 decimal places.

Bottom line? Display at least four decimal places.

Check the Frequency of Payments

Most calculations require one interest compounding per period, and, in the case of annuities, one payment per period. However, some calculators come from the factory set up for mortgages and the settings are 12 payments per period.

For most calculations, we need to make sure that the calculator program we are using considers only one payment per period and one compounding per period.

HP10B	1 ■ P/YR
TI-BAII	P/Y 1 ENTER
HP12C	*Frequency of payments are not programmed.*
HP17B	FIN TVM OTHER P/YR 1 INPUT
TI-83/84	P/Y = 1

For simple lump sum problems, when you are calculating a present value given a future value or vice-versa, the setting of the frequency of payments does not matter because there is no payment (PMT) specified—so it is set at the default setting of zero. But if you are working with a payment, as is the case with any annuity, you risk altering the valuation (in other words, making an error) if you do not set the payment frequency correctly.

There are some applications, such as mortgage payments, when you may want to set the payment frequency (e.g., 12 for mortgages). This works well as long as you specify the other parameters—the number of years and the interest rate—appropriately.

We do not recommend that you set the payment frequency to anything other than one per period. The reason? When you clear the time value of money registers (e.g., CLR TVM in the TI-BAII calculator), you don't clear or change this setting. In other words, a change in the P/Y remains until you reset it to the next value.[1] Therefore, you may get subsequent calculations incorrectly—and not realize it.

Bottom line? Set the P/Y to 1 no matter what the problem.

TI-83/84: P/Y AND C/Y

The TI-83/84 financial program has both a P/Y and a C/Y key.

The P/Y setting is the number of payments per year.

The C/Y setting is for the number of times interest compounds in a year.

This is different than the HP10B, TABAII and HP12C calculators that have only a P/Y setting. In these calculators, if the P/Y setting is 12 but the periodic payment is set to zero, the P/Y key acts as the equivalent to the C/Y key in the TI-83/84.

---

[1]If you set P/YR to 12 and then turn off the calculator, the next time you pick it up and turn it on, the payment frequency is still 12.

Clear the Financial Function's Registers after Each Problem

The information you input and the results of the calculations you perform are stored in the computer's registers (its memory for the bits and pieces of information). Clear your registers before starting a new calculation. If you fail to clear the registers in your calculator, you will find that the next problem you do will use data left over from the last problem, even if you had turned off your calculator since the last problem. To clear your calculator:

Calculator	Clearing Operation
HP10B	CLEAR ALL
TI-BAII	CLR WORK
HP12C	f REG
HP17B	CLEAR DATA

Each calculator has its own set of programs and clearing the registers that use these programs will differ. Some examples:

- *TI-BA II* has a specific clearing function for the time value of money registers, CLR TVM. However, this clearing does not clear the cash flow registers that we use in the NPV and IRR calculations; you will need to perform the more general CLEAR WORK to clear these registers.
- *TI-83/84* You are filling in a screen and will change all entries to the appropriate values, so if the calculation has no payment, you will set the payment to zero: PMT = 0.
- *HP17B* allows storage of individual cash flow data; you need to clear the cash flow information separately: ∎ CLEAR DATA YES

A couple of warnings:

- Keep in mind that clearing the display window on a calculator does not clear any registers.
- Turning off the calculator does not clear any registers. The calculator will remember the last calculation you performed. You can turn off your calculator today and then turn it back on, assuming the batteries are still good, in two years and the calculator will remember your last calculation.

Bottom line? Learn how to clear your calculator's registers.

THE BASICS

The manufacturers design most calculators so that many keys serve double- or triple-duty to keep hand-held calculators small, but useful, for many different types of calculations. For example, in the HP10B calculator the key labeled y^x is used for both multiplication ($\times$) and raising a value to a power (y^x). How do you raise some value to a power? You first strike second-level key, and then y^x).[2] The second-level key tells the computer to use the second function (y^x) of this key, much like a Shift key on a keyboard.

Access to the double or triple level functions differs among calculators. For the HP10B, we access the alternate function of a key by using the colored key. In other models, the alternative function may be accessed through, for example, a 2nd key or a g key. You need to refer to the manual that came with your financial calculator to see how to access these second or third level functions.

In addition to access to different levels through a single key, some calculators, such as the Hewlett-Packard HP17B and HP19B models, have a set of unidentified keys (just below the display) that perform a function assigned to them based on the screen shown in the display. For example, if you select the time value of money screen (by striking the ■ key below the FIN in the display and then the ■ below the TVM in the display), these keys are assigned to represent PV, N, FV, and so on.

In the examples that follow, the keys are described by the label corresponding to the function you are using. For example, to calculate 3^4 on the HP10B, the key strokes are indicated as:

3 ■ y^x 4 y^x

which we represent as:

HP10B
1.05
■ y^x
4 y^x

The basic math calculations (such as addition, subtraction, multiplication, and division) are similar among the different brands and models. With the exception of the HP12C, the math is performed much like you

---

[2]The second-level keys in most calculators are indicated as colored (e.g., orange or blue), or simply 2nd.

would if you were doing it without the calculator. Consider the problem of multiplying 3 by 4:

All models except HP12C:

HP10B
3
×
4
=

You perform division, addition, and subtraction in a like manner.

The HP12C uses reverse-Polish notation, which is tough to get used to but becomes a time-saver in complex calculations.

HP12C
3
ENTER
4 ×

Example

Solve the following using the calculator: 1.05 to the fourth power, or 1.05^4. The answer is 1.2155:

HP10B	TIBAII	HP12C	TI-83/84
1.05	1.05 y^x	1.05	1.05
■ y^x	4 y^x	y^x	^
4 y^x		4	4
			ENTER

Solve the following using the calculator: fourth root of 1.05, or $\sqrt[4]{1.05} = 1.05^{1/4}$. The answer is 1.0123.

HP10B	TIBAII	HP12C	TI-83/84
1.05	1.05 y^x	1.05	1.05
■ y^x	.25 y^x	y^x	^
.25 y^x		.25	.25
			ENTER

FINANCIAL FUNCTIONS

In addition to the math functions, financial calculators provide two types of financial programs within the calculator.

1. Time Value of Money Keys

A row of keys that we use to input the variables in a time value of money problem:

N	I/YR	PV	PMT	FV
↑	↑	↑	↑	↑
Number of compounding periods	Interest rate per compounding period	Present value	Periodic payment	Future value

We input values by typing in the value and then striking the appropriate TVM key. Once we input the known values, we then strike the value we seek to solve.

2. Cash Flow Keys

A set of keys or second-level keys to use to input cash flows to solve for the net present value (NPV) or the internal rate of return (IRR).

CF	I/YR	NPV	IRR
↑	↑	↑	↑
A period's cash flow	Interest rate per compounding period	Net present value	Internal rate of return

To use the cash flow program, we enter the cash flows in chronological order, and then either solve for the IRR or enter the interest rate and solve for the NPV.

TVM Functions

Let's look closely at an example using the time value of money functions to solve a future value problem.

If an investor deposits $1,000 today in an account that pays 5% interest each year, how much will be in the account at the end of 10 years?

We are given the following in the problem description:

Present value, PV = $1,000
Interest rate per period, $i = 5\%$ per year
Number of periods, $n = 10$ years

and we want to solve for FV. The answer is $1,628.89.

In the financial calculators, the financial functions are on the face of the calculator. In the TI-83/84, you need to access the financial applications through its applications.

TI-83/84 FINANCIAL APPLICATIONS

In the TI-83/84, you need to first enter the financial functions and then input the data into the screen. For example, TVM Solver screen on the TI-83/84 has everything set up and you simply enter in the values for n, etc.

Accessing the financial programs:

APPS
1: Finance
ENTER
1: TVM Solver
ENTER

Using the TVM Solver screen, entering the known values:

$n = 10$
$i\% = 5$
PV $= -1000$
PMT $= 0$
FV $=$ ALPHA SOLVE
P/Y $= 1$
C/Y $= 1$
PMT: END BEGIN

When the cursor is at the FV= entry, use the ALPHA SOLVE to solve for the future value.

For presentation, we represent the inputs for the TI-83/84 for all the values that are necessary for the problem at hand.

The future value calculation is the following:

HP10B	TI-BAII	HP12C	TI 83/84
1000 +/−	1000 +/−	1000 CHS	N = 10
5 I/YR	5 I/YR	5 i	I% = 5
10 N	10 N	10 n	PV = −1000
FV	CPT	FV	*Solve for*
	FV		*FV*

Let's try another calculation.

Suppose you have a goal of saving $1,000 by three years from now. If you earn 6% on your savings, what is the amount you need to deposit today to reach this goal?

We have the following information:

FV = $1,000
  n = 3
  i = 6%

and want to solve for the present value, PV. The present value is $839.62. Using the calculators,

HP10B	TIBAII	HP12C	TI-83/84
1000 FV	1000 FV	1000 FV	N = 10
6 I/YR	6 I/YR	6 i	I% = 6
3 N	3 N	3 n	FV = 1000
FV	CPT	FV	*Solve for*
	FV		*FV*

You will notice that the calculator reports the present value as a negative number, −839.62. This is the way the calculators are programmed. The correct answer is $829.62: if you invest $839.62 today, you will reach your goal of $1,000 at the end of three years.

Cash Flow Functions

The cash flow functions in financial calculators are separate from the TVM functions. We use the cash flow functions when we are valuing a set of uneven cash flows or determining a return, referred to as the internal rate of return, on a set of cash flows. In the case of these types of problems, the most challenging part of executing this on a calculator is inputting the cash flows correctly.

The basic idea is to enter all cash flows in chronological order. If there is a period that does not have a cash flow, you must enter a zero in the sequence; failure to include the zero will result in an incorrect valuation or return.

The calculators differ somewhat in terms of how you enter the initial cash flow, and some calculators allow or require you to indicate the frequency of the cash flow. How you enter the cash flows is what really sets the financial calculators apart.

Consider the following set of cash flows:

Period	Cash flow
0	−$10,000
1	$1,000
2	$2,000
3	$12,000

And suppose we want to calculate the present value of these cash flows using a discount rate of 10%, as well as the internal rate of return. The net present value is $1,577.7611 and the internal rate of return is 16.1659%.

First, ignore the dollar signs. These cash flows may be dollars, yen, euros, or any other currency—it doesn't matter within the calculator. Second, ignore the commas that we typically use to help us view amounts; in other words, $1,000 is 1000 for calculator purposes.

We will treat the TI-83/84 separately because its method is quite different than the financial calculators. Using the three calculators, let's calculate the net present value and internal rate of return. We can see that the entry of the cash flows is different:

HP10B	TI-BAII	HP12C
10000 +/− CFj	CF 10000 +/− ENTER	10000 CHS
1000 CFj	↑ 1 enter	CF_0
2000 CFj	↑ 1000 enter	1000 CF_j
12000 CFj	↑ 1 enter	2000 CF_j
10 I/YR	↑ 2000 enter	12000 CF_j
■ NPV	↑ 1 enter	10 i
■ IRR	↑ 12000 enter	f NPV
	CPT NPV	f IRR
	10 enter	
	↑↑↑ *(to find NPV=)*	
	CPT	
	IRR CPT	

There are a few subtle differences among the methods of inputting data:

- The HP10B entry is the simplest.
- The TI-BAII requires indicating the frequency of each cash flow, which is rather tedious, and we must manage the data by using arrows; think of these arrows and changing cells in an imaginary spreadsheet, one that you cannot see.
- The HP12C has a different entry for the initial cash flow than the other cash flows, but otherwise it is similar to the HP10B.

The TI-83/84 requires us to input the cash flow by placing it in a list. Once these cash flows are in a list, we use the NPV and IRR programs with this list.

Option 1	Option 2
2nd {	STAT
1000,2000,12000	*Select* 1:EDIT ENTER *and then enter*
2nd {	*the cash flows in the list. To leave*
STO L1	*the list entry,* 2nd QUIT

Once you have cash flows saved in a list (using whatever list name you wish, including default names of L1, L2, etc.), you use the financial programs that you access through APPS and then selecting 1:Finance. There are two programs we use: 7:NPV and 8:IRR. In the NPV program, the interest rate (in whole numbers) is the first argument, the initial cash flow is the second argument, and the list is the third argument, each separated by commas:

TI-83/84
NPV(10,−10000,2nd
L1
ENTER

For the internal rate of return, there are two arguments: the initial cash flow and the list:

TI-83/84
IRR(−10000,2nd
L1
ENTER

TIPS

Use Shortcuts Whenever Possible

Many calculators allow you to key in a value and then key in how many times that value is repeated. For example, if you have to input six consecutive cash flows of $1 each in your HP12C, for example, 1 g CF$_j$ 6 g N$_j$, the sequence 6 g N$_j$ tells the calculator's program that the one dollar cash flow is repeated six times.

Consider the following problem. We want to calculate the net present value, using a 10% interest rate, and the internal rate of return for the following cash flows:

Period	Cash Flow
0	−€ 10,000
1	€ 1,000
2	€ 1,000
3	€ 1,000
4	€ 12,000

The net present value is € 683.0135 and the internal rate of return is 12.0896%. We can use the shortcuts for the series of three cash flows that are the same:[3]

HP10B	TI-BAII	HP12C
10000 +/− CFj	CF 10000 +/− ENTER	10000 CHS
1000 CFj	↑ 3 enter	CF$_0$
3 ■ Nj	↑ 1000 enter	1000 CF$_j$
12000 CFj	↑ 1 enter	3 g N$_j$
10 I/YR	↑ 12000 enter	12000 CF$_j$
■ NPV	CPT NPV	10 i
■ IRR	10 enter	f NPV
	↑↑↑ *(to find NPV=)*	f IRR
	CPT	
	IRR CPT	

---

[3]In the case of the HP17B and the HP19B, the shortcut for cash flows is the prompt #TIMES that corresponds to a period's cash flow.

Check the Timing of the Cash Flows

Check to see whether your calculator is set up to assume cash flows at the end of the period or the beginning of the period. Many calculator brands allow you to specify when cash flows occur (beginning or end of the period), which is useful for annuity due calculations. However, like most registers in the calculator, the calculator remembers the last way you specified the cash flows, so you must change this register if you, say, switch from an annuity due to an ordinary annuity calculation.

To change the setting from end-of-period to beginning-of-period, for example:

HP10B	■ BEG/END
TI-BAII	2nd FORMAT 4 ENTER
HP12C	g BEG
HP17B	FIN TVM OTHER BEG
	EXIT

Check Your Work

Always check for the reasonableness of your calculations; it's very easy to hit the wrong key—especially when taking tests. Learn to do your problem with your calculator and then either check your answers using another method, such as with the basic math. Also, use commonsense checks for reasonableness. If the interest rate is greater than zero (which should be the case), then:

PV	<	FV
FV	>	PV
PV of a series of cash flows	<	Sum of series of cash flows
FV of a series of cash flows	>	Sum of series of cash flows

TROUBLESHOOTING PROBLEMS

A.1. I keep getting smaller present values and larger future values than what I should each time I try to replicate one of the examples.

Check whether the calculator TVM settings are in the beginning of the period mode or the ending period mode.

Check the P/Y setting to make sure it is equal to one.

Check to make sure that you cleared the calculator before performing the calculation.

A.2. When I calculate the net present value of a series of cash flows, I sometimes (but not always) get a value less than what the value should be.

Check to see whether you entered zero for periods in which the cash flows are zero.

A.3. When I calculate the internal rate of return for a series of cash flows, I sometimes (but not always) get a value less than what the value should be.

Check to see whether you entered zero for periods in which the cash flows are zero.

A.4. When I calculate the net present value of a series of cash flows, I always get a value much larger than what the value should be.

Check to see whether you entered the interest as a whole number instead of in decimal form. That is, if the interest rate is 10%, you should enter 10, not .1.

A.5. When I calculate the present value or the future value, I sometimes get an incorrect value, but there doesn't seem to be a pattern in these errors.

Check to see whether you are clearing the calculator between each problem.

A.6. I get "no Solution" or "Error 5," or "ERR: NO SIGN CHNG" in the display window.

Make sure that you have entered the present value as a negative value.

A.7. I am doing a simple lump sum problem (that is, converting a present value in to a future value or vice versa), and the present value is equal to the future value.

Check to see whether you entered the interest rate.

A.8. I use the HP12C and the values displayed have commas instead of decimal places.

You have somehow changed the display to European notation. To change the display to U.S. display, first turn the calculator off and then turn it on while holding down the decimal point key.

A.9. I was performing a problem that required two steps, and my final answer is off by a few cents.

If you calculate the first step in the calculator, write down the values, and then input these values in the calculator for the second step, you will have lost the precision from the first step. In other words, by using the displayed values in the first step as inputs to the second step, you did not consider that the displayed value is merely a few of the many decimal places that the calculator uses. Either tolerate the small imprecision, or figure out how to perform both steps sequentially in the calculator.

Using Spreadsheets in Financial Calculations

There are a number of spreadsheet programs available for computers and mobile devices that can perform financial calculations. We focus on one spreadsheet program, Microsoft Excel, which is an application in the Microsoft Office productivity suite.

However, if you don't have Microsoft Office, you can use the free Google spreadsheet, found by checking out Google's Docs programs at docs.google.com. You can perform the same calculations in the spreadsheet in Google Docs, using commands similar to those in Microsoft Excel. You can even upload your Microsoft Excel spreadsheet to Google Docs to share with others. Another free program is to use the Calc software available free at OpenOffice.org.

THE BASICS

Spreadsheets give you the ability to perform math operations. For example, if you want to calculate 1.05 to the fourth power (that is, 1.05^4), you use the caret, $^\wedge$, to work this problem:

$$=1.05^\wedge 4$$

where $=$ indicates that you are entering a formula or function. You can perform most any mathematical operation as long as you know the spreadsheet's operations or functions:[1]

---

[1]You will notice that we do not need to specify the function in uppercase letters. The spreadsheets to not distinguish between upper- and lowercase characters.

Operator or Function	Use	Example	In the Spreadsheet
^	To take a value to a power.	1.05^4	=1.05^4
EXP	To take e (that is, Euler's e), to a power.	e^1	=exp(1)
LN	To find the natural log of a value.	ln 2	=ln(2)
SQRT	To find the square root of a value.	$\sqrt{2}$	=sqrt(2)
POWER	To calculate the result of taking a value to a power.	1.10^4	=power(1.1,4)

TIME VALUE OF MONEY FUNCTIONS

Aside from the ability to use the basic math functions in a spreadsheet, most spreadsheets provide built-in financial functions. These functions allow you to perform basic financial calculations, including calculating a present value, calculating a future value, or solving for the number of periods.

The functions that perform financial calculations include the following parameters:

Notation Used in this Book	Abbreviation Used by the Spreadsheet Functions	What Does it Mean?
N	NPER	Number of compounding periods
i	RATE	Interest rate per compounding period
PV	PV	Present value
FV	FV	Future value
PMT	PMT	Periodic payment

In Microsoft Excel, there are a number of basic financial functions. In terms of the notation that we use in this book, these functions are:

Function	Arguments	Use of Function
FV	=FV(i,N,PMT,FV,type)	Solve for the future value of a present value and/or series of periodic payments.
PV	=PV(i,N,PMT,FV,type)	Solve for the present value of a future value and/or series of periodic payments.

Function	Arguments	Use of Function
NPER	=NPER(i,PMT,PV,FV,type)	Solve for the number of periods or payments necessary to equate the present value with the payments and/or future value.
RATE	=RATE(N,PMT,PV,FV, type,guess)	Solve for the rate of interest that equates the present value with the future value and/or periodic payments.
PMT	=PMT(i,N,PV,FV,type)	Solve for the payment that is equivalent to either the present value or the future value.

We should note a few things about using these functions:

1. *Specifying the interest rate.* We specify the interest rate in decimal form, not a whole number as is the case with financial calculators. If the interest rate is 5%, the interest rate argument has a value of .05.
2. *Ordering the arguments.* In all cases, the order of the arguments is crucial; switching the order of even one argument will cause an incorrect value or will cause an error response from the spreadsheet program.
3. *Signing the present value.* In problems in which one of the arguments is the present value, you must specify this present value as a negative value. If both the PV and the FV are positive, there is no solution and you will receive an error message. You could, of course, enter the FV as a negative value and the problem will work, but we do not advise this because this will cause problems in more complex problems, such as those involving PV, PMT and FV values.

   When we solve for the present value, we will receive a negative number for the present value from the function. Multiplying this value by negative one will provide a more readable, interpretable spreadsheet.
4. *Using 0 to hold the place.* Each function has a number of arguments. In the function =FV(i,N,PMT,FV,type), for example, there are five arguments: i, N, PMT, FV, and type. In the case of an argument that is PV, FV, i, N, or PMT, a zero *must* be used to hold the place of any value not in the problem. For example, if we want the present value of 1000 to be received in three years and the interest rate is 5%, we specify the function PV as:

$$=PV(.05,3,0,1000,0)$$

which is $863.84. If we had specified this incorrectly, leaving out the 0 for PMT:

$$=PV(.05,3,1000,0)$$

we would arrive at the *incorrect* answer of $2,723.25, which is the present value of a series of payments of $1,000, not the single lump-sum as the problem requires.

5. *Specifying the timing of the cash flows.* The argument "type" to indicate whether the cash flows are end-of-period (TYPE is 0) or beginning of period (TYPE is 1). If we leave this out of our specification of the function, the program assumes that the cash flows are end of period. For example,

$$=PV(.05,10,1000,500)$$

is equivalent to

$$=PV(.05,10,1000,500,0)$$

6. *Guessing.* When we use the function that solves for the interest rate (e.g., RATE), we have the option to specify a guess. The reason we do this is that solving for a rate for uneven cash flows requires iterations to reach the rate (i.e., trial and error). When we do this, the spreadsheet's program will use trial and error to converge upon the solution. In some cases, this can be quite time consuming, so you can speed this up by providing a guess, which will be where the spreadsheet begins its trial and error. Without the guess, Microsoft Excel assumes a starting point of 10%. In rare cases, the spreadsheet will not reach convergence within the default settings (that is, the number of trial and errors in the convergence), so providing the guess may be practical.[2]

Entering the Data

You have two choices when it comes to entering the data. You can use the function directly, or input the values of the arguments into different cells in the spreadsheet and then use cell references. Consider the following problem. What is the present value of $6,000 that will be received at the end of 10 years, if the discount rate is 5%?

---

[2]Google Docs is similar, but the default parameters in Microsoft Excel are set so that you are more likely to converge in Excel. You may encounter some problems in convergence in Google Docs by using the defaults in cases in which Excel converges just fine.

We can input the elements directly in to the PV function,

$$=PV(.05,10,0,6000)$$

or create cells and use the cell references and refer to these cells:

	A	B
1	Interest rate	5%
2	Number of periods	10
3	Payment	0
4	Future value	6000
5		
6	Present value	3683.48

← =PV(B1,B2,B3,B4)*−1

Unlike calculators, you can specify that a cell involves currency, and you can also specify that commas separate values into thousands, millions, and so on.[3] So in this example, you could specify that cells B4 and B6 are dollars, with commas, and the function will work fine:

	A	B
1	Interest rate	5%
2	Number of periods	10
3	Payment	0
4	Future value	$6,000
5		
6	Present value	$3,683.48

← =PV(B1,B2,B3,B4)*−1

Be careful not to include dollar signs and commas if you enter the values directly into the function. In other words, you will get an error message if you enter the incorrect function arguments of =PV(.05,10,0,$6,000).

---

[3] You would do this by using the Format > Cells > Number commands, specifying Currency for the cell type.

CASH FLOW FUNCTIONS

The spreadsheets have functions that you can use to calculate the net present value and the internal rate of return for a series of values. Using CF_t to indicate the cash flow occurring at the end of period t:

$$= NPV\,(i, CF_1, CF_2, CF_3, \ldots)$$

$$= IRR\,(CF_0, CF_1, CF_2, CF_3, \ldots, \text{guess})$$

There is a subtle difference in the setup of these functions. The NPV function uses the cash flows starting at the end of the first period, whereas the IRR uses the cash flows starting at time 0, or today.

Let's consider an example and then demonstrate how to set this up in the spreadsheets. Consider the following cash flows:

Period	End of Period Cash Flow
0	–$10,000
1	1000
2	2000
3	12,000

1. What is the internal rate of return for these cash flows?
2. What is the net present value of these cash flows if the discount rate is 5%?

In the case of the net present value, we can either enter the values as arguments into the function, or we can use cell references. Using the NPV function directly, we calculate the net present value of $3,132.49:

$$=NPV(0.05,1000,2000,12000) - 10000$$

In the case of the internal rate of return, however, we must use cell references.

Using cell references, we input the values into the spreadsheet, using column A and row 1 cells to label our values and using Column B cells for our values:

	A	B
1	Period	End of Period Cash Flow
2	0	-$10,000
3	1	$1,000
4	2	$2,000
5	3	$12,000

Using the NPV and IRR functions with cell references:

	A	B	
1	Period	End of Period Cash Flow	
2	0	-$10,000	
3	1	$1,000	
4	2	$2,000	
5	3	$12,000	
6			
7	NPV	$3,132.49	← =NPV(0.05,B3:B5)+B2
8	IRR	16.1569%	← =IRR(B2:B5)

OTHER USEFUL FUNCTIONS FOR FINANCIAL MATHEMATICS

The spreadsheets include a number of additional functions that are useful for financial mathematics. We don't cover these specifically in this book, but you may find these useful in more advanced applications:

Function	Purpose
IPMT	Calculates the interest paid on a loan for a specific loan payment.
PPMT	Calculates the principal paid on a loan for a specific loan payment.
YIELD	Calculates the yield on a security that has even, periodic payments, such as interest or dividends.
YIELDMAT	Calculates the yield to maturity on a security.

Formulas

NOTATION

APR	Annual percentage rate
CF	Cash flow
CIF_t	Cash inflow in period t
COF_t	Cash outflow in period t
D	Dividend per share
D_t	Dividend per share in period t
e	Euler's e
EAR	Effective annual rate
FV	Future value
g	Growth rate
HPR	Holding period return
i	Rate of interest
IRR	Internal rate of return
i_t	Interest rate in period t
M	Maturity or face value of a bond
n	Number of compounding periods
N	Number of payments
NPV	Net present value
P_0	Price per share of common stock
PI	Profitability index
PMT	Periodic, even payment
PV	Present value
r_d	Required rate of return on a bond
r_e	Required rate of return on equity
r_p	Required rate of return on a preferred stock
V	Value of a bond

CHAPTER 1

Future value with discrete compounding:

$$FV = PV(1+i)^n$$

Future value with continuous compounding:

$$FV = PV\left[e^{APRn}\right]$$

CHAPTER 2

Present value with discrete compounding:

$$PV = \frac{FV}{(1+i)^n}$$

Present value with continuous compounding:

$$PV = \frac{FV}{e^{APRn}}$$

CHAPTER 3

Present value of a stream of cash flows:

$$PV = \sum_{t=1}^{N} \frac{CF_t}{(1+i)^t}$$

Present value of a perpetuity:

$$PV = \frac{CF}{i}$$

Present value of an ordinary annuity:

$$PV = \sum_{t=1}^{N} \frac{CF}{(1+i)^t} = CF \sum_{t=1}^{N} \frac{1}{(1+i)^t} = CF\left(1 - \frac{(1+i)^N)}{i}\right)$$

Present value of an annuity due:

$$PV = \sum_{t=1}^{N} \frac{CF}{(1+i)^{t-1}} = CF \sum_{t=1}^{N} \frac{1}{(1+i)^{t-1}}$$

CHAPTER 4

Annual percentage rate:

$$APR = i \times n$$

Effective annual rate, discrete compounding:

$$EAR = (1+i)^n - 1$$

$$EAR = \left(1 + \frac{APR}{n}\right)^n - 1$$

Effective annual rate, continuous compounding:

$$EAR = e^{APR} - 1$$

Interest rate implied by PV, FV and n:

$$i = \left(\sqrt[n]{\frac{FV}{PV}}\right) - 1$$

Geometric average return:

$$\text{Geometric average return} = [(1+i_1) \times (1+i_2) \times \ldots \times (1+i_n)]^{1/n} - 1,$$

Holding period return for one period:

$$\text{HPR for one period} = \frac{\text{Ending value} + \text{Dividend} - \text{Beginning value}}{\text{Beginning value}}$$

Internal rate of return:

$$CF_0 = \sum_{t=1}^{N} \frac{CF_t}{(1+IRR)^t}$$

CHAPTER 5

Loan valuation:

$$PV = \sum_{t=1}^{N} \frac{PMT}{\left(1 + \dfrac{APR}{12}\right)^t}$$

CHAPTER 7

Bond equivalent yield:

$$\text{Bond equivalent yield} = \text{6-month yield} \times 2$$

Bond valuation:

$$V = \left[\sum_{t=1}^{N} \frac{PMT_t}{(1 + r_d)^t}\right] + \frac{M}{(1 + r_d)^N}$$

CHAPTER 8

Value of a share of preferred stock:

$$P_0 = \frac{D}{r_p}$$

Value of a common stock:

$$P_0 = \sum_{t=1}^{\infty} \frac{D_t}{(1 + r_e)^t}$$

Value of a share of common stock if dividends grow at a constant rate:

$$P_0 = \frac{D_0(1 + g)}{(r_e - g)} \quad P_0 = \frac{D_1}{(r_e - g)}$$

Average annual return:

$$i = \sqrt[n]{\frac{FV}{PV}} - 1$$

CHAPTER 9

Net present value:

$$NPV = \frac{\text{Present value}}{\text{of cash inflows}} - \frac{\text{Present value}}{\text{of cash outflows}} = \sum_{t=1}^{N} \frac{CF_t}{(1+i)^t}$$

Profitability index:

$$PI = \frac{\dfrac{\text{Present value}}{\text{of cash inflows}}}{\dfrac{\text{Present value}}{\text{of cash outflows}}} = \frac{\sum_{t=1}^{N} \dfrac{CIF_t}{(1+i)^t}}{\sum_{t=1}^{N} \dfrac{COF_t}{(1+i)^t}}$$

Internal rate of return:

$$\$0 = \sum_{t=1}^{N} \frac{CF_t}{(1+IRR)^t}$$

Glossary

annual percentage rate The rate of interest stated in a borrowing arrangement that is the product of the rate per compounding period multiplied by the number of compounding periods.

annual percentage rate A stated or reported rate, which is the product of the interest rate per period and the number of compounding periods within a year.

annual percentage yield An annualized rate that considers the frequency by which interest is compounded within a year.

annuity A finite series of even, periodic cash flows.

annuity due A finite series of even, periodic cash flows in which the first cash flow occurs immediately.

APR See *annual percentage rate.*

APY See *annual percentage yield.*

balloon payment A large loan payment, usually as a lump sum at the end of the life of the loan.

basis point A measure of the difference in yields on securities, in units of 1% of 1%.

bond A debt obligation, which is a legal commitment to repay the amount borrowed and any promised interest.

bond equivalent yield The annualized six-month return on a bond.

capital budgeting The evaluation of investing funds today in order to receive benefits some time in the future.

capital rationing The situation in which there is a limit on how much you spend on long-term investments.

capital yield The return on a security from the appreciation or depreciation in the value of the security.

capitalization rate The discount rate used to convert a series of future cash flows into a present value.

cash dividends Distributions to shareholders in the form of cash.

common stock The ownership interest in a corporation, represented by shares of stock.

compound factor The term applied against a present value to convert it to a future value.

compound interest   The payment of interest on both the principal amount and any accumulated interest.

continuous compounding   The compounding of interest at every instant in time.

coupon   The interest payment on a debt instrument.

coupon rate   The annual stated rate of interest on a bond.

credit spread   The difference in interest rates between Treasury and non-Treasury securities that are identical in all respects except for their credit rating.

crossover discount rate   See *crossover rate.*

crossover rate   The discount rate that, when applied to discount the cash flows of investments, equates the net present value of the investments.

default risk   The uncertainty that the issuer of the security is unable to make timely payments of interest and/or principal when obligated to do so.

deferred annuity   A finite series of even, periodic cash flows in which the first cash flow occurs beyond one period from the present.

discount factor   The term applied against a future value to convert it to a present value.

discounting   The process of translating a future value into an equivalent present value, considering a specified interest rate.

dividend discount model   See *dividend valuation model.*

dividend valuation model   A valuation model that relates the present value of a stock to the present value of future dividends.

dividend yield   The return on a stock in the form of a dividends.

dividends   A distribution to the owners of a corporation, either in the form of cash or additional shares of stock.

dividends per share   The cash dividends paid by a corporation to its shareholders, divided by the number of shares outstanding.

dollar weighted return   See *money-weighted return.*

DPS   See *dividends per share.*

e   a mathematical constant, sometimes referred to as Euler's *e*, that is the inverse of the natural logarithm.

EAR   See *effective annual rate.*

effective annual rate   An annualized rate that considers the frequency by which interest is compounded within a year.

effective rate of interest   Another name for the effective annual rate.

face value   See *maturity value.*

future value annuity factor   The factor used to translate a series of payments into a single value at some future point in time.

geometric mean   A mean calculated as the nth root of the product of values.

Gordon model   A dividend valuation model in which future dividends grow at a constant rate, forever.

growth rate   The rate of change in values over time.

holding period return   The ratio of the change in the value of the investment, plus for any cash flows received or less any cash flows paid out, divided by the beginning value of the investment.

home mortgage   An agreement in which the borrower gives up a claim to his/her home in the event of a default on a loan.

interest   The compensation paid for the use of funds, which is compensation for both the time value of money and risk.

interest-only mortgage   A mortgage loan in which the initial loan payments consist only of interest, with the payments increasing to provide both interest and principal at some specified time of the loan.

internal rate of return   The average annual return on an investment, assuming that all cash flows are reinvested at the internal rate of return.

investment profile   A depiction of the net present values of an investment for different costs of capital. Also referred to as the *NPV profile*.

IO mortgage   See *interest-only mortgage.*

lessee   The party to a lease that makes payments to the lessor for the use of an asset.

lessor   The party to a lease that owns the asset (e.g., a car) and collects lease payments for its use.

loan amortization   The process of paying off a loan over time, such that each payment includes both principal repayment and interest on the loan.

loan amortization schedule   A chart of the payments on a loan, with breakdowns of each payment into amount of interest and principal associated with each payment.

maturity spread   The difference in yields for securities that have different maturities, but yet are otherwise similar.

maturity value   The principal amount of a debt instrument that is paid when the debt matures. Also known as the *face value.*

mortgage   An agreement in which the borrower gives up a claim to specified collateral in the event of a default on a loan.

mutually exclusive   The situation in which a decision to invest in one investment precludes the investment in another investment.

net present value   The present value of all cash flows of an investment.

nominal interest rate   A stated or reported rate, which does not consider compounding within the annual period.

normal yield curve   The condition in which the yields on longer-term maturities are higher than those of shorter-term securities.

NPV profile   See *investment profile.*

opportunity cost of funds   What could have been earned on a similar risk investment.

ordinary annuity   A finite series of even, periodic cash flows in which the first cash flow occurs one period from the present.

paper gain   The return on an investment due to the price appreciation that is not realized through a transaction.

perpetuity   A periodic cash flow stream that continues on forever, *ad infinitum.*

preferred stock   The ownership interest in a corporation that has a superior (hence, "preferred") claim on income and assets vis-à-vis common stock owners.

prepayment   An additional payment on a loan, which is generally deducted from the principal amount of the loan, resulting in fewer payments on the loan than originally scheduled.

present value annuity factor   The factor used to translate a series of payments into a single value at the present point in time.

profitability index An index of an investments value, calculated as the ratio of the present value of the cash inflows to the present value of the cash outflows.

rating agency A financial service firm that evaluates the credit worthiness of securities, communicating their evaluation in the form of a rating.

reinvestment risk The risk that you will earn less than what is expected because reinvested cash flow (coupons in the case of a bond) earn a yield different than what was expected.

required rate of return What security holders demand as compensation for the time value of money and risk.

Rule of 69 A rule-of-thumb for the combination of interest rate and number of periods it takes to double your money if interest compounds continuously. The product of the whole interest rate and the number of periods for doubling your money is approximately 69. This rule is sometimes referred to as the *Rule of 70*.

Rule of 70 See *Rule of 69*.

Rule of 72 A rule-of-thumb for the combination of interest rate and number of periods it takes to double your money. The product of the whole interest rate and the number of periods for doubling your money is approximately 72.

simple interest Interest paid only on the principal amount of the borrowing.

spread The difference in interest rates or yield.

stated interest rate See *nominal interest rate*.

stock dividends Distributions to shareholders in the form of additional shares of stock.

straight coupon Interest paid on a bond that is paid at a fixed rate over a bond's life.

time value of money The concept that a dollar today is not worth a dollar tomorrow.

time-weighted return Geometric mean return, calculated as the nth root, less one, of the product of one plus the individual returns.

yield The return on a security.

yield curve The relation between maturity and yield.

yield to maturity The annualized return on a security.

YTM See *yield to maturity*.

zero-coupon bond A bond that does not pay coupon interest, and therefore the investor instead earns interest at the maturity date when the bond's maturity value exceeds the purchase price.

Solutions to End-of-Chapter Problems

CHAPTER 1

1.1. Given:

PV = $10,000

$n = 5 \times 4 = 10$ quarters

$i = 4\% \div 4 = 1\%$ per qtr.

FV = $10,000 $(1 + 0.01)^{20}$ = $10,000 $\times$ 1.22019 = **$12,201.90**

1.2. Given:

PV = $2,000

$n = 6 \times 12 = 72$ months

$i = 12\% \div 12 = 1\%$ per month

FV = $2,000 $(1 + 0.01)^{72}$ = $2,000 $\times$ 2.0471 = **$4,094.20**

1.3. Given:

PV = $3,000

$n = 5 \times 2 = 10$ 6-month periods

$i = 8\% \div 2 = 4\%$

FV = $3,000 $(1 + 0.04)^{10}$ = $3,000 $\times$ 1.48024 = **$4,440.72**

1.4. Given:

PV = $100

$n = 20 \times 4 = 80$

$i = 2\% \div 4 = 0.5\%$

FV =$100 $\times$ $(1 + 0.005)^{80}$ = $100 $\times$ 1.49034 = **$149.03**

FV with simple interest = $100 + ($100 $\times$ 0.02 $\times$ 20) = $140

Interest on interest = **$9.03**

1.5. Given:

PV = $100

$i = 4\%$

$n = 3$

The problem requires the future value if there is simple interest, FV = $100 + 12 = **$112.**

The future value with compounding is FV = $100 × $(1 + 0.04)^3$ = $112.49.

Withdrawals are the difference between the future value with compounding and the future value with simple interest = $112.49 − $112.00 = $0.49.

1.6. Given: PV = €100

$i = 5\%$

$n = 6$ years

FV = €100 $(1 + 0.05)^6$ = €100 × 1.3401 = **€134.01**

1.7. Investment A provides the larger balance:

A: PV = $10,000; $I = 5\% ÷ 2 = 2.5\%$; $n = 4 × 2 = 8$; FV = **$12,184.03**

B: PV = $10,000; factor = $e^{4 × 0.048}$; FV = $10,000 × 1.2116705 = $12,116.71

1.8. Given:

PV = $100

$n = 12$

$i = 6\%$

FV = $100 $(1 + 0.06)^{12}$ = $100 × 2012197 = **$201.22**

1.9. Given:

PV = $100

$n = 6$

$i = 12\%$

FV = $100 $(1 + 0.12)^6$ = $100 × 1.97382 = **$197.38**

1.10. Given:

PV = $1,000

$n = 10$

$i = 7\%$

FV = $1,000 e10 × 0.07 = $1,000 × 2.01375 = **$2,013.75**

CHAPTER 2

2.1. You are given three inputs: FV, *i*, and N, and are required to solve for PV:

Case	Future Value	Interest Rate	Number of Periods	Present Value
A	$10,000	5%	5	$7,835.26
B	¥563,000	4%	20	¥256,945.85
C	$5,000	5.5%	3	$4,258.07

2.2. Given:

FV = $500,000; $i = 5\%$; $n = 10$

PV = $500,000 $(1 \div (1 + 0.05)^{10})$ = $500,000 $\times$ 0.6139 = **$306,959.63**

2.3. Given: FV = $20,000; $i = 12\% \div 4 = 3\%$; $n = 10 \times 4 = 40$ quarters

PV = $6,131.14

2.4. *Hint:* There are two different future values. Treat as two separate present values, then combine.

FV = $5,000; $n = 5$, $i = 5\%$

PV = $3,917.63

FV = $6,000; $n = 6$, $i = 5\%$

PV = $4,477.29

PV of the two future values = $3,917.63 + 4,477.29 = **$8,394.92**

Or, you can use the NPV function in a financial calculator:

In the TI-83/84, the cash flows are {0,0,0,0,5000,5000}

In the HP10B, the cash flows are 0,0,0,0,5000,5000

2.5. PV = $8,638.38 + 8,227.02 = **$16,865.40**

Note: In the TI-83/84 calculator, cash flow list is {0,0,10000,10000}.

2.6. B.

Value of A = €432

Value of B = **€449**

Value of C = €448

2.7. The two present values differ slightly:

PV = $500 $\div (1 + (\frac{0.04}{365}))^{730}$ = **$461.5602**

PV = $500 $\div e^{0.08}$ = **$461.5582**

2.8. PV = £5,000,000 $\div (1 + 0.01)^{120}$ = **£1,514,974**

2.9. PV = $6,000 $\div e^{0.6}$ = **$3,292.87**

2.10. PV = $10,000 $\div (1 + 0.05)^3$ = **$8,638.38**

CHAPTER 3

3.1. PV = [$1,000 × 0.952381] + [$3,000 × 0.8638]
PV = $952.38 + 2,591.51 = $3,543.89
Using calculator: **$3,543.89**

3.2. PV = [$1,000 × 1.1025] + [$3,000 × 1]
PV = $1,102.50 + 3,000 = $4,102.50

3.3. Using a calculator, PMT = $6,000; N = 5; i = 10%; PV = **$22,744.721**

3.4. PV = £7,513.148 + £6,830.13 = £14,343.278

3.5. Given:
CF = $1,000
N = 3
i = 5%
FV = $1,000 × FV annuity factor = **$3,152.50**

3.6. Given:
CF = $1,000
N = 4
i = 5%
PV = $1,000 × (PV annuity factor) = **$3,546**

3.7. FV = $1,000 × 3.1525 × 1.05 = $1,000 × 3.3101 = **$3,310.10**
Using the calculation function: PMT=1,000; N = 3; I = 5; solve for FV

3.8. Given:
CF_t = $350,000
N = 20
i = 5%
PV = $350,000 × 12.4622 × 1.05 = $350,000 (13.0853) = **$4,579,862**

3.9. The values should differ by a factor of 1 + 0.05 or 1.05:
a. End mode: PMT = $4,000; n = 3; i = 5% **$PV_0$ = $10,892.99**
b. Beg mode: PMT = $4,000; n = 3; i = 5% **$PV_0$ = $11,437.64**
c. PMT = $4,000; n = 3; i = 5% ⇨ PV_1 = **$10,892.99**
Then discount to the present, one period ⇨ **PV_0 = $10,374.28**

3.10. **No**, because the value of the annuity is less than $50,000.
Given: PMT = $5,000; N = 15; i = 6%. PV = $48,561.24

CHAPTER 4

4.1. If interest is compounded more frequently than once a year, the EAR will be different than the APR; the EAR will be greater than the APR except in the case in which there is annual compounding (in which case the EAR will be equal to the APR).

4.2. The EAR will become larger than the APR as the frequency of compounding increases. The largest difference between the two is in the case in which interest is compounded continuously.

4.3. APR = 5%
$$EAR = (1 + 0.0125)^4 - 1 = 5.0945\%$$

4.4. **Six months**
50%
APR = 50% × 2 = 100%
$$EAR = (1 + 0.50)^2 - 1 = 125\%$$

4.5. EAR = 16%
APR = $1.16^{0.25}$ *this takes the fourth root of 1 + EAR*
$i = 3.78\%$
APR = 3.78% × 4 = **15.121%**

4.6. EAR = $e^{0.095} - 1 = $ **9.966%**

4.7. EAR = $(1 + 0.025)^4 - 1 = 10.3813\%$

4.8. Time –weighted return = $[(1 + 0.05) \times (1 + 0.06) \times (1 + 0.07)]^{1/3}$
$-1 = $ **5.997%**

4.9. Calculate the return using the IRR, using cash flows of −$5,000, $6,000, and $5,000. IRR = **14.833%**.

4.10. EAR = $(1 + 0.005)12 - 1 = $ **6.1678%**

CHAPTER 5

5.1. Inputs: PV = $50,000; N = 30; $i = 6\% \div 12 = 0.5\%$
Solve for PMT: PMT = **$1,798.95**

5.2. Loan B has the lowest cost.
For both loans, PV = $100,000
Loan A:
- Determine the monthly rate: N = 24; PMT = $4707.34 $i = 1\%$
- Determine the EAR: EAR = $(1 + 0.01)^{12} - 1 = $ **12.6825%**

Loan B:

- Determine the quarterly rate: $N = 8$; PMT $= \$14{,}245.64$ $i = 3\%$
- Determine the EAR: EAR $= (1 + 0.03)^4 - 1 = \textbf{12.5509\%}$

5.3. Based on the inputs of PV $= \$15{,}000$, $N = 3$, and PMT $= \$6{,}000$, the annual interest rate is 9.7%

Year	Beginning Balance	Payment	Interest	Principal Repayment	Ending Balance
0	—	—	—	—	$15,000
1	$15,000	$6,000	1,455	$4,545	$10,455
2	$10,455	$6,000	1,014	$4,986	$5,469
3	$5,469	$6,000	531	$5,469	

5.4. A. Inputs:

PV $= \$30{,}000$

$N = 36$

$i = 3\% \div 12 = 0.25\%$

Solve for PMT

Payment $= \textbf{\$872.44}$

B. Effective rate $=$ EAR $= (1 + 0.0025)^{12} - 1 = \textbf{3.0416\%}$

5.5. The interest rate is based on PV $= \$100{,}000$; PMT $= \$28{,}201.28$; and $N = 4$. $i = 5\%$

Period	Beginning Balance	Payment	Interest	Principal Repayment	Ending Balance
Today	—	—	—	—	$100,000.00
1	$100,000.00	$28,201.18	$5,000.00	$23,201.18	76,798.82
2	76,798.82	$28,201.18	3,839.94	24,361.24	52,437.58
3	52,437.58	$28,201.18	2,621.88	25,579.30	26,858.28
4	26,858.28	$28,201.18	1,342.91	26,858.28	0.00

5.6. Given information: PV $= \$10{,}000$; $N = 3$; $i = 1\%$. Solving for the payment, PMT $= \textbf{\$4{,}021.15}$.

5.7. Given information: PV $= \$2{,}000$; PMT $= \$150$; $i = 5\%$. Solving for N, $N = 22.52$. Therefore, it will take 23 payments to pay off this loan.

5.8.

Payment	Loan Payment	Interest	Repayment of Principal	End of Year Loan Balance
1	$150,000.00	$12,036.39	$7,500.00	$4,536.39
2	$145,463.61	$12,036.39	$7,273.18	$4,763.21

5.9. Given: PV = $10,000; PMT = $322.14; N = 36; Solve for i. i = 0.823888%

APR = 0.823888% × 12 = **9.8867%**

EAR = $(1 + 0.00823888)^{12} - 1$ = **10.3472%**

5.10. Loan 1: PV = $50,000; i = 6% ÷ 12 = 0.5%; N = 36; Solve for the PMT. PMT = **$1,521.10**

Loan 2: PV = $50,000; i = 6% ÷ 12 = 0.5%; N = 36; FV = $10,000; Solve for the PMT. PMT = **$1,266.88**

CHAPTER 6

6.1. PV two years from now: [PMT = $5,000; i = 5%; N = 4]. PV = $17,729.75

PV today: [N = 2; i = 5%; FV = $17,729.75]. PV = **$16,081.41**

6.2. PV 19 years from now: [PMT = $5,000; i = 5%; N = 10]. PV = $38,608.67

PV today: [N = 19; i = 5%; FV = $38,608.67]. PV = **$15278.76**

6.3. PV two years from now: [PMT = $5,000; i = 5%; N = 4]. PV = $17,729.75

PV today: [N = 1; i = 5%; FV = $17,729.75]. PV = **$16,885.48**

6.4. PV 19 years from now: [PMT = $5,000; i = 5%; N = 10]. PV = $38,608.67

Solve for the payment: FV = $38,608.67; N = 19; i = 5%. PMT = **$1,264.24**

6.5. Need in account at the end of 19 years:

PV of the end-of-year 19 amount:

PMT = $100,000; N = 30; i = 15%; PV = $656,597.96

Invest today to achieve that balance: $656,597.96 $(1 + 0.15)^{19}$ = **$46,136.07**

6.6. Step 1. Solve for the value of investments as of his 60th birthday.

PMT = $60,000; N = 25; i = 5%

PV_{60} = **$845,636.67**

Step 2: Solve for the annual deposit

FV = $845,636.67; N = 30; i = 5%

PMT = **$12,728.05**

6.7. Step 1. Solve for value as of the 65th birthday:

$i = 2\%$; N = 20; PMT = $20,000

Value on 65th birthday = $327,028.67

Step 2. Solve for present value of the value on the 65th birthday:

FV = $327,028.67; N = 40, $i = 2\%$

Solve for PV. PV = **$148,108.15**

6.8. Step 1. Solve for the PV on the 65th birthday:

$i = 5\%$; N = 30; PMT = $40,000; FV = $10,000

PV = $617,211.82

Step 2. Solve for the payments necessary to provide $617,211.82 in payments for 40 years:

$i = 5\%$; N = 40; FV = $617,211.82. Solve for PMT. PMT = **$5,109.38**

6.9. **No,** this is not a good deal for you.

The value of the annuity as of your 65th birthday (one year before the first annuity payment begins), is based on PMT = $20,000; $i = 6\%$; N = 20. The value of this annuity is $229,398.42 on your 65th birthday.

This annuity is worth $95,719.95 on your 50th birthday [FV = $229,398.42; N = 15, $i = 6\%$].

6.10. Solve for the number of periods for the equivalence of $1,000 and $10,000, if the interest rate is 7%. Inputs: PMT = $2; FV = $10,000; $i = 7\% \div 52 = 13.4615\%$. N = 1520.32 weeks, which is 29.24 years, or 29 years, 13 weeks.

CHAPTER 7

7.1.

Bond	Coupon Rate	Yield to Maturity	Premium or Discount?
A	5%	4%	Premium
B	6%	5%	Premium
C	4%	5%	Discount
D	8%	7%	Premium

7.2. This is a straight-coupon bond that is selling at a discount from its face value:

Maturity value $= M = \$1,000$

Number of periods $= n = 10$

Periodic cash flow $=$ PMT $= \$40$

Discount rate $= i = 5\%$

Value $= \mathbf{\$922.78}$

7.3. This is a straight-coupon bond that is selling at a premium from its face value:

Maturity value $= M = \$1,000$

Number of periods $= n = 8$

Periodic cash flow $=$ PMT $= \$25$

Discount rate $= i = 2\%$

Value $= \mathbf{\$1,036.63}$

7.4. This is a straight-coupon bond that is selling at a premium above its face value:

Number of periods $= n = 10$

Maturity value $= M = \$1,000$

Discount rate $= i = 3\%$

Periodic cash flow $=$ PMT $= \$50$

Value $= \mathbf{\$1,170.60}$

7.5. The yield to maturity should be greater than the coupon rate because the bond is selling at a discount from its face value:

$M = 100$

$N = 16$

$V = 88$

PMT $= 4$

Solve for i:

$i = \mathbf{5.116434\%}$

　　Therefore, YTM $= 5.116434\% \times 2 = 10.232868\%$

7.6. First, identify the periodic cash flows:

Period	Cash Flow
0	−$950
1	$20
2	$20
3	$20
4	$20
5	$30
6	$30
7	$30
8	$30
9	$30
10	$1,030

Then, solve for the internal rate of return (IRR).

IRR = i = 3.15318%

After you solve for the six-month return, convert this to an annualized rate:

YTM = 3.15318% × 2 = **6.30635%**

7.7. The coupon rate is greater than the yield, so the bond must be selling for more than its face value of $500:

Maturity value = M = $500

Discount rate = i = 3%

Periodic cash flow = PMT = $20

Number of periods = N = 8

Value = **$535.10**

Alternatively, we could solve this using the bond quote:

Maturity value = M = 100

Discount rate = i = 3%

Periodic cash flow = PMT = 4

Number of periods = N = 8

Bond quote = 107.0197

107.0197% of $500 = **$535.10**

7.8. Given:

$M = \$1,000$

$i = 2.5\%$

$N = 10$

Solve for PV: Value = $\$781.1984$

7.9. Given:

$M = \$1,000$

$PV = \$700$

$N = 10$

Solve for i: $i = 3.6311\%$. The YTM = $3.6311\% \times 2 = 7.2622\%$

7.10. Using the bond quotes:

	Bond 1	Bond 2
Number of periods, N	10	14
Present value, FV	94	96
Interest, PMT	2.5	3.0
FV	100	100
Solve for i, $i =$	3.21%	3.32%
YTM	6.42%	6.64%

Bond 2 has the higher yield to maturity.

CHAPTER 8

8.1. Given:

Current dividend = $D_0 = \$10.00$

Growth rate = $g = 3\%$

Required rate of return = r = 12%

$P_0 = \$10.00(1 + 0.03)/(0.12 - 0.03) = \$10.30 / 0.09 = \$114.4$

8.2. Given:

Current dividend = $D_0 = \$1.50$

Growth rate = $g = 5\%$

Required rate of return = $r = 10\%$

$P_0 = \$1.50(1 + 0.05) \div (0.10 - 0.05) = \$1.575 \div 0.05 = \$31.50$

8.3. Given:

Next period's dividend $= D_1 = \$2.50$

Growth rate $= g = 1\%$

Required rate of return $= r = 12\%$

$P_0 = \$2.50 \div (0.12 - 0.01) = \$2.50 \div 0.11 = \mathbf{\$22.73}$

8.4. Given:

Current dividend $= D_0 = \$2.00$

Growth rate $= g = -5\%$

Required rate of return $= r = 12\%$

$P_0 = [\$2.00 \times (1 - 0.05)] \div (0.12 + 0.05) = \$1.9 \div 0.17 = \mathbf{\$11.176}$

8.5. Calculate the dividends for periods 1 through 3,

$D_1 = \$2.40$

$D_2 = \$2.88$

$D_3 = \$3.456$

Calculate the terminal value:

$P_3 = \$3.456(1.07)/(0.15 - 0.07) = \$3.69792 / 0.08 = \mathbf{\$46.224}$

Then solve:

Period	Cash Flow	Present Value
1	$2.40	$2.08696
2	$2.88	2.17769
3	$49.68	32.66541
Total		$36.93006

$P_0 = \$36.93$

8.6. Cash flows:

Period	Cash Flow
2009	−$20
2010	$3
2011	$25

The internal rate of return is **19.555%**

8.7. Identify the inputs:

PV = $0.055

FV = $0.09

$n = 4$

$i = g = 13.10\%$

8.8. Using the equation for the return,

$$\text{Return} = \frac{D_1}{P_0} + g$$

and substituting the known values, we can solve for the return:

Return = $2/$50 + 0.03 = 0.07 or 7%

8.9. Company A stock has the higher value:

Company A: Price per share = [$2.50 × 1.05] ÷ [0.10 − 0.05] = $52.50

Company B: Price per share = [$4.00 × 1.02] ÷ [0.10 − 0.02] = $51.00

8.10.

End of Year	Dividend Yield	Capital Yield	Total Return
2011	$3 ÷ $50 = 6%	($60 −50)÷$50 = 20%	[$60 − 50+3] ÷ $50 = 26%
2012	$3 ÷ $60 = 5%	($55 − 60)÷$60 = −8.33%	[$55 − 60+3] ÷ $60 = −3.33%

CHAPTER 9

9.1. The net present value of this investment is −$90.91. In other words, you would lose money if you invested in this investment.

9.2. The IRR of this investment is 4.881%.

9.3. NPV = $21,372.25 and the PI = 1.2137

IRR = 15.001%

9.4. NPV = $19,272,82 and the PI = 1.1927

IRR = 15%

9.5. NPV = $59,526.15 and the PI = 1.2976

IRR = 18.719%

9.6. NPV = $19,459.74 and the PI = 1.1946

    IRR = 15%

9.7. You would choose **B**, because it has the higher net present value:

    $NPV_A = \$71.90$

    $NPV_B = \$73.55$

9.8. The decision changes at the crossover point:

	Cash Flows		
Year	A	B	Difference
Today	−£100	−£100	£0
1	£80	£0	£80
2	£120	£210	−£90

The IRR of the differences is the crossover point: 12.5%. You can see this in the investment profile of the two investments:

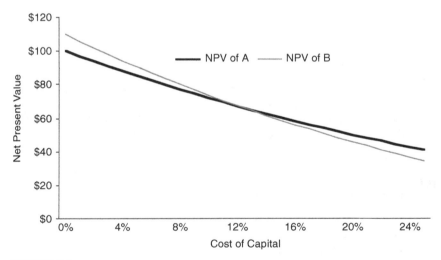

EXHIBIT E.1

9.9. If PI = 1.25 and the denominator (the PV of the outflows) is $1,000, the numerator (the PV of cash inflows) must be $1,250.

    Therefore, NPV = $1,250 − $1,000 = $250

9.10. At an 8% cost of capital, the NPV of C is greater than the NPV of D:

	C	D
NPV at an 8% cost of capital	$3.084	−$0.771
PI at an 8% cost of capital	1.0308	0.9923
IRR	9.701%	7.722%

Therefore, Investment C is preferred because it is more profitable.